For Bob —
Happy Birthday!
Fond regards
Peter

Oct 2, 2013

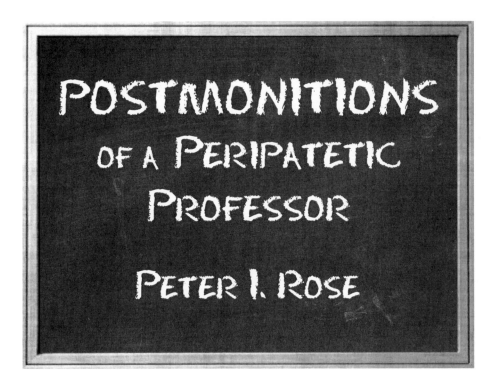

POSTMONITIONS OF A PERIPATETIC PROFESSOR

PETER I. ROSE

WITH A FOREWORD BY

ANDREA HAIRSTON

Published by *Levellers Press*, Amherst, Massachusetts

Printed in the United States of America

ISBN 978-1-937146-34-4

My object in living is to unite my avocation with my vocation as my two eyes make one in sight.

Robert Frost

For Hedy

For sixty years she has been my partner in all my endeavors, vocational and avocational.

Contents

Foreword • *ix*
Praisesong, by Andrea Hairston

Preface • *xv*
On Postmonitions

Chapter I • *1*
How My Twig was Bent

Chapter II • *31*
The 1960s: Behind and Beyond the Grécourt Gates

Chapter III • *87*
The 1970s: Fully Booked

Chapter IV • *133*
The 1980s: Flood Tides

Chapter V • *175*
The 1990s: Transitions

Chapter VI • *205*
The 2000s: Moving On

Chapter VII • *247*
The 2010s: Miles to Go...

Foreword

PRAISESONG

Václav Havel said, "Education is the ability to perceive the hidden connections between phenomena."

As I meditated on the forty years I have known, appreciated, and been inspired by Peter Rose, as I considered our parallel interests in community and identity in this nation of nations and our mutual passion for understanding immigrants, refugees, and the journey from self to other, I had to admit that in 1973, I didn't take his course "Ethnic Minorities in America" because I knew what a visionary sociologist Peter was. I didn't realize that he would help me fulfill a childhood dream to fly through space to new worlds or offer me the magic to shapeshift into aliens. I definitely had no idea that he would guide me to the hidden connections between phenomena. I just needed a fourth course.

In my junior year identity crisis, I was lost somewhere between the delicious uncertainties and sublime contradictions of theoretical physics and the dizzying chaos and unrelenting paradoxes of theatrical imitations of life. I took the course to be close to my best friend, Jackie Ponder, who was much more interested than I in what this Peter Rose would have to say about race and ethnicity in America.

So this praise poem for Peter is also from Jacqueline Renee Ponder who decided the first day James Meredith attempted admission to the University of Mississippi that she would be a lawyer and change the world into a better place than she found it. And if Peter Rose was going to be bold enough to throw out a challenging course like "Ethnic Minorities in America," we would sit in his class, Jackie with her long legs draped over the chair in front of her, and challenge him back.

"What you got, Mr. Man? TEACH ME!"

I sat next to her, thinking, "Yeah."

I try to imagine what we must have looked like. Jackie was fierce—almost six feet tall, dark-skinned, with a short Afro and an incredible voice. She sang and acted and threw herself at you with diva force. I looked like I do now—except I weighed fifty pounds more then and I could put all that weight behind my show-me smirk. Jackie and I were quite a pair.

I don't actually know what we looked like to Peter, trying to stare him down, trying to catch him in a false step. I had yet to see myself. Still, who did he think he was?

Peter lived up to our challenge. To quote from his book *Seeing Ourselves*: "All good social research comes down to one thing: Observation. Ways of looking, of seeing, and interpreting are what make the sociological perspective unique. Many people look. Some see. Only a few have the skill to put it all together and understand why we or they behave in a particular way at a given time."

We students stood on the shaky ground of a diverse society not comfortable with its complexities, breathing tension, spitting fire at one another. We were spoiling for a fight, but as the course pressed on through difficult material, Peter forced us to use our passion to uncover the truths and power of our unique cultural perspectives. He had us explore the limits of our insights, assumptions, and biases. We quickly realized the impossibility of explaining the whole world in the limits of our skin with only the range of partial vision.

Again, to quote from *Seeing Ourselves*, "What is most important [for the sociologist] is the rare gift written about by the Scottish poet Robert Burns, the gift of being able to see ourselves as others see us."

Peter convinced us that if we were going to change the world, or if Jackie was, we had to escape the limits of our particular *Weltanschauung*. Flying off into someone else's skin, we could live and think from others' perspectives. As shaman shapeshifters inhabiting alien bodies, we could ask, "Who are all these wonderful, aggravating, inspiring, disturbing, intriguing people who live next door yet we've never really seen? What does the world mean to them?" In our journeys from self to other, we came to understand what our world meant to us. Needless to say, Jackie and I were hooked. Peter Rose fans. His sociology informed the nature of our lives.

Jackie, though suffering from lupus—a debilitating disease that causes the immune system to attack not only outside pathogens but also one's own organs—went off to law school.

After graduation, she called me from the hospital and confessed that just the night before, she had thought to let go and die. As she was slipping away from herself she realized, "I haven't passed the Kentucky bar!" Jackie had always seen herself as a lawyer, so she guessed it wasn't quite her time after all. She held on to be one of the "natives challenging the outsider's description of things," to quote Peter.

A few days later, Jackie slipped out of the hospital for the day, took the exam, and became the second black woman to pass the bar in Kentucky. She died shortly thereafter.

I would also take law boards, apply to and get into law school, work as a math book editor, but the fact is that I only romanced the idea of becoming a lawyer, or a physicist, or a sociologist. In "Minorities," in lieu of a final paper, I persuaded Peter to let me write a theater piece based on the work we were doing in class. Called *Einstein*, it was my first full-length play. In it I pulled together my emerging insights on race, diversity, and stereotypes, my love of relativity, uncertainty and fuzzy mathematics, and my passion for story, for embodied knowledge and entertaining ideas. (I got Jackie to play one of the leads—a singing scientist.) That play set the tone for my career as a theater artist.

While researching and writing *Einstein*, I recognized what good sociologists, consciously or not, artists had to be. As Peter wrote, sociology should stimulate us to "ponder what it would be like to transport ourselves into another social context, to have lived in, say, Haight Ashbury several years ago instead of in Scarsdale, to have been white instead of black. [Sociologists] should help in the understanding of movements that swirl about in society but make little sense and are often mocked because of our reluctance [laziness? anxiety?] to find out more about them."

Artists hold the history and wisdom of a culture in their images; they reflect, create and recreate the ideas we have of ourselves; they let us see who we are and who we might be; they show us the roads we have taken and offer us alternate routes. Artists shape the characters we play in life and allow us the possibility to transcend.

Over the years I have worked with African-American, white, and Latino/a inner city youth who were so cowed by media impressions of perfection that bombarded and excluded them, they were afraid to do anything, most especially imagine a world not contained in those images. I have conducted workshops with women refugees from Africa, the Middle East, and eastern Europe who found themselves marooned in the new Germany. They, too, felt locked out of the world imagination as they struggled to create communities and new identities in a scramble of cultures. I have spoken with skinheads and ultraconservatives about the negative images of Germany that abound in the world. They were eager to set the record straight. I have worked with diverse American actors who were afraid to play characters different from themselves.

Creating stories with or about these people, I am always struck by an artist's necessary sociological sensibility. To paraphrase Peter: Maybe nobody knows the troubles I've seen, but somebody, perhaps anybody, can imagine them—if they work at it. At the end of his essay "Nobody Knows the Troubles *I've* Seen," Peter says, "I now feel very strongly that much of our work is like that of the Japanese judge in *Rashomon*, the one who asks various witnesses and participants to describe a particular event as seen through their own eyes."

We—sociologists, lawyers, and artists—must put the witnessing together.

Years ago Peter challenged us to imagine people we'd dismissed because we disagreed with their actions, their views of reality, to look for the hidden connections between beliefs and actions as well as the sometimes tragic irony of the disconnections. According to the Romans, *Ars est celare artem*, the nature of art is to conceal art. But as a student of Peter Rose, I think art is about revealing, showing us what we couldn't see in what we always see.

As I look back through these forty years, I can almost see a young Jackie Ponder and myself sitting in Smith's Wright Hall, bright with potential in Peter's eyes, shapeshifting, setting off to change the world and, thanks to Peter, making it a better place.

Andrea Hairston

SALZBURG GLOBAL SEMINAR

**INTERNATIONAL
STUDY PROGRAM 26**

GLOBAL CITIZENSHIP

AMERICA AND THE WORLD

Preface

ON POSTMONITIONS

I HAVE SPENT MOST OF MY ADULT LIFE THINKING, talking to, teaching, and writing about people on the move and their interactions with others. Over the years I have researched the experiences of natives and newcomers, explorers, colonists, immigrants, slaves and their descendants, refugees and, since the mid-1980s, tourists and travelers, too. My primary focus has been on America's diverse people, particularly on the competitions and conflicts among various ethnic groups and on the often-halting steps toward making ours "a more perfect union." This has meant probing the meaning of alienation in its most literal sense and considering the functions of marginality, not only the disadvantages of being a minority but also some of the advantages of having to live in two worlds and surviving.

My principal anchorage has been the United States—Northampton, Massachusetts—to be more precise. But I have had the privilege of being able to spend time as a visiting professor on a number of American campuses and at universities in England, Japan, Australia, Austria and The Netherlands, and as a lecturer at more than a hundred other universities, some in those countries, many in other places in Europe, Asia, the South Pacific, and Africa.

Ever intrigued by how other social scientists, historians, and journalists address the main issues of my primary social and political concerns, early in my career I was delighted to accept an invitation to become consulting editor in sociology for the publisher Random House/Knopf where I also developed my own series "Ethnic Groups in Comparative Perspective" and served in that capacity and as a general editor from 1965 to 1980. The opportunity to see what people with similar interests but often very different perspectives were doing and thinking before others got to read their works also was made possible by years of serving as a regular book reviewer for the *Christian Science Monitor* and *New York Newsday*, and the less frenetic demands of *Present Tense* and *Congress Monthly* and a variety of academic journals in the social sciences and in history. Finally, having a secondary career as a travel journalist and quick-take ethnographer sharpened my eyes while tempering my proclivity toward always having to probe everything in depth.

If there is a *leit motif* that runs through almost all my work it is the awareness of a persisting dichotomy between insiders and outsiders, between *we*, that is, people like us, and *they*, the others—minorities, foreigners, even naïve tourists, all falling under a single rubric: strangers. It was a distinction starkly made in a poem by Rudyard Kipling I read when I was a small boy. Despite the fact that I would later learn that Kipling was a dyed-in-the wool imperialist and racist who coined the phrase "the white man's burden," he was still a very perceptive observer who conveyed a sad reality of social life.

> The Stranger within my gate,
> He may be true or kind,
> But he does not talk my talk—
> I cannot feel his mind.
> I see his face and the eyes and the mouth,
> But not the soul behind.
>
> The men of my own stock,
> They may do ill or well,
> But they tell the lies I am wonted to,
> They are used to the lies I tell;
> And we do not need interpreters
> When we go to buy or sell.

As painful as it was to apprehend then accept what Kipling was saying, I was intrigued by his clarity of expression and its no-frills candor. This was further confirmed when I found and read his poem "We and They," which, in a few words, make the fancy term "ethnocentrism" come alive.

> All good people agree,
> And all good people say,
> All nice people like Us, are We
> And everyone else is They.

I found it even more interesting that the poem ended with these lines:

> But if you cross over the sea,
> Instead of over the way,
> You may end by (think of it!)
> Looking on We
> As only a sort of They!

There was in that last stanza an important sociological truth, something another favorite poet, the Scottish bard Robert Burns, had also said so pointedly many years ago. "Oh wad some Power the giftie gie us/ To see oursels as ithers see us!"

Putting oneself in another's shoes is central to anyone studying social life and human interactions. As I discovered, it is not easy to do and even trickier to write about. Still, it is important to set one's goal to become what I once labeled "an outsider within." To be sure, if one is successful in learning to play such a role, there is a risky pitfall that one needs to be aware of: insiders often resent it when others intrude and even more when they are able to get at innermost thoughts, feelings and behaviors and then reveal what they learn. Empathy is important, and sensitivity to biases is most essential but seeming to expose others' secrets, as many ethnographers and sociologists have learned, is often inflammatory. I have witnessed this resentment a number of times over my career, but never as dramatically as the reaction in Mexico when Oscar Lewis first released his book *Five Families: Mexican Case Studies in the Culture of Poverty* in 1959, and that of many African Americans—also numerous whites—when Daniel Patrick Moynihan published his report "The Negro Family: A Case for National Action," in 1965.

Some of these epistemologically and politically charged issues—including the "Moynihan Report"—are discussed here. There are others that also might be seen as threads running through my attempts to relate particular experiences and their contexts and to share what I call my "postmonitions."

Why "postmonitions," a word I made up?

Why not?

If premonitions are things—exciting, challenging, and sometimes foreboding things—that we anticipate, I think of postmonitions as those ideas, acts and events we look back upon. They are at once both cognitive and affective—not just visualized memories but matters we can still feel. At least mine are, as I explained in the introduction to an earlier collection of essays, *Guest Appearances and Other Travels in Time and Space* (2003). That book was mainly about my nonacademic—or extracurricular—life. This one is mainly about my professional career.

There are seven chapters here. The first begins with a quick synopsis of some of the things I've written about previously—my early life, family, and education through college at Syracuse University, and how I met my Dutch wife, Hedy—but then quickly moves on to my graduate school days at Cornell (1954–58) and my first jobs in the latter half of the 1950s. The rest of the book is partitioned by decades, from the 1960s to the 2010s, each chapter a potpourri of postmonitions about interests, involvements and activities. I describe what I did, what I taught and what I wrote about during each of those surprisingly easily partitioned periods.

I came to Smith College and Northampton from Baltimore in 1960 and—though officially retired since 2003—am still here. That was the beginning of a whirlwind decade when our children, Dan and Lies, were born, and when I would write my first book, *They and We* (on race and ethnicity in the United States) and several more; become an editor for Random House; spend a year as a Fulbright professor at the University of Leicester in England; devote many weekends to demonstrating against the war in Vietnam and serve one brief stint as a consultant at, of all places, the Pentagon (addressing ways to enhance the mobility of civilian minorities working for the U.S. Navy); moonlight as a visiting professor at Clark University and at Wesleyan; lead a year-long graduate seminar at Yale; and teach in the summer school of the University of Colorado.

The 1970s began with my first trip to visit and teach about race and ethnicity in the United States in Japan, then in Australia. These trans-Pacific tours would be followed by others to Asia and the South Pacific as well as to Europe and Africa—and, more recently, to South America—sometimes to lecture, sometimes for research.

The 1980s began with fieldwork in refugee camps in Indochina in the aftermath of the war in Vietnam. This signaled a major shift in my research orientation as I began to explore the making and implementing of U.S. refugee policy. It was also a time when I spent two years at Harvard, had a study leave at the Rockefellers' retreat in Bellagio, Italy, and began reviewing books on a regular basis. The 1980s also represented a milestone for Hedy, a Cornell graduate with an M.A. from Smith, who had long served as a faculty member at every level from pre-school, which she taught while we were in Baltimore, to high school to college—at Smith and Hampshire College. In 1986 she received her doctorate from the University of Massachusetts. Shortly thereafter she joined the faculty of Wesleyan University as associate professor of education and director of its graduate master of arts in teaching program.

The final decade of the twentieth century opened for me when, as the president of the Eastern Sociological Society, I focused my program for the annual meeting on themes that had become central to my academic work: the politics of rescue, the sociology of exile, and the psychology of altruism. A few years later I would publish *Tempest-Tost* (1997), a book of views, interviews, and reviews on race, immigration and the dilemmas of diversity, completed when I was a visiting fellow at Stanford University.

The millennial year, 2000, was for many most memorable as the start of the new century. For me it was the beginning of Hedy's courageous fight against cancer. It was a time of reflecting on what life was really all about and what ours might be like after I retired—and discovering that "permanent sabbatical," at least for me, meant not slowing down but once again branching out. I found myself organizing symposia and seminars in Northampton and in Salzburg, Austria, on immigration and the rise of nativism in this country and nationalism in Europe, and serving twice again as a Fulbright professor, first in Vienna in the fall of 2003, then in Middelburg in the Netherlands for the fall of 2008. One notable change in my writing was that my involvement in book reviewing, at least for a time, was overshadowed by the challenge of travel writing, an endeavor that continues today.

The beginning of the current decade was marked by the release of my book *With Few Reservations: Travels at Home and Abroad* (2010), a compilation of many of the stories I wrote in the early years of the twenty-first century, and by more travel, more teaching, more writing and editing, including preparation of the seventh—and fiftieth anniversary edition of *They and We*, first published by Random House in 1964.

Each chapter—indeed, this entire book—while chronologically linear in a general sense, has a spiraling character because so many things that happened were the result of something earlier that had to be connected or explained, sometimes interrupting the narrative, sometimes introducing material that just as easily have been placed elsewhere. Each chapter is augmented by concrete and unredacted, usually brief but sometimes lengthy, examples of what I was thinking, teaching and, especially, writing about at particular times over those decades. Most of these inserted materials are excerpts from articles or essays previously published in my books or in academic journals or newspapers or travel magazines. In several cases the full text is reprinted. I also include several profiles of people, a few poems, a very short story, "Dante, the Athlete," never seen in print before and an assortment of photographs of people and places. Many of the stories and some of my pictures are period pieces.

That is the format.

As for the style: I hope this book will be a counter to readers with the preconceived notion that those in my guild and in other social sciences can write only in arcane argot, or to fellow sociologists who feel it absolutely necessary to crunch numbers lest they not be taken seriously as real scientists because of the belief that "if you can't count, it doesn't count." I say this because to too many people a *sociological writer* is an oxymoron. I always believed it needn't be so. In fact, with the chutzpah of youth, long ago I decided that, if I ever did any writing of my own, I would try to prove that plain talk wouldn't diminish the credibility of the social scientist but might actually enhance it.

Readers of my postmonitions will have to judge whether or not I have succeeded in realizing that subversive goal. I do have to say that, although some of my colleagues thought I was being giddy over just a few words at the end of a review of a recent academic book of mine, the comments meant the world to me. What were those words? "Informative, thoughtful, moving...and he doesn't write like a sociologist."

The review appeared a few months before I published a short essay on my long war against abstruse writing in the monthly magazine of the American Society of Journalists and Authors in March, 2007. Here is what I wrote:

> Early in my academic career I decided that the reason so many sociologists had such bad press was that they wrote their own copy. Reactionary that I was, I thought we would all do better if we simply used plain English in our classrooms, public presentations, and writings, instead of arcane, insider argot.
>
> Over the next four decades I had ample opportunities to effect some changes. Occasionally I was successful.
>
> As a consulting editor at Random House for fifteen years, I did my best to turn the often convoluted prose of my fellow sociologists into simple, straightforward sentences. I also tried to persuade authors to replace flat titles with ones that were at once relevant and evocative. For example, I once recommended publishing a manuscript about what it was like to grow up in an all-black, ten-story low-rent building in an inner-city neighborhood in the Midwest. Although it read like a doctoral dissertation (which it had been not so long before), Random House's inside editors were able to help the writer transform it into a fascinating ethnography, without, I hasten to note, losing its sociological essence. However, the author insisted on keeping its lengthy title. It was something like, "Longitudinal Perspectives on Socialization, Culture Conflict, Anomie, and Social Entropy among African Americans Residing in a Multi-Storied Public Housing Project."

Just as the book was set to go to press, I suggested something briefer. After much hand wringing, the writer reluctantly agreed.

The Vertical Ghetto did very well within the academic community —and well beyond its ivied walls.

Wearing another hat, as chairman of Smith College's sociology and anthropology department, I once invited a distinguished Israeli sociologist to come to the college to speak about her research. She was delighted and sent me a title: "Social Structure, Sex Role Differentiation and Gender Discord Among the Members of a Uniquely Israeli Communal System." I sent out posters announcing that Yonina Talmon of the Hebrew University would speak on "Men and Women on the Kibbutz." The turnout was terrific.

I still savor the memories of the times my insurrections against jargon paid off.

But, truth to tell, I lost more battles than I won—sometimes even with myself.

On not a few occasions, when asked to replace my own punchy title and narrative text with "something more staid, more scientific, more, you know, sociological," I found myself waffling. I wanted the piece to come before my peers, after all, so I tried to be accommodating. This usually meant adding some highfalutin adjectives and putting in more tables as well as bits of multi-syllabic socio-babble at strategic points.

Musing about this recently, I reflected on what it would be like to come before a meeting of learned colleagues to offer a sociological interpretation of the re-election of George W. Bush. As I prepared my paper in my mind, I first checked voting statistics against a variety of variables: gender, race, religion, region, class, age, educational attainment, socio-economic status. I looked over opinion data. I read what other social scientists had concluded based on their surveys, focus-group interviews, and exit polls. While finishing my analysis, my imaginary hosts then asked me to come up with a name for the talk. Once again, feeling the urge to set aside my knee-jerk revulsion to tortuous titles and to prove that I hadn't forgotten my roots, I conjured up a good one that seemed to say it all: "Value Homophily Among a Cohort of Voters Who Scored High on Scales of Religiosity and Patriotism and the Failure of the Opposition to Effectively Respond to the Multi-faceted Challenge of Their Neo-Conservative Appeal."

Then, still day-dreaming, I scrapped it and came up with a better title: "Kerry Blew It."

In the spring of 2003, on the occasion of my retirement after nearly forty-five years on the Smith College faculty, I called my valedictory speech, "Postmonitions." What follows is a lengthy reprise and a considerable extension of that talk, adding ten more years of anecdotes, research summaries and passages from other presentations, articles and books.

I want to offer a special thanks to Bill Oram, who patiently read through an early draft of this book and offered his critical advice; kudos to Amanda Heller, an editor's editor whose painstaking work made me realize once again how much I still have to learn about sentence structure and bad spelling; and grateful appreciation to Steve Strimer of Levellers Press, a true partner in what became a joint venture.

The closest reader of all was my wife, Hedy, to whom, like several of my other books, this one is also dedicated. It is also dedicated to our children, Lies and Dan, Dan's wife, Susan, and our grandsons, Jordy and Robert, and to the memory of a number of individuals who had an impact on my life course, not least the man who first brought me to Smith College in 1960 and not long after became my first editor, Charles Hunt Page.

In 1982, a few years before Charles died, the University of Massachusetts Press published a book of his reflections on an academic life, *Fifty Years in the Sociological Enterprise*. His subtitle was "A Lucky Journey." *Postmonitions of a Peripatetic Professor* is about mine.

Peter Rose

The officers of the 1936 Campaign of The American Jewish Joint Distribution Committee extend their heartfelt appreciation to

Aaron Rose

for cooperation and leadership in the Campaign for aid to the distressed Jews of Germany and of Eastern Europe. Your name is hereby added to the honorable record of our distinguished co-workers in the great humanitarian program of bringing reconstructive service, relief and hope to the Jewish people in many countries overseas.

December 31, 1936

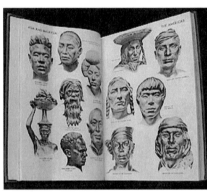

I

How My Twig Was Bent

MY LUCKY JOURNEY BEGAN EIGHTY YEARS AGO in Rochester, New York, the City of Optics.

I was the only child of very active social workers, Aaron and Lillian Rose, whose immigrant fathers' occupations, religious convictions, and political preferences were as different as their wonderful mammalian names: Bear and Wolf. Dark-haired and mustachioed, Russian-born Barney Rose, whose Hebrew name was "Dov" (meaning bear), was a highly successful and innovative self-made entrepreneur who came to this country nearly penniless, made his initial stake by reselling beer bottles to a local brewery, began turning broken shards of glass into magnifying glasses, and ended developing, owning and operating Projection Optics Company, supplying lenses to the budding movie industry. He was a community leader, a founder of Rochester's Conservative synagogue Beth El, a Mason, an Elk, a Teddy Roosevelt Republican and a super-patriot—the sort of character that E. L. Doctorow might have invented.

My maternal grandfather was completely unlike his furry counterpart. Blond and clean-shaven, Polish-born Wolf Feld was a tailor all his life. His American odyssey took him from New York City to Albany to Rochester where for many years he was a coat maker at Hickey Freeman, Rochester's leading manufacturer of men's clothing. He was an avid socialist who shunned organized religion—save for that of his personal faith in organized labor.

Their wives were also very different from each other. Tillie Berger Rose came to Rochester from Lithuania as a very young child and attended school to the eighth grade. She was a pint-sized, politically active dynamo, with three principal causes: workers' rights, women's suffrage, and the safety of Jews. (It is a family legend that the organization, Hadassah, established in New York City in 1912, was named in the living room of their large home at 376 Harvard Street.)

Celia Gutentag Feld was even smaller than Tillie; her world was smaller than Tillie's, too. An unschooled homebody who came to America with her husband around the turn of the twentieth century, she often did piecework on the coats he designed and made. She rarely left the confines of their modest house on Bismark Terrace in a predominantly Italian and Jewish working-class section of Rochester.

While the Roses had a housekeeper and an open touring car and, for a time, a summer place on Lake Ontario, the Felds had very little. But they, like the Roses, were bound and determined that each of their children should receive a college education. And they saw to it that they did.

My father had four sisters. My mother had two brothers. All, except my Aunt Toby, graduated from the University of Rochester. This was something in which both sets of grandparents took special pride. Among the first group was Sadie, a highly successful writer, starting with her prize-winning book *The Adventures of K'tonton*; Toby, a graduate of a teacher's college near Rochester, taught physical education and began a community leader; Frieda, a wealthy housewife who lived most of her adult life in Canada, and Anna, a social worker like my father. Anna's husband, Warner Victor, originally from Berlin, was one the first refugees she had met while assisting the resettlement of escapees from Nazi Germany in the early days of World War II.

The two uncles on my mother's side were Harry, an Eastman-trained violinist, and Sam, a teacher who spent a career with his Oklahoma-born Cherokee wife, Mildred Glass, in the Indian Service in the Dakotas.

I don't know if either set of grandparents or any of my aunts and uncles had any direct influence on my becoming a sociologist, one of whose main interests would be on natives and newcomers, but I know that the experiences of the Bear and the Wolf in my family were prototypes of two different pathways to fulfilling the proverbial American Dream.

I confess to never having thought much about this in such personal terms until sometime in my fiftieth year, when the editor of *The New England Sociologist* asked me to write about how I came to be a social scientist. I responded by writing a piece titled "Mid-Course Corrections," for the request came at a time when I was shifting the focus of some of my research from race and ethnicity in the United States to problems of immigrants and refugees. Today I know it was all of a piece.

In my article I described the major influences in my life that seemed to have set me on my particular career trajectory and the shifts that took place as I sought or found new challenges over my years of travel in both time and space.[1] Rereading what I wrote then as I started work on this memoir, I realized that I still hold to most of what I thought thirty years ago.

I began by noting that I was sure that the way my twig was bent all began in my home. My father and mother, who graduated from Syracuse University and the University of Rochester, respectively, spent their early careers in what was then called "group work." They worked in and led settlement houses and community centers and were also involved in organized summer camping. The camps they ran—first for others, later one they started on their own at the end of World War II, Camp Chateaugay—were very important to me. They were where, from the year of my birth, 1933, I would spend every summer of my childhood, youth, and young adulthood. It was at Camp Chateaugay when, in 1953, I met Hedy. We were married in 1956. Two years later, right after she graduated from Cornell and while I was getting ready to defend my doctoral dissertation there, my father became very ill and we assumed the direction of the camp. We would run it for ten more years.

Compared to the situation of many of my contemporaries, our home life had a very different character. Ours was an environment suffused with liberal ideas about an open, pluralistic society, populated by a string of visitors who reflected that diversity. In fact, my parents were into "multiculturalism" and "globalism" years and years before those expressions entered public discourse.

---

[1] From "Mid-Course Corrections," *New England Sociologist*, 4 (1982), 13–20.

In my mind's eye, I can still see our home—actually homes, for we moved several times, first from Rochester to Syracuse, where we lived in four different parts of town over a span of twelve years, then in the northern Adirondacks, where I would spend my last two years of high school. I can recall even now the variety of people I met while growing up in each of those places. Some who came to our house were quite wealthy, mainly members of the boards of various agencies, each a doctor or lawyer or businessperson; others were quite poor. Most were middle-class: teachers and social workers like my folks. They were black and white, native born and immigrant. And some were refugees from war-torn Europe, four of whom lived with us for extended periods in the late 1930s and early 1940s.

I always think, too, of the importance of a gigantic poster on the wall of my bedroom in the last of those houses in Syracuse. The poster was from an exhibition of Malvina Hoffman's bronze sculptures in Chicago's Field Museum, collectively known as "The Races of Mankind." On it were photos of many of her figures scattered about a map of the world indicating their places of origin. I can still see myself staring at the poster in the twilight of late spring, looking at photos of the Navaho and the Kalahari Bushman, the indigenous Australian, the Malay, and many, many others. While I surely wouldn't have expressed it this way at the time, I know now that there was some sort of inchoate compulsion to find out all I could about the very different looking people portrayed by the sculptor and the shared concerns of those who sat in our living room. That conundrum—summarized in a marvelous essay written by one of my first professors of anthropology, Douglas Haring, and titled "Racial Differences and Human Resemblances"—had a lasting effect.

For as long as I can remember I have been fascinated by ethnic differences and cultural expressions of common human needs, wants, and fears. (Disclosure: Ever since I was first asked to fill out forms with a checklist designating "Race," I always marked "Other," and then, if there was a request to specify, I'd write "Human." Despite the fact that I have often needed such information from others for my own research on dominant-minority relations, I still answer the race question the same way!)

When I was about ten years old, over a big Zenith radio in our living room, I heard a young crooner sing these words, written by Lewis Allan.

What is America to me?
A name, a map, or a flag I see
A certain word, democracy
What is America to me?

The house I live in,
A plot of earth, the street,
The grocer and the butcher
And the people that I meet
The children in the playground,
The faces that I see,
All races and religions,
That's America to me.

—

The house I live in.
My neighbors, white and black.
The people who just came here
Or from generations back.
The town hall and the soapbox,
The torch of Liberty,
A home for all God's children—
That's America to me.

At the time the United States was at war against fascism and Frank Sinatra's rendition of Allan's lyrics made me swell with patriotic pride. This was the house *I* lived in. This was *my* country.

In time I would learn that the fabulous land conveyed in the stirring anthem was in many ways quite different. Nothing could illustrate this more dramatically—or ironically—than the stanza of a poignant poem written by the very same Lewis Allan (aka Abel Meerapol) also set to music and made popular by the African American singers Billie Holiday and Josh White.

> Southern trees bear a strange fruit
> Blood on the leaves and blood at the root,
> Black bodies swinging in the southern breeze,
> Strange fruit hanging from the poplar trees.

This, too, I was beginning to discover, was my country.

What about other countries, other people?

Much of what I thought about them was doubtless shaped by what I read and saw portrayed in the *National Geographic*. There were stacks of them at home. Every month we received a new one in the mail. I savored each issue of the yellow-bordered, shiny-paged magazine with its revelations about wondrous places and exotic peoples. From preadolescence I was especially intrigued by boobies—and, as I once explained, not just those of the voluptuous females so often featured in the magazine. I wanted to go to the Galapagos to see the giant tortoises, the lumbering albatrosses, and all those red- and blue-footed, masked and unmasked boobies in the wild; to Africa to see the lions and elephants, giraffes and gnus; to India to see the Ganges and the Taj Mahal, and perhaps even to climb the soaring peaks of the Himalayas. I wanted to spend time in the Alps and the Andes. I wanted to sail the seven seas. But most of all I wanted to meet Hoffman's people in every corner of the world. Everything I read triggered my ambition to study geography, natural history and anthropology, and to roam the globe.

I would later learn much about the narrow ethnocentricity and downright racism of many of the National Geographic Society's early editors, writers and even some of its photographers. Yet there is little question that their stories and pictures not only evoked excitement among the ranks of Kiplingesque romantics, but also stimulated delusions of grandeur among hordes of hearty adventurers, professional cartographers, travel writers and wide-eyed little boys like me.

During that childhood of moving from place to place, I attended seven different public schools: four in the city of Syracuse; a one-room school on the lower slope of what the local people called Panther Mountain, in the hamlet of Merrill, New York; one in the mining town, Lyon Mountain, in the northern Adirondacks; and, finally, Chateaugay High School, just a few miles from the Quebec provincial border. The last three were all close to the children's camp my parents had opened in 1946.

Being a skier, I was thrilled that we were moving to the North Country, an area known for its extreme winters and very low temperatures. I figured that that would mean lots of time on the slopes. I was frankly disappointed when I found that most of my schoolmates had absolutely no interest in going out in the cold. And cold it was. Sometimes down to thirty below zero, the reality imitating the folk poem learned during my first winter up there. It was about a traveler heading north in an old horse drawn Hartford coach. Rolled up in a big blanket and "as snug as a roach," he was still worried about the weather. As they rode through ever-deeper snowdrifts, the driver kept telling him that he could tell from the sky that they would soon get Chateaugay thaw.

The weather worsened and the traveler, freezing and frightened cried out, "Driver, speak, e'er my vengeance I wreak/What d'ya mean by a Chateaugay thaw?"

> Then the old gossips say, he arose in the sleigh,
> And extended his hand o'er the scene,
> And he laughed and then shrieked,
> And the sleigh groaned and creaked,
> And he said, "I will tell you just what I mean.
>
> "When the north wind doth blow and it's forty below,
> And the ice devils nibble and gnaw,
> When the snow fills your eyes and the drifts quickly rise,
> This is known as a Chateaugay thaw."

Is it any wonder that I became a lone skier? Doggedly I would continue to pursue my passion out on the frozen hillocks around the lake where we lived and on nearby mountains while my schoolmates played basketball in the warmth of the gym. I was once again an odd man out. But this was nothing new.

In those years of living and going to school in many diverse places I, almost always the outsider, was already fascinated by ingroup and outgroup distinctions often made by those in my classes. Like the visitors who came to our home, the students were of highly varied backgrounds. In the Syracuse schools the main differences were those of race, ethnicity and social class; in the ones up north they were of religion and nationality: Catholic or Protestant; "old American" or French Canadian, Polish or Irish, the other prevailing identities.

I was often the only Jew or one of very few Jewish kids in school—except when I briefly attended a suburban high school in Syracuse. All the others were either Protestant or Catholic. I can't remember ever meeting or knowing anyone at school or in our communities who was Muslim or Buddhist or Hindu—people whose faiths, rites and rituals I had read about in the *National Geographic*. But I did have several friends who were Seventh-day Adventists. They were intrigued that we shared the same sabbath.

My own relative marginality—and curiosity—was something that increasingly came to interest me. Within a decade, I would begin to study and write about it.

When I was fourteen or fifteen I read the poem "Two Tramps in Mud Time" by Robert Frost that contains the lines "My object in living is to unite/My avocation with my vocation/As my two eyes make one in sight." I liked the sentiment and the phrase became a sort of personal precept.

In those days I thought of a number of ways of making a living *and* enjoying life, mostly centered on skiing and the out-of-doors, or doing some sort of archaeology. I never heard the word "sociology" when I was a child, but if I had, I would have thought it a variation on "socialism," the religion of my very secular mother, or "social work," her profession and that of my father. Now, of course, I know what sociology is and like Moliere's bourgeois gentleman who late in life realizes that he has always been speaking prose, I know that I have been "doing" sociology from a very early age.

I graduated from Chateaugay High School on the night the Korean War broke out in June 1950. Too young to be drafted—the fate of many of my classmates—I worked at camp that summer and then set off for my father's alma mater. My principal reason for choosing Syracuse had little to do with family loyalty. It was the fact that I had been told it had a bigger ski program than either Dartmouth or Middlebury, the other two schools high on my list.

Horseback riding and skiing were my teenage obsessions. At the age of twelve or thirteen, I worked as a stable boy, exercised show horses for the privilege of riding them, and talked my folks into giving me a horse for my very atypical bar mitzvah present. But my passion for riding waned considerably after my filly, Cindy, was killed in a freak accident while in the care of a friend during my first year of college.

My love of skiing persisted and for a time I had dreams of getting a college degree only as a fallback in case my desire to become a professional skier didn't work out. So when, as I once described it, "with the acknowledgment of my acceptance (at Syracuse) came a questionnaire inquiring about my interests," it is not surprising that I remember checking off 'Ski Club,' 'Outing Club,' and so on, but nothing more cerebral on the questionnaire."

At Syracuse I spent my time shuttling among three venues: the zoology department where I started out, mainly interested in natural history and field zoology; the Maxwell School of Citizenship where two years later I would begin a double major in anthropology and sociology, and the ski slopes, where I quickly joined the ski club, SUSKI, and the freshman ski team. This proved to be a bit of a comeuppance when I found out that compared to some of my teammates, really terrific skiers, including some veterans who had been in the army's Tenth Mountain Division (as had our coach, architecture professor George Earle), I was not such a hotshot after all. Although it sounds very odd to say, I found my niche by turning pro.

I quickly learned that I was a better ski instructor (at least for beginners and intermediates) than a racer. Along with some other pretty good but hardly Olympic quality skiers who also got certified by the New York Ski Association and the USEASA (United States Eastern Amateur Ski Association, later to become the Professional Ski Instructors Association), I spent December through March of my sophomore, junior and senior years teaching skiing for the university's department of physical education during the week and for the city's department of recreation most weekends.

Heavily influenced by my adviser Nathan Goldman, a clinical psychologist with a Ph.D. in sociology from the University of Chicago, and by Kenneth Kindelsperger, a professor of social work, I also volunteered as a part-time group worker at a settlement house in a run-down neighborhood in town. What struck me most forcefully during my afternoons there was the fact that no textbooks could adequately convey the real needs of the troubled teenage boys with whom I worked. They needed empathy not sympathy, to feel wanted, to be loved. It was a special kind of learning experience.

Yet when I look back on what was most important to my university education, aside from finding that *I wanted to teach even more than I wanted to ski*, I have to say it was a required first-year course in the Maxwell School known as "Problems of Democracy" (or something like it) that really focused my attention on social science and, especially the study of minorities. In the course we considered three case studies: the Sacco-Vanzetti trial, the relocation of the Japanese Americans which had taken place less than a decade before, and the Peekskill Riots, when human rights advocate Paul Robeson was attacked by American Legionnaires and others, many spouting anti-black and anti-Semitic epithets, one the occasion of a series of concerts in Peekskill, New York, on his return to the States from the USSR in the late summer of 1949.

I was appalled when I learned of the apparent injustice in the tribulations of the poor shoemaker and fish peddler anarchists Nicola Sacco and Bartolomeo Vanzetti. (One of my most treasured possessions is a signed print of Ben Shahn's iconic portrait of Sacco and Vanzetti given to me by Hedy on my fiftieth birthday). I was outraged by the attacks on Robeson, one of my idols. I can still hear his great basso voice amplified on our Victrola, singing "The Songs of Free Men" and John LaTouche and Earl Robinson's "Ballad for Americans."

As angry as I was about those two cases, I remember being even more upset at what I was learning about the fate of 110,000 Japanese Americans and their experience in internment camps to which they had been sent in the early years of World War II. One of the books about their plight that we read and discussed was *The Governing of Men*, written by the psychiatrist-anthropologist Alexander Leighton, who had been the medical director of the camp in Poston, Arizona, one of the few such places located on Native American soil and operated under the authority of the Bureau of Indian Affairs.

At the time I read his book, Leighton was a member of the anthropology faculty at Cornell. I was only a freshman in college but I decided that someday I wanted to learn more about this and maybe even study with him. Three years later, after I'd read much more in the field of cultural anthropology (some of it, incidentally, focused on social change among the Navajo and written by anthropologists named Tom Sasaki, Toshio Yatsushiro, and Roger Yoshino—who all turned out to have been internees in Poston, initially trained by Leighton), the continued pull of anthropology and, especially, Leighton's work, led me to apply for admission to the Ph.D. program at Cornell. I was admitted and decided to go there instead of attending Columbia University in sociology where I had been offered a junior fellowship in the Bureau of Social Research.

I regret to say I never got to work with Alex Leighton. As fate would have it, although I met him a few times, he was always "in the field"—in Nova Scotia, West Africa, or New York City. I now realize that he may have been known among his colleagues by a phrase that some of my more waggish friends at Smith College would later use to refer to me as "our only tenured *visiting* professor."

While at Cornell, in what was then a combined department of sociology and anthropology, I did take courses with a number of other well-known anthropologists, including Allan Holmberg, one of the finest human beings I've ever met. He had done remarkable if highly controversial fieldwork with the indigenous Siriono people of Bolivia and later with Quechua Indians in the highlands of Peru and, equally important, he was a most sensitive exemplar for generations of students, those he took into the field with him and those, like me, who stayed in this country.

Holmberg was a member of my doctoral committee chaired by another model and mentor, Robin Williams. No, not *that* Robin Williams —the sociologist Robin M. Williams Jr. Holmberg had invited me to join the Cornell Peru Project, an exercise in what was then called applied anthropology, but, while intrigued, I was eager to do research on intergroup relations in the United States, and although he continued to serve as a sounding board for my ideas, Williams, along with another sociologist, John Dean—not *that* John Dean—were my principal advisers. John P. Dean died not long after I received my Ph.D. in 1959, but I stayed in close touch with both Allan Holmberg (who also died quite young, in 1966) and Robin Williams (who died in 2006, living to be ninety-one).

When Robin was eighty, many of his colleagues and former graduate students held a three-day symposium at Cornell in his honor. I was asked to give a sort of keynote address and spent the summer before going over everything I could find that Robin had written. I also spoke at length to his wife, Marguerite, and to many of our mutual friends in order to gather material on his most interesting and productive life growing up in rural North Carolina, attending NC State College in agricultural economics, becoming a sociologist and an astute commentator on American culture and character and, especially, race relations in this country. Here are a few of the things I said:

> "Mild-manner, courtly, jet-black hair with a fine
> mustache and a soft-southern voice...."

I was describing the sociologist Robin Williams to a European colleague as we were walking down the hall in a hotel at a meeting when we were both on the way to hear Robin present a paper. As we approached the open door to the hall, there was considerable commotion inside. Somebody had his ire up. It was a courtly looking fellow all right, but the gentleman at the podium was wound up like a top, trembling a bit and steaming mad. He seemed ready to take on all challengers. It was Robin.

I immediately realized that I should have added a bit more to my word-portrait, something to the effect that the subject of my friend's curiosity had a very strong moral conscience and, though slow to burn, was quite capable of expressing high dudgeon about sloppy thinking, perceived inanities, or social injustice. This, we discovered, was precisely what he was doing. And in regard to all three. What accounted for this? Let me tell you....

Speaking of the Depression, Robin once said "Everyone was out of money; everything was out of whack." Fresh out of college, he was one of the lucky ones, he obtained a part-time job working for one of the federal agencies and, in his own words, "found myself being increasingly radicalized."

He went back to Raleigh where he obtained a position as a researcher to the sociologist C. Horace Hamilton, whom he described as "a dust-bowl empiricist." Finding sociology more creative and more challenging than economics, he gradually shifted fields and, as he said, "never looked back."

He moved to the University of North Carolina in Chapel Hill from which he received a master's degree and, at the urging of one of his professors, spent the academic year 1935–36 studying at Cornell. I am told on good authority that he hated the snowy climate and swore he'd never come back to the frozen northland again. Yet a few years later he moved to New England, this time for further study in the slightly more temperate climate of Cambridge, Massachusetts. After only a single year in residence, he left Harvard bearing the status of an "ABD" (the title had yet to be invented) and the marker of "a Harvard man," a label he would carry with him throughout his career even though he always saw himself quite differently.

Robin served for several years as a member of the faculty at the University of Kentucky before moving to Washington where he joined the Office of War Information in 1942 as a statistician and research analyst. His main assignment was to address the situation of black soldiers in our still-segregated army. From 1943 to 1945 he was at ETO Headquarters overseas, much of the time involved in those few experiments in integration. The findings were summarized in third of the four volume series, *The American Soldier*, published at the end of the war.

In his thoughtful review of *The American Soldier*, Nicholas Demerath claimed that "not since Thomas and Znaniecki's *Polish Peasant* has there been a socio-psychological work of such scope, imaginativeness, technical rigor, and important results." This was not hyperbole. The studies of American soldiers, their recruitment and training and experiences in combat, surely oriented toward a very applied goal, were to have a profound impact on what became known as "middle-range theory" as well as both quantitative and qualitative research tools—attitude scales, innovations in interviewing techniques, experiments on social control—that became a part of many sociologists' and, especially, Robin Williams' conceptual and methodological arsenal. They show up again and again in his subsequent research activities.

Despite his earlier vow never to set foot in that god-forsaken Siberia ever again, Robin returned to Ithaca, New York in 1946 as a member of the Cornell faculty.

Early in his days in the combined department of sociology and anthropology, he helped to develop and then taught a course on "The

Structure and Functioning of American Society," A few years later he published *American Society*. When the book first appeared in 1951, it received considerable critical acclaim as the first major sociological analysis of American social structure and culture. Robin then turned back to his narrower focus on intergroup relations.

When I asked Robin why his own principal research interest took the turn it did—away from the economics of farm tenancy toward the broader issue of race, he gave me a two-fold answer: the first was ethical; the second, intellectual. They were combined for him in a simple question. Speaking of the bigotry he had seen so often, he said he asked himself, "Why do those crazy people act the way they do?" He then spent a lifetime seeking the answer.

It is clear that experiences in his early years, long before Harvard, gave Robin grounding for the sort of sociology he would pursue throughout his career. He came into the field having grown up in a dichotomous, black-white rural southern society rather than the more ethnically heterogeneous urban northern one that was to influence many others of his generation in their particular takes on American society. I am thinking here of so many immigrant scholars who had fled Hitler and many more second-generation, northern—though hardly Yankee—social scientists and commentators such as Arthur M. Schlesinger, Sr., Oscar Handlin, Max Lerner, Nat Glazer, Milton Gordon, Marty Lipset, Ben Ringer, Gabriel Almond, and Larry Fuchs. Like Alfred Kazin, most of those in the latter group had grown up as "walkers in the city." For them, dealing with hyphenation, marginality and the complex variations on a theme of ethnic stratification was a part of their personae, their politics and their sociology.

Robin's world was very different from theirs and so, at least early on, was his *Weltanschauung*. In many ways it was closer to that of other progressive southerners, most of them black. A partial roster of such individuals would have to include Charles S. Johnson, Allison Davis, Bertram Doyle, J. Saunders Redding, Benjamin Quarles, John Hope Franklin, Ira Reid, and Hylan Lewis. Among the whites were Robin's mentors back in North Carolina.

Through such teachers as Horace Hamilton and Rupert Vance, Robin was introduced to a kind of grass roots, regional sociology long before he was exposed to either immigrant America or to the grand system theories of the imported European tradition. It should be clear that while Robin is often portrayed as a simple farm boy who left Hillsboro and suddenly emerged as a Harvard *Wunderkind*, his own view, evident in much of his work, indicated that, while the boy may have taken himself out of Hillsboro, no one ever took Hillsboro out of the boy. Nor did he ever forget the things he learned in North Carolina's public universities or on the job. His intellectual pursuits represent a melding of experience and several rather distinctive sociological orientations into a unique amalgam that is distinctly Williamesque.

Indeed, if there is a recurrent theme running through that book and almost everything Robin would subsequently write it is the notion of trying to achieve an integration of various elements; not homogeneity but a sense of cohesion or, in his words "a unity of diversity" involving "overlapping identities and multi-group membership" (*American Society.* 1951, 514–19). He saw hope for such integration being achieved not only through mutual dependence, external pressures, and common value-orientations (which, in the case of this society, would clearly have to recognize the strength of pluralism) but also through what he would later describe as "mutual accommodation," a device for minimizing strains and cleavages and, though he never used the phrase, relieving the pressures for what I would later call "polarizing particularism," an understandable but unfortunate reaction to two phenomena he noted in several of his writings: the increasing salience of minority identity and the tendency to become more defensively chauvinistic. Both, he saw, as predictable outcomes of categorical discrimination. The first one Robin referred to as "true isolation" (that is, being left out); the second involves various rules of ritualized hierarchical behavior, the sort of "racial etiquette" elaborated upon by Gunnar Myrdal that kept certain people "in their place."[2]

Rereading Robin's writings and those of his critics—and discussing his ideas with him directly—in preparation for that tribute was a most rewarding experience. It brought me back to the days when I first read him and then, a few years later, met him and became his student. I was impressed anew about how much he had to say about this society, its institutions and organizations, values and norms, its persisting contradictions and endemic problems, not least the racial tension that Tocqueville

[2] The address was published in short form as "Long Time Passing: Race, Prejudice and the Reduction of Inter-Group Tensions," in *A Nation Divided: Diversity, Inequality and Community in American Society* (Phyllis Moen et al, eds.) Ithaca: Cornell University Press, 1999, 277–303, and in a much longer version "'Toward a More Perfect Union': The Career and Contributions of Robin M. Williams, Jr.," *American Sociologist*, 70:2, (Summer 1999), 60–74.

had argued "would perpetually haunt the American imagination, like a painful dream."

A slender SSRC Bulletin, *The Reduction of Intergroup Tension* (1948), like all of the writings that were to follow, is characterized by a remarkable clarity of language. There, and in all of his four succeeding books on intergroup relations, Williams offered complex analyses of social issues in the United States in straightforward, readily accessible prose. And the same can be said for his last book, a comprehensive, disturbing, timely—and like *The Reduction of Intergroup Tension*—amazingly prescient *tour de force*. Robin called it *The Wars Within: Peoples and States in Conflict* (2003).

Those who know my own work can now see how much I owe to that mild-mannered, courtly gentleman with the soft-southern voice and a belly full of passion, Robin Williams. While I often disagreed with him, there is little question that exposure to his ideas and his values way back in the 1950s had a profound impact on my approach to whatever I studied and whatever I taught.

During my own years in Ithaca, I began doing some teaching, some research on my own, and some serious writing, too. Actually, I should have said "serious *academic* writing," because I was already a published author. My first piece, which appeared in 1953, was an article titled "The Roots of the New American Ski Technique." There I contrasted the down-up-down "Arlberg approach" of the Austrian skier Hannes Schneider with the up-down-up method of the French ace Emile Allais. I can't remember if that piece was "peer-reviewed"—but one that was, an article on student preferences on and opinions about the presidential election of 1956, was published in the *Public Opinion Quarterly* the following year.

In its pages I reported that while two-thirds of the students surveyed were Eisenhower supporters, and one-third said they favored Adlai Stevenson, close to 100 percent were convinced that Ike would win. And they were right. It led me to speculate a great deal about "self-fulfilling prophecies," an expression I had just learned from reading an essay by Robert K. Merton (coiner of the expression "role-model") in his book

Social Theory and Social Structure (1949).[3] (I thought of this idea and the impact of anticipatory decision-making six decades later in the run-up to the presidential election of 2012.)

The voting preference study came out of one side of my quantitative/qualitative split personality, one part of which led me to take courses with three methodologists who had all worked at Columbia University's Bureau of Applied Social Research under Paul Lazarsfeld. Those three, Edward Suchman, Norman Kaplan and Manny Rosenberg, were the yins of my slowly developing yin/yang academic persona.

Although Ed, Norman, and Manny all became friends with whom I stayed in touch until each of their too early deaths, while I never completely abandoned using quantitative techniques, I have to admit that the pull of the more qualitative methods came increasingly to dominate my approach rather than number-crunching positivism. While still in Ithaca, I conducted research on small group behavior and on the effects of forced proximity on friendship patterns—something that would later have implications for studies of integration in the armed forces and in schools and communities. I worked as a research associate on a study of the careers of nurses—some of whom saw what they did as a job, some as profession, and many as a calling. The telling trichotomy was something that I would remember three decades later when I was studying the motivations of workers in a number of refugee camps in Southeast Asia after the end of the wars in Indochina. It again proved to be a key factor in how individuals defined what they did, played out in their actual commitment and performance.

I also served as an investigator and analyst on the famous "Elmira Study" being carried out by social scientists at Cornell while I was there. Elmira, an urban hub south of Ithaca, was one of four pilot cities—the others were similar sized towns in the South, Midwest, and Far West— in what would later become a nationwide survey of race relations, culminating in several books written by Cornell researchers and edited by several professors. The best known was *Strangers Next Door* (1964) written by Robin M. Williams Jr, John P. Dean, and Edward Suchman.

---

[3]See "Student Opinions on the 1956 Presidential Election," *Public Opinion Quarterly*, 30, 1957, 371–376.

Fellow graduate student Katie Huggins and I spent many days interviewing teenage "Negro" boys in Elmira and evenings driving back to Ithaca comparing notes and asking whether our respective "races" (Katie is African American) and our different genders were a help or a hindrances in the interview process. It was another portent. Years later I would give the Engel Lecture at Smith College on the political aspects of such an epistemological question.

I wrote my master's thesis on the concept of the "exemption mechanism," a fancy term for saying "Well, some of my best friends are..." and then conducted two studies of isolated minorities (in this instance, small-town Jews) and their neighbors in non-metropolitan counties of New York State and across the state lines in western Vermont and northern Pennsylvania in an attempt to test the nature and effects of exemption. The latter studies became the basis for my doctoral dissertation, a follow-up study almost twenty years later, and a book, *Strangers in Their Midst* (1977).

We often ask our students why they decided to work on one topic rather than another. I realize now that my doctoral research may already have been germinating when my parents and I moved to a very rural area in northern New York State. In the village of Chateaugay where I finished high school, we were only the third Jewish family to live thereabouts.

I remember I found it strange that I was often called David. Either the townsfolk assumed that all Jewish boys were named David or, more likely, they mixed me up with David Pearl, the literally fair-haired scion of the family who owned a small emporium called "Pearl's Department Store," and the only other male Jewish teenager in town. David was very tall and blond; I was short and dark-haired.

In graduate school I decided to test out some of my ideas about the nature and role of exemption in challenging stereotypes and perhaps influencing intergroup relations. What follows is a flashback of how I conducted some of my early fieldwork.

I am off on my first series of interviews with small-town Jews—those I had "operationalized" as living in communities of fewer than 10,000 persons with less than five Jewish families in rural counties of New York State, Vermont, and northern Pennsylvania. My primary objective was to establish contact and to spend time with at least forty such individuals in at least twenty different towns over the next year. I was hoping to reach at least one hundred more by mail.

I remember sitting in a dingy motel reviewing my strategy. I have been conducting interviews early in the mornings and in early afternoon, then returning to my room to write up my notes. I am frustrated because I don't think I'm getting the full picture. It is time to go out for another quick meal at a roadside eatery, usually a diner and gas station combo (the sort that has a sign "EAT HERE—GET GAS"). I decide that something has to change on the research front and on the gastronomic one, too. I revise my plan. I will make my appointments only in the late afternoon and meet the "head of household" at his office or place of business. (I soon learned that there is a kernel of truth in many stereotypes. Most small-town Jewish men were either merchants or doctors.)

My new plan works like a charm. Almost invariably, because the subjects are so eager to tell their stories, the sessions drag on for several hours. Around 6:00 o'clock there is a phone call. The man to whom I'm speaking says into the phone,

"Oh, it's that young man from Cornell. You know, the one who is writing about Jews in small towns."

Pause.

"I'll ask him."

He then turns to me. "Do you have plans for dinner? My wife and I would love to have you join us."

While I'm dying to say yes, I answer "Oh, you're very kind but I don't want to inconvenience anyone." And, not surprisingly, he says, "No problem," and I go.

I can report that the ploy—for this is what it became—proved to have a triple function. First, I got a decent meal; second, I was able to do some quick-take visual ethnography—getting a sense of the place, the lifestyle, the magazines and papers people read, a sort of "living room index." Most of all, the mealtime colloquies also gave me the opportunity to engage whole families in what the man of the house and I had been discussing. The conversations often revealed sharp differences of opinion about the attitudes of neighbors and feelings of marginality.

I carried out more than fifty formal interviews with the heads of households and, as a result of my ingratiating technique, informal ones with other members of many Jewish families.

The second part of my study focused on the would-be "exempters." It involved asking non-Jews—half of them in ten towns with a few Jewish residents (about whom I already knew a great deal) and half in ten towns that I knew had no Jews—questions about backgrounds and interests which were identical to those in the first part of the study. But I also asked other questions, especially about perceptions of "others," such as Jews, Negroes, and foreigners. My interviews and questionnaires with several hundred such persons were directed toward having these subjects tell their stories as well and discuss any changes in their towns and their thoughts about various groups of people. I let them define for me what "foreigner" meant. The answers, which proved to be a rough guide to ethnocentrism, varied from "Well, there are lots of Italians around here"—people who, it turned out, had been in the village for fifty years—to "Foreigners?" One man in the same town said to me, "The only foreigners I know are those refugees from Hungary who came here a year ago." (This was two years after the Hungarian uprising of 1956.)

As for perceptions of Jews: people in all of the communities held many mental images, some based on their experiences shopping in the local Jewish-owned store or visiting a Jewish doctor (most often a refugee from Europe who had been placed in the town by a Jewish agency). Other ideas about Jews were far cruder and highly caricatured. What became apparent was the influence of direct contact. In those small towns that had a few Jewish residents, whether they were merchants, cattle dealers, doctors or those in other walks of life, exemption was widespread and, equally important, seemed to allow for the questioning of certain stereotypes, leading, perhaps, to the thought, "Well, not all Jews are..."

Nearly two decades after the study was completed, Liv Olsen Pertzoff, a "mature" religion major at Smith (back in school after a long hiatus) read my dissertation and asked me if I ever did a follow-up on my prediction that very soon, other than those who lived in college towns and little villages that had become engulfed in suburban sprawl, small-town Jews would be very hard to find. I told her, being involved in many other projects, I hadn't found the time to return to study. Liv was very persuasive and soon she'd gotten me to agree to do it and together we embarked on a quest to re-interview the Jews in the first study and to question their now-grown children.

When the book *Strangers in Their Midst* was published in 1977, although mainly based on my doctoral dissertation, it included a new chapter written with Liv called "City Lights." There we reported that, as predicted, almost every child whose parents I'd interviewed in the late 1950s had left the hamlets for urban areas. Even more interesting and quite unexpected was that, contrary to what their parents had told me, very few said they ever felt completely at ease in their villages.

The last chapter of *Strangers* began with the following direct quote from the daughter of one of the small-town Jews interviewed in the late 1950s: "Revelations through discussions of the questionnaire [with my family] had a profound effect on me...." She then described many of her ambivalent feelings as a minority of one in a small town and ended by saying, "The subject of research was changed in some ways by the research itself."[4] (Her comment about the role of the researcher reminded me of the answer to a quiz question I'd learned years earlier while studying cultural anthropology and the influence of outsiders. Question: "Describe the Navajo nuclear family." Answer: "Mother, father, children and anthropologist.")

In the spring of 1958, with my dissertation completed and defended, I accepted an instructorship at Goucher College. In many ways, it was another turning point. I was becoming increasingly concerned about racial discrimination and so gave up an offer from Dartmouth, a dream job for a skier like me, to go to Baltimore, a city in the early throes of the desegregation struggle.

While at Goucher, as a member of a tiny, three-person Department of Economics, Sociology, and Anthropology, I taught everything but

---

[4]*Strangers in Their Midst* (Merrick, New York: Richwood Press, 1977).

economics, offering courses from introductory sociology to physical and cultural anthropology to social psychology to what in those pre-politically correct days was called "Social Pathology."

Moonlighting from my day job, I did some contract research on "unreached youth" (a then-favored euphemism for delinquent boys) for the Council of Social Agencies. This involved a study of white boys who had gotten in trouble. (A black social worker was interviewing African American ones.) It proved to be a sort of precursor to a nationwide investigation, for just as we were winding down that project, I was asked by the Anti-Defamation League to do a pilot study of an epidemic of swastika-scrawling that had just taken place in a number of cities, including Baltimore.

Among those I interviewed for the new project were several of the same young men I had been talking to just a few weeks before. For the record I should note that my conclusions and, later, those of the larger study, showed that contrary to the fears of the ADL and other human rights groups, there was little evidence of an organized, neo-Nazi plot. Instead, it seemed that what had started as a prank—doubtless triggered by someone who knew how to upset people—had become a sort of epidemic of "timely" vandalism, no less insidious but far less scary than what had been feared to be a campaign led by the American Nazi George Lincoln Rockwell or some other anti-Semitic group that was "out to get the Jews."

In those days Baltimore was still very much a divided city. We lived very near the line separating the black and white parts of town and became friendly with several fellow academics at the "historically black" Morgan State College which was quite close to our apartment complex, a place that housed mostly young professors, interns and residents at Johns Hopkins, public health officers and other outsiders. We were shocked at the reaction of nearby neighbors when our African American friends would come over to see us.

Rejection of other sorts of integration as well was apparent also within the white majority. This was made very clear when Hedy and I started looking for a bigger place, especially in one attractive and seemingly affordable neighborhood and were told by the realtor, "You wouldn't be happy there. You'd like it much better in Pikesville" (a predominantly Jewish suburb). Later I learned that the area we preferred had strict covenants against renting or selling to "Jews and coloreds." The codicils—some in writing, others implied—reminded me of the movie *Gentleman's Agreement* and of the anti-Semitic policies at many resorts in New Hampshire and the not so subtle signs I had seen in the late 1940s at the ski center at Mont Tremblant in Quebec that read: RESTRICTED CLIENTELE. (For Hedy, who spent the war years as a hidden child in her home city of Amsterdam in The Netherlands, hearing such things brought back painful memories of signs posted by the Nazi-dominated authorities that said VOOR JODEN VERBOTEN.)

Sometimes the lessons I taught came out of such personal experiences; at other times they were the unpredictable result of what I now think of as my rather freewheeling lecture style. Here is another flashback, a brief sample of the latter, a class session I will never forget.

It was the winter of 1958–59, the fourth or fifth day of my second term at Goucher. I had just read and reviewed anthropologist Edward T. Hall's new book, *The Silent Language*, for the *Baltimore Sun*: it would be one of the first of some two hundred reviews I would write for newspapers, magazines and academic journals over the next fifty-five years.

I decided to start my class by discussing Hall's thesis that culture "speaks." It is what he calls a "silent language," in which culture sends messages that convey rules about roles and relationships, about what is right and good and pleasurable, and about time and place, too, that societal members quickly internalize. I did it, beginning with Hall's example of how proprietary we Americans are about both time and space; how we treat the former as a commodity—spending it, saving it—and treat the latter with a sense of ownership, of territoriality.

My comments were interrupted by a late-arriving student. I paused as she rushed to the front of the room then stopped abruptly. From the look on her face it was obvious that she was upset to see someone sitting in her seat, the one she had occupied the previous two meetings, although no seats had ever been assigned. A bit chagrined, she looked for another seat and sat down.

I was not the only one aware of the timeliness of her entry, action and reaction. The entire class seemed to have noticed, and many of her fellow students began to chuckle. The object of their laughter was baffled. Trying to explain why people were laughing, I gently told the latecomer what we had been talking about just before she arrived. She was embarrassed. I told her not to worry. She smiled wanly and blushed. Then she said, "But she is sitting in my seat."

Culture was still talking. And now the whole class was listening. Very carefully.

During those two years in Baltimore, in addition to my teaching responsibilities and my extracurricular work in town, I also did a stint as a workshop leader at a fascinating conference on children and youth sponsored by the Eisenhower White House.

When I returned from Washington, Hedy said that someone named Charles Hunt Page of Smith College had phoned and wanted to talk to me. Page was very well known and, when she told me that he'd called, I thought it was a local friend pulling my leg. But it was *the* Charles Page. When I reached him he explained that he was about to leave Smith for Princeton to chair its sociology department and that Smith was looking for a sociologist to take his place (but, alas, not his rank) and that he had been urged by Melvin Tumin of Princeton to call me. (Mel Tumin and I had gotten to each other on several projects for the Anti-Defamation League.)

It gave me considerable pause to think about leaving a city I had found such a treasure trove of sociological interest, but I agreed to send in my credentials and some recommendations. Shortly thereafter I found myself in Northampton for an interview. Intrigued by those I met, the setting of the college, and the city itself, I left hoping I would be offered the position. Within a matter of days I was. I accepted the appointment and, a few months later, moved to New England. Northampton became our home, and Smith became my base of operations. More than fifty years later, it still is.

There is an interesting sidebar to the story of my departure from Goucher.

At the time when I was a young faculty member there, the president of the college was Otto Kraushaar, a gentle, soft-spoken and rather formal person, known to both faculty and students as "Dr. Kraushaar." He was a man I admired but with whom I had little contact, even in that small place.

After my soul-searching and the decision to move to Smith, I went to see the president to tell him in person that I was leaving. I knew it would be hard for me because only a month before I had received a great vote of confidence from the first-year students, who had selected me to be their class dean. (Always chosen by members of the first-year class, the class dean stays with them for the next three years.) Dr. Kraushaar had come to the rather raucous ceremony of installation. At a reception afterwards he'd told me how pleased he was that I was willing to take on the job. Now I had to tell him I was abandoning ship.

Ever the gentleman, he took what I told him with an even-tempered if pensive expression. He asked if I might reconsider. When I said, "No, I've made up my mind," he then asked if I might tell him where I was going.

"Smith College," I said.

To my surprise, the president blanched a bit and swore under his breath. (Actually, I think he said, "Shit!") Then, composing himself, he told me that he hoped I would love it as much as he had. It was then that I learned that Otto Kraushaar had come to Goucher from Smith and that he still missed it.

I have to say I was beginning to have second thoughts when, after it was announced that I was leaving, a number of faculty members I had gotten to know and even more members of "my" class—the class of 1962—came to tell me they were sorry to see me go. But the die had been cast and in late May 1960 Hedy and I packed our household possessions for shipment up to Northampton, loaded our little Peugeot 403 to the roofline, leaving only a small space for our six-month-old baby daughter, Elisabeth (whom we would always call by the Dutch diminutive, Lies— pronounced "Lees"), and set off for our new lives in New England.

Because the flat I had rented at 49 Dryads Green wouldn't be ready for another week, we stayed at the home of my new colleague, Ely Chinoy, but not with the Chinoys. Ely and his wife, Helen, were away and our host, who was also in transition, was none other that Charles

Page. Over several evenings, Charles briefed me on the amenities of Northampton and gave me a list of sources for repairs and the like, with a note: "If you have any trouble with your hi-fi, call Jess Josephs." A year later I called Mr. Josephs, asking him if he could come over and fix our stereo. Surprised, he said, "I'm not a repairman, where did you get my name?" I said, "From Charles Page." Jess laughed and said, "I'll be right over." He turned out to be a physicist on the faculty and a specialist in acoustics, and became one of our first close friends at Smith.

Once our things arrived in the moving van, we ran over to our new apartment, showed the movers where to put the furniture, unpacked some things, and left town. We were off to Chateaugay to get set for another summer of directing our camp. This meant painting and putting out the docks; checking out the fleet of canoes, rowboats, and two sailboats; stocking supplies of staples; ordering meat and produce, athletic and aquatic equipment and camping gear; overseeing last minute repairs in any of our fifteen buildings, and running a week-long institute for our crew of forty counselors and specialists and kitchen staff, all before the kids, ages seven to sixteen, arrived for their eight-week stay.

While this now meant that we were not only caring for 120 campers and the staff and our own little girl, reassuming our roles as directors was far easier than it had been two summers before when my father had suddenly become ill and my mother withdrew from direct involvement to take care of him. Not only had we needed to step immediately into the positions where the buck always stopped, but also I had to assume a new role at our opening "Indian ceremony" where, in place of my father, I became the receiver of gifts instead of the giver.

I wrote about this *rite de passage* some years ago in an article in Northampton's *Hampshire Life* (2000). The editor called it "Good Intentions," but when I reprinted it in my book, *Guest Appearances and Other Travels in Time and Space* (2003) it bore my own original title, "Indian Giver." Here's the story:

> From the start, Camp Chateaugay, established by my parents in 1945 in the northern Adirondacks, bore their progressive-school stamp of "creative camping." There were all the regular activities—water and land sports, arts and crafts, overnight hikes and canoe trips;

but there were also a number of program innovations that clearly reflected their liberal attitudes. There were all sorts of projects on folk life and politics and on such subjects as the dignity of labor and comparative religion. There were special days to celebrate the spirit of the United Nations and to appreciate Mankind itself. Among the most memorable of our traditions were the Indian ceremonies at the beginning and end of each season.

Back in those days, Indians and their stereotyped nobility and resourcefulness were an integral part of programs at many summer camps, the basis for activities like basket weaving and lacrosse and ideas about Man and Nature. At Chateaugay, as at various camps my parents had directed before, the season was opened and closed with an enactment of a dramatic meeting between those representing the indigenous people of the area and the intruders who now occupied their ancient land.

With the entire camp community waiting on the beach behind a roaring campfire, the blanketed and feathered representatives of the Tribe of Panther Mountain (a real place), would suddenly appear out of the waning light of dusk, paddling toward them in torch-lit canoes. They would land their crafts, then silently walk to the edge of the gathering and one of them, the Chief, would greet my father, to whom he referred as The Great White Sachem, with a stern-faced "How!" Sachem would reply, "We are pleased to greet our brothers from across the waters."

Then the chief would continue. "We have waited many moons to hear the voices of children echo from the far side of Shat-O-Gay, the lake that is the source of our strength and sustenance, and from the land of our forefathers where deer run wild and pines grow tall, where the sunshine sparkles on the rocks and icy water reflects the purple mountains and the glories of the Earth Mother.

"And now we come to lend you several of our most important possessions, each to be used with care so your campers can become more conscious of their surroundings, stronger and healthier, and more creative, too.

"In two moons we will return to recover these items."

It was always at this point in the ceremony that some wise-cracking thirteen-year old would whisper loud enough for all to hear, "Indian giver!" and his buddies would start to laugh only to be hushed by a counselor who could hardly suppress his own giggles.

After that almost predictable interlude, the visiting party would present its gifts: a sheaf of wheat symbolizing food and health; a beaded moccasin for arts and crafts; a canoe paddle for aquatics, and a bow and arrow for sports and good sportsmanship.

My father would solemnly accept each item, promising that his campers would use it well and that he would return it at the end of the season for safe-keeping over the long winter months. True to his word, each year for two decades he did precisely that.

It never surprised any but the youngest campers that the Panther Mountain Indians were our staff members and that their leader was the head counselor or program director, outfitted in a beaded Sioux headdress of eagle feathers and wearing buckskins. Yet, most went along with the fiction, enjoying the pageantry and understanding the symbolic character of the ritual.

Given my father's plan that I would succeed him as the camp's director, I was destined to work my way up from paddler to torch bearer to chief of the Panther Mountain tribe and, in the future, to take his place on the other side of the beach.

When I became Chief, I decided it was time for some innovation. Instead of coming in canoes for the final ceremony, I suggested we hide behind the docks, light kerosene-soaked torches and then, swimming underwater with flames above, rise from the depths and walk onto the beach where the entire camp family of 180 awaited us.

My fellow "tribesmen" reluctantly agreed. Because it was cold I suggested we coat our nearly naked bodies with grease. It was a big mistake.

Things started smoothly enough. Slathered in Crisco and decorated in war paint, we lit our torches, swam around the docks with only the flames exposed, then rose up and waded ashore. We stood silently. My father and I exchanged greetings and he gave back each present—with that inevitable snickering Greek-chorus murmuring about "Indian-givers" in the background. He kept his composure as he solemnly explained to us how each item had been used while we tried to stand still without shaking from the cold or twitching from the swarms of mosquitoes apparently attracted to our tasty torsos. It was a night to remember.

While the ethnographer in me now shudders at our repeated violation of a host of native American traditions and at our creation of rituals based on naïve stereotypes, I must say that the sentiments that underscored the inauthentic pageantry were as genuine as the artifacts that were used—the headdresses and horsehair roaches, moccasins and the bow and arrow had all been given to us by my mother's brother and his wife who spent their lives working with the Lakota Sioux in the Dakotas.[5]

In 1958, when illness forced my father to retire and my wife and I took over the directorship of the camp, I changed roles. I was now the one to receive and protect the gifts. It was then that I knew that I was really in charge.

We sold the Camp Chateaugay in 1968, and when the spring semester ended, instead of heading north as we had always done, we went west to spend the summer in Boulder, where I taught in the Department of Sociology at the University of Colorado, and where we spent our free time hiking in the Rockies and touring Colorado and parts of New Mexico.

The next summer we spent some time in Eastham on Cape Cod. It was to be the first of what is now nearly forty-five summers on the Cape, the place where much of this memoir was written.

The rest was written in Northampton, our hometown since I first accepted a job behind the Grécourt Gates of Smith. (The gates were named for those given by the grateful citizens of Grécourt in France, where a corps of Smith women had driven ambulances during World War I.) It was also a haven, for it was Smith—and the city of Northampton—that became my Kansas when, like Dorothy, I would travel to weird and wonderful and sometimes very troubled places over the next five decades—and think of home.

---

[5] "Good Intentions," *Hampshire Life*, August 25, 2000; reprinted as "Indian Giver" in *Guest Appearances and Other Travels in Time and Space* (Swallow Press, 2003) 61–63.

II

The 1960s: Behind and Beyond the Grécourt Gates

WHILE TRYING TO PACK UP MY OFFICE to move to a much smaller one in January of 2004, after forty-three years in Wright Hall 103 at Smith College (and after winning the dubious award for having "the messiest desk in the Pioneer Valley" the spring before), I came up with some interesting memorabilia from my early days in Northampton. The first item I found was my letter to the editor of *The New York Times,* published on July 27, 1964. Although it was dated four years after we left Baltimore, in many ways it summarized what I had been thinking about throughout my time there while I participated in and observed the ever-changing civil rights struggle as our society entered one of its rockiest period. What triggered my decision to write at that time was the mayhem that was happening in cities across the country, including my hometown, Rochester, New York. *The Fire Next Time,* a sorrowful meditation by James Baldwin, written just the year before, proved to be prophetic. Addressing the rioting in Rochester specifically, I wrote:

> As a native of the area, I have been appalled by the wanton riots, the pillaging and the total disregard for law and order exercised by some members of the community in the past few days. As a lifelong advocate of integration, I am deeply troubled for I see in the streets of the city the acceleration of the "boomerang effect" that responsible civil rights leaders have so assiduously tried to avoid. But as a social scientist, I am not at all surprised by what is happening. There have

been changes but, in too many instances, they have been token measures that have done little to alleviate the basic malaise.

For years there have been warnings of the consequences of continued denial and exclusion, of the real possibility of violent upheaval, of dislocation and civil strife. And now the predictions are the frightening facts of daily life.

No one wins in these skirmishes. The police may succeed in maintaining or restoring order, but only at the expense of greater alienation and repeated charges of brutality (many real, many fabricated). The white community may say that this merely proves that Negroes are unfit for entry into their sanctum sanctorum, but they do so only by failing to recognize that the hatred and deprivation that pervade the ghettos is not mainly the Negroes' problem but their own. The rioters may thrill at the power they wield as they run amok through the streets striking their blows for freedom as they give "whitey" his comeuppance, but even the satisfaction gained is short-lived and, too frequently, off target.

The urban riots that occurred in the summer of 1964 hit close to home—at least emotionally. Parts of the city of my birth, and the place where my grandmother still lived, were in flames. I felt I had to speak my piece. In some ways the letter presaged the fuller expression of thoughts that would dominate much of my involvements and writings throughout that second decade of my career.

Another document I came upon was clearly related. It was the text of a brief talk I gave on October 16, 1963, before the entire student body at the Smith president's weekly assembly. I'd titled it "Radical Pacifism and the Negro Revolt." This was four months after the civil rights leader Medgar Evers was murdered by the white supremacist Byron De La Beckwith in Jackson, Mississippi, and two months after the great March on Washington when the Reverend Martin Luther King Jr., gave his famous "I Have a Dream" speech, a time when the upheaval I would write about the following summer was already simmering in cities across the land.

In another file folder I found a photo of the huge sign that we faculty members carried in a large protest march against Alabama governor George Wallace when he came to the campus during his presidential campaign the following fall. The sign read "WE DENY NOT YOUR RIGHT TO SPEAK, WE DETEST WHAT YOU STAND FOR."

Civil rights was not the only hot issue on the campuses and in the streets in the early 1960s, the beginning of a decade of violence and upheaval, important tests of American leadership, the rapidly accelerating war in Southeast Asia, and a sea change in cultural styles, political expressions, and sexual attitudes. It was also the beginning of a period of political assassinations of our leaders, first the killing of President John F. Kennedy in Dallas, and, several years later, the murders of Martin Luther King Jr. and the president's brother, Robert F. Kennedy.

Like most Americans, I have distinct memories of where I was when each of those horrendous events occurred. The first took place when I was in The Quill, the campus bookshop. Someone entered the store on Northampton's Green Street and shouted "The president's been shot." With others I ran out of the place to join throngs of people leaning on cars parked along the street with their doors open and the radios blaring the news from Dallas.

Hedy and I spent the next few days glued to television sets, first watching the replays of the shooting and the inauguration of Lyndon Johnson aboard Air Force One, then the capture of the prime suspect in the crime, Lee Harvey Oswald, his killing by Jack Ruby, and the funeral with its indelible images of John Jr. saluting, the devastated Jacqueline Kennedy and JFK's brothers, and the procession of notables walking behind them, including nineteen heads of state and other dignitaries. Most memorable to me were four figures: Eamon de Valera, the President of Ireland; Golda Meir, then Foreign Minister of Israel; the diminutive Emperor of Ethiopia Haile Selassie; and the towering President of France, Charles de Gaulle.

When I first heard of the murder of Dr. King, on April 4, 1968, I was in my office, going over notes for my course on American minorities. Unlike my colleagues who immediately passed the word that they were cancelling their classes, I kept my group together and held a lengthy discussion on the event that had just occurred in Memphis and what might happen next. One student asked me who I thought would take over the leadership of the movement for integration. "Would it be Ralph Abernathy or Fred Shuttlesworth or Joseph Lowery?" I said that I felt it was too early to say which of King's lieutenants would take his place heading the Southern Christian Leadership Council but would bet that the one person who could be counted on to rally Americans to the cause MLK lived and died for would be Bobby Kennedy. Kennedy, former Attorney General, then a senator from New York who had become a civil rights advocate both in this country and around the world, was to suffer King's fate—and that of his brother—only two months later, in the early hours of June 6, 1968.

The night of his assassination, I had spent the evening with the city planner and public administrator Edward Logue in the study of the home of the Smith College president at 6 Paradise Road in Northampton where there was a special dinner honoring him, the next day's commencement speaker, and several honorary degree candidates. I remember him sheepishly asking our host, President Mendenhall, if there was a place to which he might sneak away after dinner to watch the returns of primaries in which RFK was competing with Eugene McCarthy. The president suggested he go upstairs to his private den. Logue invited me to join him and together we watched the early reports of what was happening in South Dakota and California then staying on into the wee hours of the next morning when we watched the victorious candidate move through the kitchen of the Ambassador Hotel in Los Angeles where he was shot and killed by Sirhan Sirhan.

Among my files I found many clippings of those three murders, that of Medgar Evers, and several others, all carefully saved in a single folder. I also came upon many reminders of campaigns against the war in Vietnam, including pictures of several marches through local streets which I had helped to organize.

Although never as active as many other academics, I was involved—as were many people in Northampton and Amherst and what we still call the hilltowns—in the grassroots antiwar movement. While we were concerned about the nuclear weapons ninety miles off America's shores and grateful for the fact that the Russians backed down and withdrew their missiles from Cuba, there was a gnawing sense of an even greater threat of war in places much farther away as our leaders seemed to buy into the idea of stemming the tide of communism in divided Vietnam.

Ironically, the demonstrations against the buildup of American forces in the former Indochina began just as my students and I were finishing a study on "Citizens' Opinions on Civil Defense," examining the whole idea of building fallout shelters and the debates not only about their probable effectiveness in protecting people from radiation in case of a Soviet nuclear attack on this country, but also about whether building shelters or being willing to do so made our resolve to wage war more credible. One paper summarizing the research was published in 1963 in a special issue of the journal *Social Problems* titled "The Public and the Threat of War," which Jerome Laulicht and I had been asked to edit. Another report on our study would appear in *The Committee of Correspondence Newsletter* at the urging the sociologist David Riesman.

Along with others in Northampton, Hedy and I participated in a number of peace vigils where we met many remarkable people from all walks of life whose strength of commitment became the backbone of the antiwar movement. Among the most impressive of the true stalwarts was Frances Crowe, a remarkable local pacifist and adviser to generations of petitioners for conscientious objector status. (Frances, now in her mid-nineties, is still pressing her peace agenda, even when it means going to jail—which she has done on numerous occasions.)

Three other personal involvements in the antiwar movement took place a bit later in the 1960s. The first occurred when Richard Unsworth, a Protestant minister and member of Smith's Department of Religion, was the college chaplain. Dick and I organized a protest march against the war from the fairgrounds near the outskirts of Northampton through center of the city. We were able to mobilize hundreds of marchers from all around the Pioneer Valley—and, as it turned out, an equal number of opponents, many shouting slogans and carrying signs reading "COMMIE LOVERS" and the like. Their ire was directed particularly at several of the men in our group who were recent returnees from Vietnam and wore their military uniforms as they marched with us.

Riot police had been brought into town and kept in the old Northampton fire station (now Woodstar Café), but they never had to go into the streets. At the end of our planned march, worried that a riot might break out, we decided to lead our troops onto the sanctuary of the Smith campus. Unexpectedly, many of the counter-demonstrators followed. There was a very tense denouement, a shouting and pushing match between some members of the Students for a Democratic Society (SDS) and a young man named, Kenny Brandt, the leader of the anti-antiwar protesters, followed by some skillful mediation by Dick Unsworth and a colleague of mine in the sociology department, Mickey Glazer. They succeeded in getting the two sides to cool it and agree to send their respective representatives to local churches to argue the pros and cons of the war. It proved to be quite a positive ending to what could well have become a very ugly scene.

Early in June of 1967 a different form of protest against the war was mounted in response to the knowledge that Nicholas Katzenbach was coming to Smith to deliver the commencement address. The senior class had invited him the year before because of his critical involvement in quelling the protests of segregationists resisting the admission of the African American air force veteran James Meredith to the University of Mississippi when Katzenbach was Lyndon Johnson's attorney general. Yet, by the time of the country's mobilization of troops and his visit to the campus, Katzenbach had changed jobs and was now Undersecretary of State and a key spokesperson for the government's foreign policy, including in Southeast Asia.

Despite the fact that many of us saw him as a genuine hero in the civil rights struggle, we felt he was fair game because of his new position. I agreed to draft a statement which started out, "To the President of the United States and the members of Congress: Owing to the presence of the Under Secretary of State, Nicholas Katzenbach, we, all members of the Smith College, faculty wish to convey to him and to you our profound opposition to the war in Indochina." It continued with a brief explanation of why we were speaking out and trying to persuade the Johnson administration to change course.

In a very short time over 150 colleagues (close to two-thirds of the faculty) signed the open letter. Then my good friend Elliot Offner, sculptor, artist and printer, designed and published a simple broadside containing the statement and all the faculty signatures. Despite considerable objection and some harassment by the local authorities when we tried to distribute the statement around town, we did manage to get copies into almost every commencement program and into the hands of thousands of attendees.

I know exactly when this was: one of those unforgettable dates like November 11, 1918, December 7, 1941, June 6, 1944 (D-Day), April 12, 1945 (the day Franklin Delano Roosevelt died), November 22, 1963, and a half-century later, September 11, 2001. It was June 4, 1967.

At my table at a pre-commencement luncheon at the president's house, I was seated between Mary Elizabeth Switzer, the head of the Vocational Rehabilitation Agency in Washington and one of those to be given an honorary degree, and Undersecretary Katzenbach. Believing he should know what was going on, I gave him a copy of our statement. He read it carefully, mused a bit, and then smiled and said that our eighteenth-century-looking document seemed a bit more reasoned and controlled sort of protest than what he had faced at Ole Miss—an understatement to be sure! I then asked him to tell me about that momentous confrontation.

During our conversation he was interrupted by one of his security people several times and, after each tug on his sleeve, he would leave the table for a few minutes then return, each time looking more upset. Note the date I just mentioned. I later learned that he was being called about the outbreak of war in Israel.

At the end our brief encounter over salmon and salad and before I went back out to protest, I said that we had never been able to get anyone from the administration to sit down with us and discuss the war and its rationale. To my surprise, especially with all that was then on his mind, Katzenbach said he would do so after the commencement ceremony. And he was good to his word. He spoke in a campus auditorium and took questions, most of them unsurprisingly quite hostile. Though I'm sure he was disappointed that he didn't change many minds, I was pleased. At least he was willing to take on the criticisms of me and my colleagues and debate with us.

The third war protest-related episode occurred a bit later in the 1960s, when I was the vice president and program chair of the Eastern Sociological Society. We were meeting in New York City. It turned out to be the weekend of a huge peace march in the city in which Martin Luther King Jr. was one of the key figures. A number of our members wanted to participate—as did I.

We added a general session to the first day's program and spent time debating not only about the war but also about whether we, as a nonprofit academic society, could speak with a corporate voice on a political issue. A compromise was reached. It was based on a ploy I had learned from my experience organizing the Katzenbach protest at Smith. If we began our statement "We, members of the ESS,..." instead of "The Eastern Sociological Society...," we would be better able to persuade many on the fence to join us. We also managed to change the program to try to accommodate those who wanted to march, though not without a bitter struggle, including a threat from the very conservative incoming president who said he would resign if we continued to politicize the meeting and the organization. In the end a number of us did march. And, as in the case at Smith, we did manage to send our message to Washington with many signatures.

As I look back, I realize that much of my teaching in those early years at Smith was related to the two matters that preoccupied so many of us during the turbulent 1960s: the struggle for civil rights and the war in Vietnam. But there were other subjects, too.

Shortly after I arrived at the college in 1960 I was asked to develop and then direct a new social science research center. It still exists and is now called the Jahnige Social Science Research Center, in memory of my successor as director, political scientist Tom Jahnige, who died of leukemia not many years after he assumed the position.

During the time I ran the center I also offered a course, "Methods of Social Research," in which I tried to interest the students in ways they might learn to become researchers by getting their hands dirty from the start, while focusing on a single agreed-upon topic. Together the students and I would plan and carry out a study on a particular subject often combining techniques of observation, interviewing, and survey research. Over time we studied a host of issues ranging from shelter building and the threat of war, to the effect of the social climate of colleges on the political attitudes of students, to themes in teaching about race relations.[6]

The course was mainly for sociology majors but some students in the other social sciences did enroll. In many ways the early design and syllabus were variations on a team-taught core course that had been required of all social science graduate students at Cornell. But there was one major difference. While the Cornell course, like mine, required lab sessions, each was on a different subject, whereas my whole course was designed so students could learn to work both independently and together on a single, manageable and socially relevant project from start to finish, first learning, then applying the techniques appropriate to the questions they sought to answer while concentrating their background reading on the subject of the project instead of on the methodology textbooks. Although there was much discussion of epistemological questions, sociological theory, research techniques (participant observation, focused interviews, surveys and others) and the standard issues of reliability and validity, it was the problem itself on which we focused.

Thinking about it more than fifty years later, I still recall that teaching the course was exhausting and time-consuming, especially with no lab assistants, but it was exhilarating for me and rewarding for most of

---

[6]Several publications resulted: "The Public and the Threat of War," *Social Problems*, 11, 1963, 62–77; "The Myth of Unanimity," *Sociology of Education*, 1963, 129–148; and a book, *The Subject is Race; Traditional Ideologies and the Teaching of Race Relations* (New York: Oxford University Press, 1968).

the students—and for many of our subjects, some of whom I came to call our "clients." On three occasions we did *pro bono* contract research for local groups: once for the college on the issue of coeducation, and two for outside, non-profit groups, the Northampton Public Schools and the United Way.

Each fall I would start the first semester by suggesting three or four topics I thought the students might study. A caveat: I proposed only those that were of interest to me. Each subject was presented and the students in the class were then asked to decide which they would like to tackle. We would then focus all our attention on that subject.

Over the next fifteen years, members of succeeding classes would conduct research on campus, in town, in the wider area, and once all across the nation on a number of disparate critical local or national issues reflected in such titles as "The Social Attitudes and Political Convictions of University Students," "Local Agencies and Their Funding" and "Teaching Race Relations in Colleges and Universities in the United States." (The last-named became the triggering subject of the first of three books of mine published by the Oxford University Press. It came out in 1968 under the title *The Subject is Race: Traditional Ideologies and the Teaching of Race Relations*.) Some topics were related to extant political debates, including the study of shelter-builders I mentioned earlier.

Here is how that project developed:

> It was 1962, the Cold War was getting hotter, and a big campaign is being waged to get private citizens to build bomb shelters. The Kennedy administration was urging people to do this; the Rockefeller administration in New York State was even more emphatic. And these were the liberals! I thought it would be interesting to do some preliminary reconnaissance in the immediate area around Northampton, Massachusetts, a city that was said to be on the periphery of a primary-target area, the Westover Strategic Air Command (SAC) base in nearby Chicopee, where, according to government literature, a shelter could protect you from a direct hit by a ten-megaton-bomb. Halfway into our research we learned that it was all very academic in more ways than one: our planes were already carrying twenty-five megaton bombs and, presumably, Russian planes had similar payloads, if not even bigger ones. Still, we went ahead with the study.

Early on, the students and I quickly learned that only a handful of people in the area had built shelters. Bowed but not broken, we devised a study that would compare hypothetical shelter-builders with refuseniks. All interviews and questionnaires began with the query "If the government supplied each family with sufficient funds to build a shelter..." This was to avoid the response "I might but I could never afford to build one."

We then decided to write to a large random sample of all household heads listed in the Northampton city directory, not only to ask whether or not they would build a shelter but also to inquire about their general attitudes about the threat of nuclear war. In the course of planning the study, I asked the student researchers to consider whether people were building shelters because there was plenty of information available in the post offices and libraries urging them to do it and telling them how, or whether they thought that only those already inclined to build would seek out information. It generated a useful classroom discussion about dependent and independent variables.

As we developed a questionnaire, we put in a number of questions relating to personal information: age, gender, social class (through an index based on income, occupation, residence and self-designation), education, military experience, political affiliation and political beliefs, and religion and religiosity. Nearly finished with the development of the survey instrument, I asked the group assembled as a team if they thought that those who said they would build a shelter if the money were provided would be more or less religious than non-builders. Immediately, one young woman said, "More religious, because religious people tend to accept the dictates of authoritarian bodies. They accept the directives of the Church; they will accept those of the Government."

"Nonsense," one of the young men in the class blurted out. "Religious people are fatalistic. Shelters won't help them."

"Ah," said a Smith senior sitting next to him, with a twinkle in her eye she said he should remember that "God helps those who help themselves."

We found that those who scored high on religiosity, in fact declared themselves much more willing to build than the others. In a great example of multivariate analysis, we also learned that a high level of religiosity was related in significant ways not just to religious affiliation, but also to social class, level of education and military experience as well. We were beginning to put together a portrait of the sort of person most likely to be a shelter builder: a working class Catholic combat veteran.

The old admonition among sociologists about the dangers of the single-case analysis ("Women are crazy, you should meet my wife!") was never truer than in our study. The one person who showed up in the sample who had actually built a shelter did not fit the builder-profile. He was an upper-middle-class Protestant professional. A graduate of an ivy-league college who did not seem to be very religious, he had been in the service with an ROTC commission but had never seen combat. It was a great lesson for the class and especially for the student who said, "Why are we doing all this? Why don't we just interview the guy who built the shelter?"

In 2001 I agreed to review a new book, *One Nation Underground*, by Kenneth Rose (no relation). It was an interesting volume and one that took me back to what we at Smith had been doing decades before. As I read Rose's analysis of the last time we'd had a great national debate on weapons of mass destruction and what to do to protect ourselves, I kept wondering if the author had ever seen the published report on our research. I found the answer in his last chapter. He noted that ours was the first systematic study on the building of fallout shelters in the United States, and that Northampton's story and what we learned from it turned out to be the norm.[7]

In many ways, "Methods of Social Research" was quite innovative. But what about my more conventional teaching?

When I first came to Smith College in 1960. I participated in a team-taught variation on the standard introduction to sociology and anthropology I had offered on my own taught at Goucher; a course called "The City," on urban sociology; another on "The Origins of Scientific Sociology," and a new one I labeled "Ethnic Minorities in America." That new course would be the basis of much of what I would teach for the rest of my days at Smith and on many other campuses in this country and abroad over the next fifty years.

---

[7]My review, "A House for Dr. Strangelove," appeared in the *Christian Science Monitor*, August 2, 2001.

As I organized my initial syllabus for "Minorities," I looked for a small book that might serve as a framework for discussion. I wanted to find something that was not a standard formulaic text but more a series of essays on such subjects as prejudice, discrimination, and the nature of minority status that would raise the critical issues in a more literary and compelling manner than most introductions then extant.

At the time, the man who had brought me to Smith, Charles Page, was editor of the *American Sociological Review*, then based at the College. He was also the editor of a series of excellent books of one hundred pages or so on various aspects of sociology published by Doubleday and Sons.

I asked Page why there wasn't a book on intergroup relations in his series. Misunderstanding my question and thinking I was offering to submit a proposal for a volume on the subject, he told me that we were on the same wavelength, and that he'd been thinking of asking me to consider writing one.

While I was clearly delighted that Page would deem me qualified to take on such a project, my first thought was that I shouldn't even consider it. At the time, I had all I could do to keep my head above water and my health intact. In June 1958, on top of my new responsibilities at the college, Hedy and I had taken over the operation of Camp Chateaugay, the sole source of income for my parents. While that was a labor of love—and, I suppose, duty—like every newly-minted Ph.D. I knew, I was also hoping to find some time to start turning my doctoral dissertation into a book.

Still, the challenge Charles Page put before me was too enticing to pass up. Within a few months of his expression of interest, during which Random House had bought the series and Page had become the consulting editor for that larger company, I submitted a proposal to him with a copy to the editor-in-chief, Charles D. Lieber. A few weeks later, the two of them sent me a joint letter accepting my proposal. After a bit of negotiating about the terms of the contract, I signed on. It was the beginning of a wonderful relationship. But it was not without further contretemps.

After two years of writing and rewriting, I sent the manuscript of what I wanted to call *They and We* (an inversion of the title of the Kipling poem, "We and They") off to Charles Page, now at Princeton, and eagerly awaited his enthusiastic kudos for a job well done. Two weeks later I received a letter from him. Tearing it open, I stopped dead in my tracks when I read this terse sentence: "I really like everything about your manuscript except for some problems with the tone, the style and some of the content."

I was devastated. But after a hiatus of several months, I dragged myself back to the old Royal typewriter and restructured and rewrote nearly the entire thing, while being sure to avoid such openers as the one I used at the beginning of a chapter on protest which, in the draft, had read "Two four six eight, we don't want to integrate," and was followed by a line about the "drum-beat cadence of hate." (Today I think I should have fought to keep such telegraphic outbursts in the text.)

The second version was far more acceptable and, I admit, far better organized and better written, too. The book came out in 1964.

By its third edition, I was far surer of my own writing and more certain how I wanted the book to read and nobody stopped me. For example, in the first section of a chapter titled "Patterns of Discrimination," which I called "Insult and Injury," now began with these lines:

"Eenie, meenie, miney, mo.
Catch a nigger by the toe."

Not a tiger, a "nigger." Until very recently, the bit of doggerel chanted by children throughout the English-speaking Western world contained that explicit racial epithet. It may have been an unintended indiscretion but it was clearly an insult.

Insults are but one in a range of actions we call discriminatory. In this chapter various expressions of behavior that fall under the rubric of *discrimination,* the singling out of people for separate and unequal treatment, are examined. The treatment itself is often institutionalized, an accepted part of every day life. Examples include pejorative language, the denial of the franchise, selective hiring practices, restrictive neighborhoods, and exclusive social clubs and other forms of segregation. It may involve organized forms of intimidation and physical abuse as well.

Patterns of discrimination may be *de jure*, grounded in law, or *de facto*, part of a tradition or custom. Moreover...those who discriminate may do so because they believe they are superior to others or simply because they think, "that's the way it is." Too many acceptors of the status quo are reluctant to change what, to them, are economically, psychologically, and socially acceptable or necessary arrangements. It is not surprising to find that many Americans are fair-weather liberals who more often do what is "expected" than what is "right."[8]

My candid statement did raise some hackles, though not from where I might have expected trouble to come. Shortly after the fifth edition of *They and We* came out in 1997, the editor of the student newspaper at Smith, the *Sophian*, received a letter from a professor at a southern university warning that there was a rabid racist on the faculty (namely yours truly) who used such proscribed words as "nigger" in his writing. He mentioned other politically incorrect transgressions, charges that were as misguided as his assumption about my intention in using the derogatory "n" word. In my rebuttal to a portion of his attack published in the paper, I said that I wondered if he'd ever actually read what I had written. I was not the only one to say so.

It turned out that the editor had asked a random group of students who were then studying with me and an African American faculty member who had once been my student to weigh in about the controversy. All said that my detractor was way, way off base. The faculty member said, "How do we deal with such issues as racial epithets if we don't address them."

I later learned that my accuser was a very angry black professor of education who had frequently attacked white professors for deigning to write about *his* experiences. It was a subject that I had tried to address in a public lecture[9] and in subsequent publications in the late 1970s.

---

[8]See *They and We*, 3rd ed. (New York: Random House, 1974). The same chapter opener is to be found in the four subsequent editions of the book, which was originally published in 1964.

[9]See *Nobody Knows the Troubles I've Seen: Some Reflections on the Insider-Outsider Debate* (Northampton: Smith College, 1978)

Within several years, Charles Page and Charles Lieber, each of whom had decided not only that I had learned some lessons about writing but also might not be a bad critic myself, invited me to join them as a second consulting editor in sociology at Random House, where, in addition to my general responsibilities, I would focus my attention on social issues and social problems and especially race and ethnic relations. To this end I read many proposals, did some recruiting of manuscripts, and edited a number of books, most, but not all, on those subjects and a few on the social sciences more generally. These included Inge Bell's *CORE and the Strategy of Non-Violence* (1968), Lewis M. Killian's *The Impossible Revolution? Black Power and the American Dream* (1968), William Moore's *The Vertical Ghetto: Everyday Life in an Urban Project* (1969), Richard Schermerhorn's *Comparative Ethnic Relations: A Framework for Theory and Research* (1979), Minako Kurokawa's, *Minority Responses* (1981), and nearly twenty others. At the same time I was developing a series called "Ethnic Groups in Comparative Perspective." Among the books we published under the Random House imprint were volumes on American Jews, Chinese Americans, Italian Americans, Japanese Americans, Mexican Americans, and white southerners (as an ethnic group and a quasi-minority), as well as a special volume on minorities in the United Kingdom. All were written and most were completed in the late 1960s and all were published between 1970 and 1975.

I had persuaded a young sociologist, William Julius Wilson, to prepare the textbook for the series on the subject of African Americans. When it came in, it turned out to be more a treatise on race and social class than an introductory overview of the African-American experience. The Random House editors felt it did not fit with the others, mainly because it didn't follow the rough guideline for content I had mapped out. I agreed but then said that it was by far the best book I'd commissioned and urged that it be done as a separate publication. The inside editor hemmed and hawed. In the end, the book, called *The Declining Significance of Race*, was published in 1978 by the press of the University of Chicago, the institution to which Bill Wilson would move after several years at the nearby University of Massachusetts (where we had first met and worked together). He later became a University Professor at Harvard and author of several more major works, including *The Truly Disadvantaged* (1987), *When Work Disappears* (1996), and *More Than Just Race* (2009).

Each of the volumes in the ethnic-group series that Random House did publish began with a two-part foreword. The second part was always a specific commentary on the particular volume but the first part was the same for all books in the series.[10] In a few words I tried to set the stage for what the readers might expect.

> Nation of nations or Herrenvolk democracy? Melting pot or seething caldron? How does one describe the ethnic character of the United States?
>
> The conventional wisdom, reflected in traditional texts on American history and society, tells of the odyssey of one group of newcomers after another who came to these shores, some of their own free will and others in the chains of bondage, some to escape religious persecution, others fleeing from political oppression, and many seeking their fortunes. "Rich and poor," goes the story, "mighty and meek, white and black, Jew and Gentile, Protestant and Catholic, Irishman and Italian and Pole, a motley array who, together, make up the Great American Nation."
>
> Although many a school child can recite the litany, even they know that it has a rather hollow ring. For most people there are at least three kinds of Americans: whatever one happens to be, the members of the dominant group (viewed differently depending where one stands in the status hierarchy), and everybody else. And if one happens to see oneself as a member of the dominant group, the number of alternatives may be reduced to two: they and we.
>
> For a variety of reasons, writers of textbooks and teachers of American history have tended to overlook or underplay this essential fact of American life. While acknowledging the pluralistic character of the social structure and celebrating the extent to which "our differences make us strong," they rarely convey the true meaning of membership in an ethnic group. And none know this better than those whose life experiences belied the notion of tolerance for all. Recently, a common plea has arisen from various quarters: "Give us equal time."

---

[10] *Ethnic Groups in Comparative Perspective* (New York: Random House, 1970–1975).

In response to such demands there have been attempts to alter the rather lop-sided image of American history and of the American people. Historians and social scientists have begun to respond to the call for a more accurate and meaningful view of race and ethnicity in America. Many have sought to "redress the balance," as they say, by upgrading the status of one group or another and rewriting their history to parallel that of the dominant group. One finds new volumes that appear to make the same strategic errors as those they wish to complement, i.e. placing emphasis on great events and prominent figures while avoiding in-depth descriptions of patterns of social organization, cultural traditions, and everyday activities.

Fortunately, there have been some other approaches tried recently, most notably studies seeking to reassess the entire ethnic experience not by playing the mirroring game (we have a hero, you have a hero; we have a holiday, you have a holiday; everybody has...) but by getting to the core of the social and economic and political realities of existence for the various people who came and stayed. The work of the latter scholars is far more important and, by its very nature, far more difficult. It involves new ways of looking, new perspectives. It encourages the examination of history and biography, of episode and event as before. But it also requires careful study of culture and community and character, the examination of everyday life.

Those who have and use such an imagination—C. Wright Mills called it "the sociological imagination"—must possess a willingness to challenge the old homilies, to get away from stereotypes and deal with real people, and to relate that which is revealed with both detachment and compassion.

For the student to truly understand the nature of group life in the United States and the relevance of race, religion, and nationality as meaningful social categories and critical social variables, he should receive two kinds of messages: those that help him to know, and others that help him to understand. This means that, if truly successful, writers of articles and books on the Irish in America, or the Jews, or the Black experience should be able to evoke in their readers some sense of empathy, some visceral response to what it means to read a sign IRISH NEED NOT APPLY, or to hear the echo of "Sheeny, Sheeny, Sheeny" ricochet off the walls between two old-law tenements, or to know what it is to be called "boy" by some and "brother" by others.

For more than fifteen years Random House was my part-time employer as well as my publisher. (At professional meetings someone would invariably say to me, "I know of you, you're with Random House.")

In the late 1960s I published two anthologies with them. The first, *The Study of Society: An Integrated Anthology*, was widely adopted in sociology courses around the world. (Random House published the first edition in 1967 and three more editions, the last in 1977.) The second book was *The Ghetto and Beyond: Essays on Jewish Life in America* (Random House, 1969). At the end of my introductory essay in that book, I made some predictions about American Jews, especially in terms of their attitudes toward others, toward the war in Vietnam, and to what had just been going on in the Middle East.

> American Jews, delighted at Israel's victory in the Six-Day War have evinced much less enthusiasm for their own country's protracted conflict in Southeast Asia and its stalemated War Against Poverty at home. Other groups in America share this frustration. In the search for scapegoats that may ensue, Jews may find themselves most vulnerable to attacks from Right, Left, and below. By seeking reform and compromise on most issues instead of radical change, they may increasingly come to appear too white for the black militants, too red for the white conservatives, and too yellow for their own children. Jews are not unaware of such possibilities. They know that latent anti-Semitism can be revived in America, as it has been in the past. But they do not seem worried. They feel they can ride out the coming storms. Like their forebears who came to settle on the Lower East Side, most Jews still believe in America and its people.
>
> As for their dissident children, they feel (rightly or wrongly) that they have heard it all before. New Left protest, at least when voiced by Jewish youth, sounds strikingly familiar. Irving Howe sums up the sentiment in one succinct sentence when writing about dissent in the 1930s. "You might be shouting at the top of your lungs against reformism or Stalin's betrayal, but for the middle-aged garment worker strolling along Southern Boulevard, you were just a bright and cocky Jewish boy, a talkative little pisher."
>
> The same is being said today—though the cause, the occupation of the listeners and the boulevard area different. Today's young Jewish

activists will grow up, too. When they do, they will probably find themselves radical in thought, reformist in action, and bourgeois in manner—and still Jewish. Just like the rest.[11]

Several other books followed almost immediately, including *Seeing Ourselves*, published by the Random House partner, Alfred A. Knopf (1972; second edition, 1975).

During those crazy days of writing and editing my own books, editing those of others, running the camp and, with my wife, getting used to parenting our daughter, Lies, born in Baltimore in 1960, and son, Dan, born in Northampton in 1962—I continued teaching and started a course of involvement in international education. I also began the almost routine overseas travel that continues to this day.

My segue into working closely with those from other countries and then spending a good deal of time overseas may be said to have begun in the 1961–62 academic year when I was invited to serve as a member of a committee to consider the establishment of a small graduate program for non-American "Americanists." Its chair was Daniel Aaron, a professor of English and one of the leading figures in the slowly growing new field of American Studies, something he would later describe as being promoted for both intellectual and political objectives. The first goal, he said, was to look at this society by examining the interplay of literature and history, a subject in which Dan Aaron, who later became the founding editor of the still growing *Library of American Literature*, had pioneered. The second goal was clearly related to Cold War concerns contributing to a campaign to counter to what were seen as distortions by America's adversaries through exposure to the true nature of our society and culture.

While in sympathy with the first objective and very skeptical of the second, worrying that it smacked too much of propaganda, I was still intrigued by the idea of looking at American society and culture from an interdisciplinary perspective, and even more by the idea of bringing foreign graduate students to study at Smith.

---

[11]See the introduction to *The Ghetto and Beyond: Essays on Jewish Life in America* (New York: Random House, 1969), 17.

The college already had a very long tradition of sending a number of its students abroad in their third year. This went back to the heady days when the Scots-born educator, William Allan Neilson, served as Smith College's third president from 1917 to 1939, during which time he initiated many programs to further an understanding of others. Neilson was also a forceful progressive voice and an active leader not only in the academic world but also beyond its ivied walls. To cite two examples: Neilson joined the board of the National Association for the Advancement of Colored People (NAACP) in the early 1930s and then became the founding chair of the Committee of 100, which, in 1943 would establish the NAACP's Legal and Educational Defense Fund. He was also deeply concerned about the plight of refugees from Nazi-dominated Europe and became one of the founders of the Emergency Rescue Committee, an organization known today as the International Rescue Committee.

Alongside a small undergraduate concentration, our proposal for an American Studies Diploma Program won the support of the faculty and the president, Thomas C. Mendenhall. By the next year, 1962–63, we welcomed our first four diploma candidates. Those pioneers came from Austria, France, Italy, and the United Kingdom.

I stayed on the committee for several years and, then, after co-leading a rather difficult campaign in the late 1960s to establish a Department of Afro-American Studies which finally received the endorsement of the faculty and administration, I agreed to be seconded to help organize, develop the curriculum and teach in the new Afro-Am department on a part-time basis. At the time I was also wrapping up some research in Puerto Rico that I had begun six or seven years earlier.

Stretched very thin for almost a decade, I had little to do with the Diploma Program, which in those days was rather loosely organized with rotating chairpersons running it. Then, sometime in the early 1970s, I was asked to join history professor Allen Weinstein for a three-year stint as co-director. I agreed and after Allen left the college for Washington, D.C. (and a career that would culminate with his appointment as the archivist of the United States), I was asked to stay on as director, a post I would hold for more than thirty years, ending only with my retirement in 2003.

In May of 2012 the fiftieth anniversary of the program was celebrated with a reunion in Northampton. Fifty of our 450 graduates came back to the college to celebrate "The First Fifty Years of Smith's Foreign Legion." Those returning—some from as far away as China, Japan, Poland, Iran and Israel—represented a true cross-section of what I can proudly say are among Smith's most loyal and illustrious alumnae and alumni (the program has been coeducational almost since its inception), including three ambassadors (from Austria, Finland, and Switzerland), leading journalists, artists, writers, filmmakers, businesspeople and a number of professors. On the roster of returning alumnae were two of the original four Diplomats: Mariarosa Pipperelli from Italy, who still lives in Florence, and Margaret Rawson, who came to us from the University of Manchester in the United Kingdom and is now a neighbor in Massachusetts.

When I returned to work with American Studies, in addition to my role as director of the graduate program, every spring I led the second part of a required yearlong seminar for diploma candidates. In the first semester the emphasis was usually focused on the ideas and institutions of American society from the time of the founding of the nation to the late nineteenth century. Most often it was led by a professor of literature or history. The second semester, my term, addressed the dramatic changes taking place in our rapidly industrializing society and, especially, the issues of immigration, race and social class.

Early in the decade my former professor, Ed Suchman, invited me to come to Puerto Rico where he was spending time helping the Department of Health to establish a social science bureau similar to the one he then headed in New York City. He said I might work with him on several projects relating to health and welfare. I leapt at the opportunity and the chance to be a part-time consultant—and to go overseas. While my jobs were challenging, the most memorable part of the experience was the unexpected meeting with, then having as an assistant, one of the most notorious men in America: Nathan Leopold. Later I would write about my encounter with the man, who with his best friend, murdered a young boy "just for the thrill of it" as Simon Baatz titled his excellent

2008 book on the subject. My report was far more personal. Here is a small part of it.

When I was a boy, if someone said "Crime of the Century," three words, run together as one, would pop into almost everyone's head: "LeopoldandLoeb." Trial of the Century? "LeopoldandLoeb." Millionaire Murderers? "LeopoldandLoeb."

For me, Leopold-and-Loeb meant something more. Although their senseless act of cold-blooded murder had occurred in 1924, nine years before I was born, the Crime of the Century had a very personal meaning. Their victim, Bobby Franks, was, I was told, a distant cousin of my father. That revelation was both a source of deep-seated loathing and insatiable curiosity. As I grew up, I became fascinated by the story of Leopold and Loeb.

In time, I read a good deal about how the two very rich geniuses, Nathan Leopold and Richard Loeb, students of law and philosophy, especially the philosophy of Nietzsche, thinking they were supermen, planned "a perfect crime," then actually carried out their perverse scheme. I read about how, failing to find their targeted victim, they selected another young boy they knew; how they bludgeoned him to death and then dumped his body in a swampy area some distance from the Chicago neighborhood where they lived; how they were quickly discovered when the police got the names of the manufacturer of Leopold's glasses, accidentally dropped at the place where they disposed of the body; and how the great lawyer, Clarence Darrow came to defend them, convincing the jury to give the self-confessed murderers "life plus ninety-nine years" rather than death sentences.

I read Darrow's arguments in a collection of his most famous cases, *Attorney for the Damned*, edited by Arthur Weinberg. I read Meyer Levin's *Compulsion* and Levin's "brief" that later appeared in the *Saturday Evening Post* called "Why Leopold Should Be Freed." Still later I read two autobiographical works written by and presented to me by their author, Nathan Leopold himself.

Through a quick of fate, he and I met in the early 1960s. At the time he was only partially free. He lived and worked in Puerto Rico, where he had been paroled after spending more than thirty-six years in prison. (Loeb, held in another penal institution had died in the 1930s, stabbed to death in a prison shower room.) Leopold had obtained a master's degree in social work and was employed in the Department of Health in San Juan. Needless to say, our first meeting was very awkward, at least for me.

On my first day, I breezed into the office, said hello to my friend, former professor from Cornell and now boss, Ed Suchman, and was asked if I'd like to meet the staff. I said I'd like that very much. We walked down the hall, opened the door and there he was, sitting right in front of me. I had no idea he had been paroled, that he was in Puerto Rico, or that he worked for the Commonwealth. But I recognized him immediately. (Meyer Levin's article had been accompanied by a large picture of him—and he looked just the same: a sixty-ish year-old, average-size man without any distinctive features save for piercing eyes behind thick glasses.) My heart skipped a beat and I moved forward, hearing Suchman say, "Peter, this is Nate Leopold."

Hesitantly (I now admit) I reached out to accept his proffered hand. (Reminiscing about this strange encounter as I write, I think I was about as enthusiastic as Itzak Rabin was in shaking hands with Arafat—and for a not-too-different reason. It was stained with blood. The blood of my people!).

"Pleased to meet you," the monster said.

We moved on through the office. I looked back over my shoulder a few times. "It really is him," I kept telling myself.

Two days later, after a series of meetings at the University of Puerto Rico, I returned to the office and learned that I have been assigned an assistant. It was to be Leopold....[12]

I did work with Leopold—actually he worked for me—on several projects over several years. He was helpful and efficient and very hardworking. But I could never forget who he was or what he and Loeb had done. The last time I saw him I had lunch with him and his wife in their apartment in Santurce. I described that scene in my essay, "Leopold and Me," too.

...I hadn't been to his apartment before. I was struck by two photographs, each next to a vase with a fresh flower. I can still see them. The first was on the coffee table in the living room. It was unmistakable who it was. I picked it up and, before I could say anything, Leopold said, "Clarence Darrow, the man who saved my life."

The second picture was in the master bedroom through which I had to pass to go to the bathroom. It was on a dresser. I noticed it as I

[12]"Leopold and Me," *Congress Monthly*, November-December, 1998, and reprinted in *Guest Appearances and Other Travels in Time and Space* (Athens, Ohio: Swallow Press, 2003), 189–91.

walked back through the room. It was a blown up snapshot of a well-dressed young man of, say, nineteen or twenty. At first I thought it was Leopold himself but, on closer inspection, I realized it was somebody else. I was pretty sure I knew whom it was....Looking into the room, as I squinted at the picture, Nathan confirmed it.

"Dickie Loeb," he said, "was the guy who ruined my life." He paused then added "Still, I gotta tell you something. You know what, he was really a swell guy, the best friend I ever had."

I never saw Leopold again.[13]

While Puerto Rico was in some ways a foreign place, my main preoccupation when I was in the commonwealth turned out to be interviewing people from the mainland who were residing and working there. In the mid-1960s I had my first experience living for an extended period in a truly different country myself. A year in the United Kingdom would prove to be life-changing, the first of a number of such extended overseas stays.

As with so much else in my career, a chance encounter played a key role in how I joined the ranks of the mobile dons as one of those Arthur Koestler "call girls." Here is how I explained the reference and my "Year in the Midlands," in a preface to an essay by the same name.

Several years ago I found a copy of Arthur Koestler's book, *The Call Girls*, on the remainder table of a local bookshop. Curious about why he would write about this subject, I started reading it as soon as I got home. It wasn't what I expected, but it had an odd effect on me.

As I turned the pages, I was immediately transported back to the early days of my initiation into the rites, rituals and free rides of academics. You see Koestler's call girls were folks like me. Supported by their institutions or by grants, they would go to conferences both in nearby places and those quite far: Gstaad, Copenhagen, Honolulu, Rio. There they would spend three days complaining about how silly it was to spend so much money to hear people they knew say things they'd already heard over and over at various other places. Then, on the fourth day, they would decide where to meet next year.

But of course academic meetings have other purposes. They serve as job markets and opportunities to meet fellow professors from other places, too. In fact, I shouldn't bad-mouth the enterprise because my

---

[13]Ibid., 196.

own international experiences actually began rather serendipitously at one of those meetings.

I, a very junior, untenured assistant professor, was sitting in the coffee shop of the Sheraton Hotel in Washington, D.C. sometime in the early 1960s. A stout fellow with a heavy Russian accent sat down beside me. Leaning over and reading my badge, he said, "Hello Rose. I'm Neustadt. I just read about you in *The New York Times*."

"Who, me?" I squeaked.

But it was true. An article describing a recent piece of research I had just completed was published that very day in an article on the catholicity of papers being delivered at the World Congress of Sociology we were both attending. Neustadt said he would like to know more about my study. I told him and...to make a long story very short, he ended up inviting me to spend a year at the University of Leicester in England where he was Professor of Sociology and, as they say there, Head of Department.

Within a year I received both a formal invitation and a grant to spend the year as a Fulbright Professor in the English Midlands. I was excited and quickly accepted, but not before asking for and receiving permission to take what is known in my trade as "LWOP" (leave without pay). It turned out that the Leicester stipend, even when augmented by support from the Council on the International Exchange of Scholars, was far less than expected. My wife and I and our two little kids learned to rough it during a year of adventures in merry cold (it was freezing) England—and on the continent, too.[14]

Expecting something of a classic "Oxbridge" setting for the University of Leicester, when we arrived we quickly learned that it was more a "red brick" place, the sort of institution that would be made famous by Leicester alumnus Malcolm Bradbury as well as two other popular writers, David Lodge and Kingsley Amis. And, to add to the specialness of my new temporary base, the Social Science Block where I had my office was the former Leicester Lunatic Asylum. I came to think of it as a most appropriate venue for a sociology department in the turbulent 1960s.

During the academic year I taught several general courses and a seminar on comparative race relations. Already active in the civil rights movement and antiwar movements back home, I was soon drawn into

---

[14]From "A Year in the Midlands," in *Guest Appearances and Other Travels in Time and Space* (Athens, Ohio: Swallow Press, 2003), 72–81.

several demonstrations there. Such true participant observation was a good way to get a sense of what things were like on the ground. I spent a good deal of time in cities around the country gathering impressions on the racial situation and took part in several large conferences on the subject, mainly as a commentator on the presentations of others. I didn't write anything about what I'd learned and felt for several years. Then, in March of 1967, I published a paper, "Outsiders in Britain," in the social science journal *Transaction* in which I observed:

> Until the middle of the twentieth century Great Britain might well have been called a "white little island." As recently as 1950 there were fewer than 50,000 Negroes in the country (compared to over 15 million in the United States at the same time), and the combined figures for all other non-whites probably came to even less. During the past decade the situation has changed dramatically. Close to a million colored immigrants from Commonwealth nations have entered Britain (over one half from the West Indies, some 165,000 from India, and approximately 100,000 from Pakistan). Their reception has been considerably less than cordial and, for the first time, the UK has a serious "colour problem."
>
> Although Britain played an instrumental role in the African slave trade, few slaves were taken there and of those who were many were freed upon arrival and the rest (or their descendants) were freed by the Mansfield Judgment of 1772, which proclaimed the holding of slaves illegal. Compared to whites, the number of Africans and Asians remained infinitesimal during the whole of the nineteenth century and half of the twentieth.
>
> In 1950 the majority of blacks were dockers (longshoremen) and seamen who lived in the port towns of Bristol, Cardiff, Liverpool, and London, or were students attending English or Scottish schools or universities. In addition, some West Indian workers were to be found in various parts of the country (London, Birmingham, and the West Midlands), workers who had come—or whose families had come— during the First World War or the Second. There were also some Africans, a few Indians, and even fewer Pakistanis. Far more British West Indians went to the United States than to the United Kingdom until the McCarran Act of 1952 sealed American ports of entry to those from the islands. It was then that Southampton replaced New York as the gateway to opportunity, at least in the dreams of the immigrants.

Population pressures and depressed living conditions in their homelands, the desire for more social advancement (the world-wide "revolution of rising expectations"), and the emergence of a welfare state guaranteeing at least a minimum standard of living to all, and the attraction of economic opportunities in the UK combined to encourage immigration....

The rapid influx brought with it a growing concern that without severe restrictions, the flow would soon become a torrent; soon black and brown immigrants (pejoratively called "spades" and "wogs" and other unseemly epithets) would seriously threaten the fabric of British society. Anxiety over the potential problems perceived to be created by the presence of such newcomers prompted the Conservative government to enact the Commonwealth Immigration Law of 1962, a decidedly racialist piece of legislation which limited the number and "types" of persons allow to enter the country. Fenner Brockway, commenting on this, wrote, "While it is true that the Act itself makes no mention of race or colour, there is no need for it to do so because the categories to be admitted to this country cover most white applicants and its provisions for exclusion apply almost entirely to coloured applicants." In fact, he continued, "When, during the discussion of the Bill in Parliament, it was admitted that immigration from the Republic of Ireland (an independent state for thirty years), could not be controlled, the measure patently became discriminatory against the non-white peoples of the Commonwealth...." Against his wishes, Lord Brockway's own Labour Party, once back in power, supported and tightened the very law it has so vehemently opposed.

Although the Act effectively curtailed the inflow, it did not offset resentment in many sections of the country. On the contrary, since its passage, racialism has shown a decided upsurge and the "immigration problem" has become one of Britain's most pressing political issues.

During the election campaign of the fall of 1964, for example, it was not uncommon to see the slogan IF YOU WANT A NIGGER NEIGHBOUR, VOTE LABOUR in those areas that have large numbers of immigrants. The seat in Smethwick, a constituency of Birmingham, was won by an outspoken Conservative advocate of segregation, Peter Griffiths. Race was an issue in at least five other voting districts. In bye-elections held during the winter, the issue of immigration kept surfacing in various parts of the country. And, in the spring of 1965 chapters of the Ku Klux Klan were being formed in several Midland cities.

In the same week in August, 1965, when in the United States President Lyndon Johnson signed a bill dramatically reversing a fifty-year old policy of discriminatory quotas against foreigners seeking entry (known as the Immigration Reform Act), the Wilson government in the United Kingdom reduced the number of permits to be issued from 20,000 to 8,500, and those were to be awarded only to those with specialized skills, such as physicians and ancillary medical personnel or to those with jobs already awaiting them. Referring to these new restrictions and other reversals wrought by the Labour government, one spokesman for the immigrants reported that, "There is a new mood amongst Britain's coloured people today—a mood of humiliation, of bitterness and anger." Said another, "They want our doctors. They want our nurses. They want our scientists and technologists. But the don't want our ordinary people."

Three theories have been advanced to explain the rising antipathy and distrust of the new immigrants in Britain. The first, called the "colour-class" hypothesis, suggested by the anthropologist Kenneth Little, states that, because of their past, British citizens have been deeply imbued with a colonial mentality. Although relatively few have had any personal contract with colored people, they tend to identify them with the lowest, most backward and uncivilized elements in the Commonwealth (i.e. the old Empire).... And it is true that the "white man's burden" is a phrase that is once again being echoed in the country. Benevolent paternalism is still in the air, especially evident in the comments of welfare workers about "their people," who suggest and often say, "Only we know what's good for them." One is reminded of the recent statement by Nicholas Deakin of the institute of Race Relations in London that "one of the most paradoxical characteristics of the British, both individually and collectively, is their capacity for considering themselves tolerant, even while displaying prejudice."

The second hypothesis suggest that the visibility and cultural distinctiveness of colored immigrants make them archetypal "strangers" in a society in which xenophobia has long been a latent feature of social life, a society in which, as Ruth Glass says, "social segregation is the accepted norm."

The third hypothesis, discussed by various writers including A.H. Richmond, offered the view that both prejudice and discrimination in Britain as elsewhere are related to insecurity, a fear of losing hard won ground by those most vulnerable, the old elites and especially the rising working classes....

Actually these are not at all mutually exclusive. No single factor can possibly account for all contingencies. The real explanation probably incorporates all three of the elements cited by British social scientists: racial prejudice, fear of the stranger, and status-anxiety.[15]

I went on to discuss some of the parallels and many of the differences I saw in what was happening in the UK during that period and the situation in the United States. And then I mentioned the three paths that were being recommended for how to address the problem that were coming from various factions in the UK. The first advocated a blatant policy of forced repatriation, telegraphed in the slogan "Send them back," a now-all-too-familiar American "solution" to dealing with undocumented aliens. The second was a sort of variation on what was, for a time in our own country, a policy of draconian assimilation: "If you people would drop your unacceptable foreign ways, strange religions, weird cuisine, and flashy dress and learn to speak proper English, we might accept you." The third was the idea, supported mostly by academic liberals, left-wing Labourites and spokespersons of various immigrant communities of striving for a kind of viable pluralism, or acceptable hyphenation. (This was long before *multiculturalism* became a new watchword).

While I favored the last of the three, perhaps brashly for an outsider, I made several suggestions in my paper for what else might be done to reduce the intergroup tension that was mounting in that country. In my concluding paragraphs I wrote:

> It should be pointed out that, should it choose to do so, the British government might be able to effect changes in a way that, until recently, has been extremely difficult in the United States.
>
> Here, owing to the apportionment of authority at the federal and state and local levels, each of which has particularly strong vested interests to uphold, each has worked out its own plans for social reform—or resistance to it. There, the centralized control of the Parliament and the organs of government, whose direct and indirect administrative and financial influence extends to every constituency, could be used to initiate programs to reduce discrimination and aid in

---

[15]From "Outsiders in Britain," *Transaction*, 4, March 1967, 18–22.

the adjustment of newcomers on all fronts, but, whether it [the British government] will take such initiative is difficult to predict. Should it not, colored immigrants to Britain will remain second-class—in name and in fact.[16]

Before leaving the United Kingdom and before I even started writing the article excerpted here, I had several interesting experiences relating to being asked my opinion about what was going on in the U.K.

The first happened on March 8, 1965, on *This Day Tonight*, the BBC's evening news program. That afternoon I had received a request to appear and be interviewed by Magnus Magnusson about some breaking news from the United States: a vicious attack on Martin Luther King Jr. and fellow marchers on the Edmund Pettus Bridge in Selma, Alabama. I agreed immediately and took a taxi to the nearby city of Nottingham where I would do the interview by a remote hookup in a satellite station there. When it was my turn, pictures of what was already being called "Bloody Sunday" flashed on the screen and the questioning began. Yet, soon after I began to answer, the interviewer asked me about the Black Muslims. Maybe, I thought, this has to do with the fact that Malcolm X had recently been in the U.K. I offered my thoughts about why his group and its ideology appealed to so many African Americans. I think I quoted Malcolm X's statement that "the worst crime the white man has committed is to teach us to hate ourselves."

Despite his prior assurance that the interview would be confined to the situation on the other side of the Atlantic, Magnusson then shifted the subject. Instead of continuing to ask about what was going on in the United States, in either the civil rights or black nationalist movements, he invited me to elaborate on several things I had said at a symposium in response to a series of studies about mounting racism in England and which had been reported in a number of papers from the *Guardian* to the *Times* to several very right-wing newspapers. He asked whether I had been misquoted or quoted out of context. Furious about this, but feeling trapped, I tried my best to explain and elaborate upon what I had actually said. Then it was over.

---

[16]Ibid., 24.

I will never forget the tension of that session, nor will I ever give up a treasured memento of that year in the Midlands. It is the bold headline of a column written by the pseudonymous Peter Simple in the very conservative *Daily Telegraph*: "MALCOLM X AND PETER ROSE, YANKEES GO HOME!" I still laugh, thinking that was surely the first time either of us had ever been called a Yankee!

Early in our year-long stay in the United Kingdom we drove to Scotland in a Volvo station wagon that we had purchased before leaving the United States and had delivered in Southampton when we arrived. We also took many other trips around Great Britain, most of them to London both to see the sights and, for me, to lecture at various places, including the University of London and Imperial College. It was at the latter that I spent a delightful hour with Michael Ramsey, the bushy-browed, upbeat and very liberal archbishop of Canterbury who was also speaking there that day. I spent a number of other days giving talks at other universities all over the country and during one two week period, flew to Israel at the invitation of the sociologist, Shmuel Eisenstadt, a giant in my field. Looking back on that trip some years later I wrote:

> Sometime in the spring of 1965, I received and accepted an invitation to come to Jerusalem as a guest of colleagues at the Hebrew University. I had never been there before and was eager to visit historic and holy sites and learn something about roots, mine and those of many others with a special interest in that new/old society. On the appointed day, I drove down from Leicester and picked up a Lod-bound flight at Heathrow. The El Al plane had originated in New York and was filled, so far as I could determine, with tourists of various sorts and some obvious pilgrims, Jewish and Christian.
>
> The plane landed on time and I followed the crowd to go through the entry procedures.
>
> An American couple in front of me in the line at Immigration seemed overcome with joy. They exchanged "Ohs," "Ahs," and succinct, telling phrases.
>
> "It's wonderful. Like a dream."
>
> The wife turned to her husband. "Just think," she said. "On the plane already there were Jews running things. The pilot. The stewardesses. And here they are all Jews: soldiers, immigration officers, customs officials."

A little old man was sweeping up right next to us. He was also listening to the conversation. Then, when the husband added, "And, Sadie, the cops are Jews, too," the sweeper turned, smiled, and said, "So are the crooks, mister, so are the crooks."

I chuckled to myself, then put my wallet in my front pocket and moved through immigration and customs, retrieved my luggage and caught a cab. It looked amazingly like a 1948 DeSoto, which, of course it was.[17]

I had hired the taxi to take me to Jerusalem.

It turned out that this would be the first of five trips I would make to Israel. In many ways, besides being in the only country in the world where Jews were in the majority (as fascinating to me as a sociologist of minorities as to me as a Jew), that first trip—two years before the Six-Day War—was the most memorable. Among the many impressions I took away, one day spent on Mount Zion was an eye-opener, especially for a person who would later become a travel writer interested in what goes on behind the scenes in all sorts of touristic endeavors. I had started early in the morning, leaving my one-star hostel and walking over to the posh King David Hotel, from where I wandered down the hill just below it to the narrow corridor that was lined with Israeli soldiers facing Jordanian ones on the winding road to the historic sites on Mount Zion.

Moving along at a pretty good clip, I came upon a group of Jewish tourists. They were blocking the path. I slowed but couldn't get through without trying to part them, Moses-style. Without divine assistance, I gave up fighting the crowd and joined it. It proved well worth it. They had a great guide called Ari (I knew it from his nametag) and from him I learned the first important lesson about an important rule of tour leaders: "Give 'em what they want!"

I followed the entourage and listened to what Ari had to say. When the group reached the top of the hill, I followed them into the remains of an old building where, we were told "This is where our great King David is buried."

"Ohs," and "Ahs," not heard since I'd flown into Tel Aviv. Whispers, too.

"Sam. Did he say King David?"

---

[17]From "A Tale of Two Cities," in *Guest Appearances*, 101–6.

"Yes, King David. Our King David."

We were encouraged to walk around the place for a few minutes and then were led into a nearby building. As we entered, the guide, whose English was excellent, explained that, "This is where the Christian people say Mary ascended to Heaven." He paused momentarily, looked at the faces of his audience, and then, with a sort of "if-you-believe-this-you-will-believe-anything expression," he shrugged. Then we moved to another place where we were told, "This is where the Christian people say the 'Last Supper,' took place."

The last bit of information was elaborated upon a bit by one of the men nearest to us. He explained that the Last Supper was actually a Seder. As he did, I could hear an elderly woman, who had moved ahead quite a way, loudly whispering to her husband, "It was a Seder." She knew, too.

When the tourists walked out into the brilliant noonday sunshine, it was very hot. Everyone was sweating. With jackets over shoulders and sweaters over arms, the whole gang tromped down the grade and through the corridor. I followed part way then stopped at an open-air canteen half way down the hill, ordered some falafel and a Coke and surveyed the scene.

Hot from the sun, I started to doze. Soon I realized I had been there for more than an hour. I quickly paid the check and got up. As I did, I noticed another group gathering at the bottom of the hill. Even from a distance it was clear it was different from the earlier one. Most notably there were several men in clerical collars and three nuns. They were wearing badges as were the rest of the group—Christian pilgrims on a trip to the Holy Land.

As they trudged up the hill, I saw that they had two guides: one who almost seemed a member of their group (I surmised he was the coordinator of their tour), the other was the same guy who had led the Jewish party that morning.

As they passed the canteen, the imp in me decided to abandon my plan to go to Mt. Herzl. I was going to go back up Mt. Zion. And I did, surreptitiously pursuing the new group, moving in as close as possible to hear the spiel and watch the reaction.

At the top of the hill the Israeli guide told his new charges that, "This is where the Jews say King David is buried." Then quickly added, "But, of course, it is hard to know these things for sure."

The listeners nodded and some took notes. Then, as before, he led them to the Church of the Dormition. This time it was they who did the "Oh-ing" and "Ah-ing," as he explained that they were standing on the very place from which Mary had ascended to Heaven.

By the time they reached the room of the Last Supper, the voices were hushed. As one, the pilgrims were in awe of where they were and what it meant.

As they slowly began to file out, each one glancing back as if to freeze the savored experience, the guide spotted me. A bit puzzled, he smiled and nodded rather perfunctorily. Then he sort of winked. He let everybody pass and started down behind them. I waited and fell in with him. On impulse I invited him to have a beer with me at a place near where the tour buses were lined up. He agreed.

A few minutes later he and I were sitting at the sidewalk café. We chatted a while and, after directing the conversation toward the business of tourism, I asked Ari why he had said one thing to the Jewish group and something different to the others. Without batting an eye, he looked at me, smiled and said, "It's very simple. It's a living."[18]

Ari's remarks that day so long ago, got me to thinking about the role of guides, especially on pilgrimages, and the fact I had only rarely had the opportunity to hear one speak so ingeniously out of both sides of his mouth.

The day after my personal revelations (at least about tour guides) on Mount Zion, I gave my first lecture at what is now the old campus of the Hebrew University. I happened to be there at the same time a fellow sociologist, Chris van Nieuwenhuijzen from The Hague, was visiting the country, and someone in the sociology department arranged for the two of us to have a chauffeur-driven three-day tour of the country accompanied by an anthropologist. Knowing I was Jewish and assuming Chris was a Christian, our hosts made certain we saw all the sites that were considered especially significant to both faiths. Years later I would remember the experience, feeling as if we were characters in the second volume of John Updike's wonderful Henry Bech trilogy, especially the story about the time Bech, a Jewish academic with ambivalent feelings about Israel, visits the country with his Christian wife who can't get enough of the Old Testament sites. I have often thought that Updike's plot might well have been concocted on one of my later trips to Israel

---

[18]Ibid., 103–104.

when he and I both happened to speak at the same gathering in Tel Aviv. That time I was there to discuss my research on American-style racial and ethnic pluralism in the aftermath of the Black Power revolt; Updike was in Israel to talk about his own take on American society.

Our points of view were as different as our subjects, although, it turned out, we had more in common than one might have thought from what we were saying there. Later I would write:

> Updike was well known in the country despite the fact that most of his fiction was viewed by Israeli readers—as by many of their American cousins—as something quite removed from their everyday lives. For those who read it and commented upon it, there was a rather common agreement that it was a kind of "ethnography of the other," interesting, but in a voyeuristic sort of way. There was one exception: a controversial new book about a wired-haired little man named Henry Bech, a Jewish writer clearly related to Norman Mailer, Saul Bellow, Bernard Malamud, and Philip Roth. A playful spoof and wry send-up, *Bech: A Book* (Knopf, 1970) even begins with a Roth-like ploy where the fictional character writes a letter to his creator. Signed, "Henry Bech," it begins "Dear John, Well, if you must commit the artistic indecency of writing about a writer, better I suppose about me than about you."
>
> From the start Bech is not only a composite of Mailer-Bellow-Malamud-Roth, he is Updike's Nathan Zuckerman. He is a writer with problems—problems with writing, problems with women, problems with celebrity and success, problems with failure.
>
> Updike's stories about Henry Bech are not just works of parody and tomfoolery; they are filled with insight and empathy for certain sensibilities, and they are, to me, generally on the mark. Coming from the author of *The Poorhouse Fair, Couples, Marry Me, A Month of Sundays, Rabbit Run, Rabbit Redux, Rabbit is Rich, Rabbit at Rest* and a number of other books peopled by those who eat white bread and drink lots of bourbon and scotch, this may seem a surprising achievement.
>
> For many non-Wasps, Jewish and otherwise, Rabbit Angstrom's sort of angst, and that of most of Updike's characters, is often hard to appreciate, harder to feel. But Henry Bech is, as he might say, something different altogether. Creating him was, I imagine, quite easy; making him believable for those most at home with the Jewish-American belletristic genre was much more difficult.

It is not easy to be a credible portrayer of "others." Jewish writers are well aware of the pitfalls. Many admit that, because "Wasp cool" is not their thing, it is difficult to "do" Wasps, except in exaggerated caricature. Updike, by contrast, seems to have been able to cross over. This is not only my opinion. With some notable exceptions, it is a view shared by many Jewish critics and by even more Jewish readers, including some of the members of that curious but well-read group of listeners at the auditorium in the American Embassy in Tel Aviv.

Updike and I were up on the stage. Our audience was made up, mostly, of academics, writers and politicians.

After our respective presentations, I was asked some sharply worded questions about what I had said would mean to the historic relationships between blacks and Jews. I answered each rather directly but quickly. The majority of those in the audience were clearly restless. It was obvious that what most really wanted to ask—and say—had to do with Updike's novels, not the reflections of an itinerant sociologist.

Updike was peppered with questions, some—in good Israeli style—very direct: How had he, who was known mainly as the quintessential chronicler of white, Anglo-Saxon Protestant Americans, decided to write about this Jewish guy, Henry Bech?

I do not remember Updike's responses exactly but do recall that he was a bit evasive, seeming to want to hear what they had to say rather than saying much himself. The author seemed to be at once respectful, thoughtful, and watchful, something like a fox, a literary fox. He was processing what he was hearing, filing it away. He didn't lick his chops but he smiled rather benignly.

After the session ended, we had lunch with some of the more important members of the audience. Sitting next to me, the writer, who was on his first trip to Israel, told me about the itinerary that had been carefully planned for him and his wife. It was one that highlighted visits to Christian sites. I was doing some processing of my own and thought to myself that our session, that luncheon and his tour around the country were bound to appear in some new stories sometime soon.

My prescience was realized several years later in "The Holy Land," a story that was to appear first in *Playboy* magazine, then in *Bech is Back* (Knopf, 1982).

In one lengthy scene in that hilarious yet poignant twice-told tale, Bech, having been picked up at the official city guesthouse,

Mishkenot, by the Jesuit archaeologist Pére Gibergue, is shepherded from one sacred spot to another. "I should never have married a Christian," he laments as their party fights its way up the Via Dolorosa through a throng of pilgrims.

Bech's wife, by contrast, is enthralled by everything. The Way of the Cross where they walk and all the places to which they are taken. She isn't parochial either. She is fascinated by the Jews, by Zionism. She loves Israel; she loves the Israelis. Bech is far less comfortable. To her Israel is a dreamland, evoking the past, challenging the future; to him it is "a ghetto with farms." With an obvious nod to American Jews who have written sarcastically about their chauvinistic, self-satisfied *landsleut,* Bech says to his wife "I know these people. I've spent my whole life trying to get away from them, trying to think bigger."

Yet, as much as he is put off by his fellow Jews and their own very special places, Bech has an even more uncomfortable feeling about the Christian shrines. About to enter the Church of the Holy Sepulcher," Bech resists.

"Let's go," he says to Bea.

"Oh Henry, why?"

"This frightens me." The narrator, Updike, then explains, "It had that alchemic stink of medieval basements where vapors condensed as demons and pogroms and autos-da-fe. Torquemada. Hitler, the tsars —every despot major and minor who had tried to stunt and crush his race had inhaled these Christian vapors."[19]

And lest one think it was all sightseeing for me (as it must have been for Updike), on my first trip Chris Nieuwenhuijzen and I met what seemed to be at least half of the sociologists in the country.

En route back to London I stopped off for a few days in Athens, my first time there, too. I would return to Greece many times to speak at Pierce College and at the University of Athens and for meetings of the board of a program known as "Study in Greece" and on two occasions on family vacations, the first of which included a weeklong cruise with what I would later learn were routine stopovers in Mykonos, Delos, Santorini, Crete, Rhodes, and the Turkish coast to visit Ephesus. But, as in the case of Israel, certain events of my first visit are what come to mind when someone mentions anything about going to Greece.

---

[19]"Travels with Bech," *Congress Monthly,* 66:2, March/April 1999, 15–17.

The fact is that what I always think of as nothing monumental is very revealing about lingering political differences and cultural affinities, especially gastronomic ones. On my first night in Athens I had dinner in the little hotel where I was staying. As he cleared away the dishes from the main course, the waiter, whose English was near perfect although heavily accented, asked if I would like coffee.

"Yes, please," I replied.

"American coffee?"

"No," I said, "Turkish coffee," something I had come to enjoy in Jerusalem.

He looked at me, smiled wryly, and said, *"You mean, Grik coffee!"* And then he brought me a cup of the same thing!

The other travels during our residency in England were two long family trips, the first, at Christmastime to France, Belgium and the Netherlands; the second, in the spring, to France, Switzerland (where, for the first time, this diehard skier got to ski in the Alps), and as far as Florence in Italy. On the return we drove back through Switzerland, across Germany and again stopped in Holland. Each Continental tour began with our driving south to Lydd and then flying over the Channel to the little village of Le Touquet on the French coast in a small cargo plane where we were first seated in the rear, behind the area where our car and one or two others were then driven on board. Getting to France that way was an adventure in itself.

While both cross-Channel trips involved doing many touristy things, the time in the Netherlands, especially Amsterdam, was very different. There, for the first time since she and her sister, Betsy, had left their homeland to join a group of French orphans in Marseilles for the long voyage to America, Hedy would be united with Tante Toos, the Dutch woman who had saved her life by hiding her and Betsy for almost four years in the basement of her liquor store in the western part of the city. It was also the chance for us all to become acquainted with the only other survivor of the war in Hedy's family, her cousin, also named Betsy, Betsy Kraaijpoel-Cohen, and her two children: Bert, then around thirteen years old, and his sister, Liesbeth, who was about eleven.

There is much to tell about those few days in Amsterdam, but that is Hedy's story. For me, what was particularly touching was how, despite so many barriers, including Tante Toos's utter lack of English and my and the children's utter lack of Dutch—the language in which she and Hedy communicated—we were all so warmly welcomed by her.

While in Amsterdam, we paid a visit to Joop and Maria Goudsblom, two young Dutch sociologists I had met in the early 1960s at the same meeting of the International Sociological Association where Ilya Neustadt and I had had the breakfast conversation that led to our year in the Midlands.

Because of Hedy's background, our affection for Cousin Betsy and her kids, our friendship with the Goudsbloms—and Joop Goudsblom's invitation to me to return to lecture in his department and to make his home our base in Amsterdam, what started as two homecoming visits for Hedy became the beginning of numerous trips to the Netherlands and, through a later chance encounter, my role in the creation of two Smith-like institutions of higher education in the country.

Our year in England was followed by a much shorter visit to Amsterdam later in the decade. I was totally unprepared for what happened during one of my first times lecturing at the University of Amsterdam. I had been invited there to talk about the changing character of race relations in the United States, especially the Black Power movement which was being discussed around the world.

On the evening of the lecture, Joop and I, properly dressed up in ties and jackets, as were many of the older men in the audience, went up onto the dais. After a warm introduction, I walked over to the podium and began to speak, explaining that my talk would be divided into two parts. In the first they would hear me using the term "Negroes;" in the second I would speak of "Blacks." I then proceeded.

No more than five minutes into the presentation, a young man, dressed in a T-shirt, jeans and a cowboy hat and sporting a big button that said, in English, "WHITE IMPOTENCE," with two very attractive similarly clad young women on either side of him, walked into the room, strode down the central aisle and sat atop a table against the wall in the back of the hall. The tension in the room was palpable, but I soldiered on. "And so," I remember saying, "Negroes began..." At that point the intruder shouted out, "Don't you know that word is considered pejorative?"

I was a bit surprised by the outburst, but wanting to maintain control of the situation, I said, "Sir, if you had been here at the beginning of my talk, you would understand why I am using that particular word— and why I will be using a different one in a few minutes."

He remained silent until the question period that followed a welcome break. When Joop called the meeting back to order, the first to raise a hand was the same person. He challenged me about something I'd said, though I can't remember specifically what it was.

"How do you know that?" he demanded.

I said it was well known in the research literature.

"Whose work?" he asked with increasing belligerence. And I recited the names of at least five social scientists.

He sat down and, as he did, Joop whispered something to me to the effect that the guy wouldn't know any of them anyway, or much else!

At the end of the evening, the young man came up to me and, in a most traditional European gesture, shook my hand, nodded his head, and thanked me for the interesting talk, and with his lemon tarts, to use Tom Wolfe's vivid expression, he left. I was suddenly aware that, like air let out of a balloon, the tension in the room dissipated as many of the older people said, "Whew!" or its Dutch equivalent.

It was then I was told that I had just been confronted by one of the leaders of the Provos (for "provocateurs"), a movement that was dramatically shaking up much of Dutch society in the mid-1960s, not least the traditional practices of universities. Years later I would revisit one aspect of the Provo movement and learn that many who had been so anarchistic in those early days of my first travels to the Netherlands had become very conventional rightists by the early decades of the new century.

Shortly after those days in Amsterdam, I flew to Naples as a guest of the Italian sociologist, Gilberto Marselli, to speak in his department at the University of Naples' Portici campus. While there I was able to visit the ruins of Herculaneum, visit Gilberto's wonderful villa in Massa Lubrensa, part way down the Amalfi Drive, and, accompanying my host, have my first brief glimpse of Rome (and some insight into the crazy-quilt character of Italian political proclivities).

With his gloved hands gripping the wheel of his snazzy Alfa Romeo sports car, Gilberto was heading for a meeting of the Socialist Party—and I was going sightseeing. As we passed the iconic ruins of Monte Cassino, I learned that he had gone to school as a child right there. I also learned that his father, also educated on the slopes of Cassino, had been a scion of an aristocratic Neapolitan family and a career military officer but turned against the Fascist regime and became a hero of the partisan resistance.

In 1965, back at Smith not too long after our return from the year in England, I joined an interdisciplinary team offering a series of history and social science seminars. The first one was called "The Negro in America." The two other instructors were my friends, political scientist Leo Weinstein, an expert on constitutional law, and historian Stanley Elkins, author of *Slavery: A Problem in American Institutional and Intellectual Life* (1959), one of the most important and controversial books on the subject. We offered that particular seminar twice more. The transformation of its title and the composition of the student members clearly reflected the changing times. In the second go-round it was called "Desegregation," in the third, two years later, "The Black Experience."

Each time we offered the seminar we had to select no more than sixteen students from a pool of up to forty applicants. I will never forget how much we on the faculty learned from our chosen few. While I could relate many stories about them, I will highlight only two. The first was a fabricated mini-moot court presentation by two pre-law students on a sit-in case in a Louisiana parish. They called it "Sound vs. Fury."

The second occurred in the last year we offered the seminar. By then at least a third of the students were African American (the term had replaced the previously favored word, "Negro," around 1964–65). In one session students decided to address the issues by doing some role-playing, and their professors were not allowed to exempt themselves. We drew our assignments from a passed hat, and then had ten minutes to prepare to address a common issue involving community control in New York. To watch a black student from Hartford, Connecticut, assume the role of a white cop in Brooklyn, a white professor try to internalize and then articulate the thoughts and feelings of a black mother in a housing project who wanted nothing more than to see that her kids had a better life than hers was quite astounding—and clearly memorable.

Later I would work with the political scientist Stanley Rothman, on another interdisciplinary seminar, "Comparative Studies of Race and Ethnicity," and with the European historian, Nelly Hoyt, on one we called "The Experience of Exile."

I have to say that I found co-teaching these interdisciplinary seminars stimulating, educational, and often quite exhausting (but in a different way than that experienced when teaching "Methods of Social Research"). They were stimulating because of the exchanges of ideas, and because of being forced to think out of my own box as my co-teachers and I outlined our plans and pulled together syllabi for the seminars and met to discuss various issues relating to the general topic in our offices and then in the classrooms. They were educational because I learned so much from fellow faculty members as well as from the students. And they were exhausting because there always seemed to be a high level of tension before and during each session. I'm sure there were elements of academic competition but, at least for me, the desire to hold my own with some very sharp and very smart colleagues far outweighed any thought of trying to one-up them.

Like those in the joint seminars, many of our students—both undergraduate and graduate—were challenging in more ways than one. One of them, Andrea Hairston, a young woman from Pittsburgh who came to Smith on a science scholarship, took my course "Ethnic Minorities in America" and persuaded me to allow her to write a play in lieu of a final paper. The play was called "Einstein." It was on relativity, in this instance, cultural relativity. Although that was a long time ago, some of the discussions we had back then are still relevant, especially questions about sensitivities and understanding. Andrea is now a chaired professor in the Department of Theater, a member of the faculty of the Department of Afro-American Studies at Smith, and a world-renowned prize-winning author and playwright. (An earlier version of her "Praisesong" that is the foreword to this book was a surprising—and most moving—tribute offered on the occasion of my retirement from Smith in 2003.)

My Fulbright year (1964–65) in the United Kingdom and two more Fulbright appointments (in Japan and Australia) in 1970), and, I suppose, my being a social scientist, led to a study commissioned by the Assistant Secretary of State for Cultural Affairs, Charles Frankel, and the Council on the International Exchange of Scholars to evaluate the Senior Fulbright Program in East Asia and the South Pacific. It would be the second time I was under a short-term contract from the federal government. The first was in the summer of 1964, before our departure for England, when I, an avowed opponent of the military action that was building up in Vietnam, was invited by Dick Beaumont, the Assistant Secretary of the Navy for manpower, to serve as a consultant in, of all places, the Pentagon.

After wrestling with competing personal and political feelings, I agreed to go to Washington to work with a number of what they called "COs." They were definitely not the conscientious objectors with whom I was wont to consort but rather the Navy's kind of CO: commanding officers. What persuaded me to do it was the charge "to advise Commanding Officers on creative ways to enforce a presidentially-ordered 'affirmative action program' for Negro civilian employees of the Fifth Naval District," a district that extends from Philadelphia to Norfolk, Virginia. I think it was the first time I ever heard the expression "affirmative action" in connection with a government policy.

When I got there, I was met by a young naval officer and taken to the meeting room. After an initial meeting with Lyndon Johnson's Secretary of the Navy, Paul Nitze; Dick Beaumont; and Admiral John Hogle, the senior naval officer on the project, I was to spend a full week in the belly of the Pentagon with seven other admirals—one, Hogle with three stars, ten captains, and an assortment of more junior officers and thirty very white but often red-faced (read: apoplectic) civilian senior managers responsible for implementing whatever we came up with. The Navy's Office of Manpower had done extensive research on several different bases—the Naval Air Station at Norfolk, the "Repo-Depot" where ships are repaired, and a number of others. I'd received summaries of the resulting reports prior to the meetings in Washington.

For someone who had already spent more than a decade talking and writing about the dangers of stereotyping, the whole experience was quite an eye-opener. I was exposed to a bunch of Annapolis graduates and others in crisply starched white uniforms, but very few of them fit the caricatured images I had of military leaders with pinheads and bull necks. I quickly learned that they took their mandate to do what they could to improve opportunities for minorities very seriously. They expressed their frustrations openly in the face of a Greek chorus of embittered believers in American apartheid who had to listen to how *they* were going to be forced to change their ways.

The whole story of this peacenik's odyssey through the looking glass appears in a chapter, "Wrapped in the Flag," in my book *Guest Appearances and Other Travels in Time* (2003). For now, to get a sense of what I saw, did, felt, and advised at the time, I offer a part of that essay.

> After a very awkward first session when I was introduced as a special consultant, we broke for lunch, instructed by the commandant to return at 1400 hours. Not being invited by anyone to go anywhere to eat, I set out alone, grabbed a hotdog at a little shop, and then decided to explore the halls of the Pentagon.
>
> I had trouble finding my way back through the maze of that huge building and reentered the meeting room a few minutes late. It was already filled with the straight-backed senior officers clearly miffed at my lackadaisical, civilian, academic, liberal-left style. (Those were the adjectives I imagined were racing around in their heads.)
>
> The commandant welcomed me back and pointed to the board, where he had written what he thought I had said in the previous session. It was a rather jumbled version. When I said it wasn't exactly what I'd said, he invited me to come up on the dais saying, why don't you come up and explain what you meant.

I walked up, took an eraser, and wiped the board clean. As I wrote down what I had actually said, a kind of collective gasp was heard. (Sometime later I learned that one doesn't remove what the chief honcho writes unless he gives permission.) The damage was done. My faux pas was duly noted by all assembled. To add insult to my embarrassment, the Admiral Hogle then suggested, "Since you are so skilled at organizing things, why don't you stay up here and be our recorder."

I didn't like where this was leading. I declined the offer and retorted, "What about one of those young men, pointing to the junior officers (each of whom seemed to be eager to be called upon). Surely one of them can do it." And I went back to my original set.

My first challenge paid off almost immediately. Instead of buckling under, I had asserted my independence. I felt better and, despite the knots in my belly, began to actually enjoy the charged atmosphere.

Finally we got to work. It took us five more days to reach some accord and hammer out a reasonable "affirmative action" program, modest by today's standards but quite radical then.

Things improved on the luncheon front, too. The second day one of the captains, a medical doctor who headed a naval hospital, took me with him to a little sandwich place in the building. The third and fourth days I went with two rear admirals. On Friday, just before recessing for lunch, Admiral Hogle invited me to join him in the Flag Officer's Dining Room. I accepted, we went to a top floor room where almost everyone was not only in uniform but the hats on top of the coat rack were laden with gold braid and scrambled eggs.

When we entered the room, I understood what the words "top brass" really meant. There were high-ranking officers in marine and army as well as navy uniforms, all with at least two stars on their epaulets or collars. There was also a small party of civilians. At the head of their table sat a man of about forty-five with a ruddy face, rimless glasses, and slicked-down black hair. My excitement of having arrived in the sanctum sanctorum of the Pentagon soured considerably when I realized that it was Robert McNamara, my nemesis, and the man my friend Aron Krich called "The Secretary of Death." I wanted to get up and leave. But I didn't.

I stayed and John Hogle and I talked not about the war but about our mission. We focused on the fact that, while all potential employees took tests blind, African Americans tended to do much more poorly than whites, especially in mathematics. I reminded John, as he now asked me to call him, that we had data showing that, as bad as the educational system was in many southern schools, it was poorest in the black ones. I remember suggesting to him a strategy that might prove useful, if rather unprecedented: urge the COs to consider skipping the normal chain of command and call in the greenest Academy- and NROTC-trained ensigns to recruit their cooperation as tutors, especially in math. "After all," I argued, "they are just out of college, know the latest stuff and, being 'officers and gentlemen' might well be flattered to be asked by their commanding officers to take on such a task." I didn't say it would also look good on their records. It was implied. (I was learning and using the ways of the military, in spite of myself.)

By the end of the week together, we had figured out a number of ways to provide release time for further schooling, find tutors (the commandant did use my idea and, as I had suggested to him, presented it as his own), and redefined jobs so that they would no longer be seen to be implicitly race specific (e.g. "aircraft cleaner" had meant scut work for blacks). I found, however that the toughest job was to persuade the all-white supervisory group sitting around the outer rim of our big conference table to accept the inevitability of a truly integrated work force. That, I discovered, could best be accomplished by, well, waving the flag.

"It was the President's order that established this meeting and our mission; it is your patriotic responsibility to carry it out." I didn't actually say those words, but Admiral Hogle did.

I was impressed by the sincerity with which he and the other commanders, save for the one guy who still grumbled that this was all a distraction from "our mission in Veet-Naam," now forcefully argued for fairness. One, a captain with an Italian-sounding name, who was in charge of the "Repot-Depot," later wrote an introduction to a brochure called "A Career in Shipbuilding" designed to attract a cross section of new workers. He described how his parents had come from Naples; of how, like him, there were people in the navy and working for the navy, black and white, brown and yellow, from every corner of the world—Europe and Asia and Africa. That, he said, was the American way. (I still have and treasure a signed copy he proudly sent me a few months after that week in the Pentagon.)

I came away from Washington with a somewhat different perspective on the military—and on patriotism. I didn't suddenly start saluting the flag at every street corner, but I did gain some new respect for some of those who did.

Shortly thereafter, "McNamara's War" began to escalate and I went back to the picket lines. But I cringed at the thought of burning the flag and found myself in awkward conflict when I witnessed such acts committed by my fellow protesters.[20]

Later in the decade I proposed to my old friend, Charles Lieber, who had left Random House/Knopf to start his own publishing house, Atherton Press, that I put together a book that would focus on a series of controversies about aspects of the African-American experience then being debated on campuses, in public forums, in the government and sometimes in the streets. He agreed. Indeed, he gave me the green light and a carte blanche. The result was a two-volume, one-thousand-page book, *Americans from Africa*. The first volume was called *Slavery and Its Aftermath*; the second, *Old Memories, New Moods*. Both were published in 1970.

Volume I offered readers the chance to engage in the debates by reading compelling arguments on topics such as the extent to which African languages, art and music and social structures were retained in the Middle Passage and expressed in American Negro culture; the principal legacy of slavery (a debate also known as "The Elkins Controversy," the reference being to my colleague, Stanley Elkins's book, *Slavery*, in which he discusses the internalization of disgrace as manifest in certain personality traits as well as suggesting that the concentration camp experience of European Jews was somehow comparable to that of black slavery in the United State); differences and similarities in life ways of African Americans in the South and in the North; and particular aspects of black communities in terms of social class and family life.

Those whose voices were heard and whose words were to be read and reflected upon included men and women who were both analytical in their approaches and passionate in their theses—and often subject to heated objection, like Daniel Patrick Moynihan whose report, "The Negro Family: A Case for National Action," I reprinted in full along with the writings of several of his most vehement critics. (I would return to the subject myself nearly fifty years later in a review essay on "Killing the Messenger.")

---

[20]From "Wrapped in the Flag," in *Guest Appearances*, 112–120.

Such juxtaposition of analyses and opinions was also true of Volume II of *Americans from Africa*. There the selected essays were all focused on protest and identity. They included "Who was Nat Turner?" with varied interpretations of Turner's famous revolt and other early challenges to slavery; an examination of the changing character of the civil rights movement "Freedom, Now!"; "Whither Black Power?," and, finally, "Negroes Nevermore."

In the midst of working on the complexities of issues as varied as the extent of the retention of African customs, the pros and cons of what I called soulless militancy (the move toward assimilation) and ethnocentric blackwardness, and the nationalism emphasized in the struggle for a new identity, I was invited to give a lecture at the University of Texas in Austin. In the audience was the editor of the *Social Science Quarterly* who asked if he could publish my remarks. I agreed, but only if he let me put them into better shape than I thought they were in. First published in 1969 in his journal as "The Black Experience: Issues and Images," the essay subsequently became the introduction to *Americans from Africa*.

Here, as a brief reprise of those debates, is the beginning of that essay:

> History is often written in terms of the images people, or peoples wish to project. American history, for example, was long recounted as if the English, Scottish, Irish, Welsh Protestants—and a few Dutchmen—were the only ones to have had an impact on the growth and development of the country.

> Early books and classroom lectures dealt almost exclusively with the "Anglo-American Tradition" or "our Christian Heritage." Throughout most of the eighteenth and nineteenth centuries, new comers from Northwestern Europe (whom Fletcher Knebel has recently named the "out-Wasps") were encouraged to forget about the customs of Germany or Scandinavia and to adapt themselves to the eminently superior American lifeways. Other immigrants were most often considered beyond the pale of social acceptance. In story and song the Irish Catholics, the Poles, the Italians and the Russian Jews—to say nothing about those who came from China or Japan—were referred to as "unassimilable aliens." Many politicians expressed serious doubts

about whether such immigrants would ever have the makings of real Americans. Many noted social scientists went so far as to endorse the Dillingham Commission Reports and the restrictive legislation of the 1920s.

In time, most scholars changed their views, and their histories changed as well. Pluralism became en vogue and school children and college students were then told "our differences make us strong," that "America is a multiplicity in a unity." It even became fashionable to teach about the "Judeo-Christian Heritage" and to consider Catholics as Christians, too. Indeed, as if to bear public witness to such a revisionist view, the single Protestant preacher who had always intoned opening prayers at official gatherings was supplanted by the ubiquitous triumvirate: minister, priest and rabbi, "representatives of our three great religions." (Sociologists even gave expression to this new phenomenon and America became known, at least in the parlance of the classroom, as a "triple melting pot.")

And now it is time to include yet another figure on the dais—and to add another "culture" to the heritage. Behavior rises to meet expectations and the behavior of academic historians and social scientists seems no exception. Today the bookstores are flooded with thousands of volumes on "The Negro Problem." The problem isn't new. It is as old as America. But, worried about the future, we have once again begun to look at and—to some extent—to rewrite the past.

The new books being prepared for the 1970s will indicate that these is much more to "Black History" than the slave blocks, the Old Plantation, Emancipation and the grateful darkies, Freedman's Bureaus, the Hayes-Tilden Compromise, Plessy v. Ferguson, Booker T. Washington, race riots during the two world wars, Marian Anderson, Jackie Robinson, Ralph Bunche, Thurgood Marshall and the Supreme Court Decision of 1954. Rather, to judge by the advertising copy of the books already under preparation, they will dwell on the role played by black Americans who, "under the most adverse conditions, fought and died to gain their own freedom" and who (paradoxically it seems) we enlisted in every major battle to save the Republic.

The next texts will continue to tell a story of life in the antebellum South, but the readers will learn that things were not so tranquil beneath the mimosa trees, that not all Negroes sought to emulate the ways of their masters and that none ever had good relations with them, "No matter what the romantics say." They will learn that black men didn't really move "north to freedom" but exchanged one kind of hell for another.

As more and more new histories appear, a far different picture of the black Americans will emerge. The new books will include discussions of black soldiers who fought in the Union Army; they will tell of black politicians in the turbulent days of Reconstruction; they will praise the black cowboys who helped to open the West, the black troopers who rode with Teddy Roosevelt, the black workers who toiled along the rail beds and in the factories and on the farms. Some will go further, too, extolling the virtues of blackness and the solidarity of "soul" and exposing the pallid character of "white culture" in contrast to "black."

The motivation for this latest attempt of reexamining American history and giving the Negro an honored place along with other minorities has come about as a consequence of the civil rights movement and the campaign to eliminate segregation. The demand for an entirely new view of the "Afro-American" is, however, an offshoot of that larger struggle.

Feeling that many of the hard-won victories of the 1950s and 1960s have not made that much difference, angry black spokesmen have begun to challenge a number of basic assumptions of the reform-minded civil rights advocates. First, they argue, liberal white leaders (whatever they wanted personally) could rarely offer much more than palliatives that, often as not, were viewed as programs to keep "their" cities from erupting rather than being expressly designed to help poor blacks. Second, they say that traditional Negro leaders have never been much better. They were either out of touch with the people for whom they claimed to speak (as many felt about the late Dr. King) or were too willing to play the "Establishment Game." Arguing that their people have always been deluded by whites who had taken up the "burden" and Negroes who were trying to lighten it, the new militants wanted to turn them "blackwards," wanted them to have an identity that was truly their own. They began their campaign by excoriating white liberals, "Uncle Toms" and, especially, "Honkie Society." They are crying it forward with appeals to black nationalism. They may end by making (and, in some cases, making up) history itself.[21]

The themes spelled out in that introduction—and in *Americans from Africa*—opened opportunities to share and test them at Smith and elsewhere. Over the decade, I had several visiting appointments (some on a moonlighting basis) at the University of Massachusetts, Clark University, Wesleyan University, and the University of Colorado. The last was in the summer of 1969, when for the first time in my life I was not involved in camping or camp directing.

The time in Colorado was wonderful. Not only were the summer school students outstanding, but being there also gave us a chance to experience a place where I recently had twice turned down very attractive offers, one to direct an Institute of Human Relations, the other in the Department of Sociology.

I would return to the University of Colorado on several occasions. The most memorable was a week spent as a participant in the annual crazy-quilt Conference on World Affairs, begun in 1948 by a fellow sociologist Howard Higman. Higman would bring together politicians, journalists, musicians, artists, businesspeople, activists of various sorts, and professors from the arts, humanities, sciences and social sciences for a week of cerebration and celebration, highlighted by a series of impromptu panels during the day and early evening and parties hosted by local patrons each night. In my time there, among other things, I was asked to give a talk about my forthcoming book, *Americans from Africa*, and to debate with Nobel laureate and chemist Willard Libby and a Russian scientist about whether a scientist, if called upon, should do the government's bidding even when it went against one's fundamental beliefs. The specific issue in question was the development of even more lethal nuclear weapons than already held in the arsenals of the United States and the Soviet Union. While I demurred, to my chagrin, the other two both said almost without qualification that obedience to authorities was part of being a loyal citizen. (I kept thinking of the Nuremburg defense, "I was just carrying out orders.")

On another day during the conference I was put on a panel with a Marxist economist from the United Kingdom, Joe Rogaly, and the conservative British writer, Henry Fairlie, to discuss our perspectives on race relations in their homeland. It was a great session. Fairlie claimed I was naïve and understood little about British social structure; Rogaly thought

---

[21]From "The Black Experience: Issues and Images," *Social Science Quarterly*, 69: (1969), 286–297; later expanded to become the introduction to the two volume, *Americans from Africa* (New York: Atherton Press, 1970).

I was right on target in all but one aspect of my brief take on the situation. He said I seemed to be minimizing the calculated manipulation of those in power who were quick to use the cultural threat of "the colored people" as a deflecting sop to the white workers they continued to exploit. But neither of those encounters was as interesting to me or as memorable as my several conversations at mealtimes times with two other participants, the journalist and foreign correspondent, Nora Beloff, and the Israeli ambassador to the United States, Yitzak Rabin.

During the academic year following our summer in Colorado, I offered a graduate seminar on comparative race relations at Yale. It was a time of great stress in the halls of academe and in the streets: Bobbie Seale was before the court in the celebrated Black Panther trial taking place right there in New Haven, and *everybody* was suddenly talking about race relations in the U.S. and Americans from Africa.

Thinking about all that was going on in the 1960s, especially my own attempts to address issues relating to race relations in many different settings, brought back a flood of memories of what I was doing in the streets and in lecture halls and in writing ventures and seminars and courses relating to the subject but also of particular students of mine whose lives would become consumed, in several cases quite literally, by the horrors of racial inequality and the persistence of institutionalized racism in the United States. Among them was a bright-eyed, bushy-tailed young woman, Posey Lombard, one of the first to "go south," to march and to be jailed in the notorious Parchman Prison in Mississippi. I remember Posey with great admiration, both for her courage and for staying the course. She remained active in the civil rights struggle, working in various parts of the South until her premature death not too many years after her graduation from Smith.

Another was Marshall Bloom, an Amherst College student who took one of my courses and, knowing of my own involvement in the civil rights struggle and my interest in the marginality of American Jews, asked me to serve as his thesis adviser.

Marshall was a very intense student, highly principled, eager to right historic wrongs and unsure which direction to go to achieve this. He sought several routes: as an active protester against violations of civil rights in the Deep South where he, too, was arrested for his activities; as editor of the Amherst *Student* newspaper, bureau chief for a summer for the independent *Southern Courier* in Montgomery, Alabama, and co-founder, with Ray Mungo, of the *Liberation News Service*, and as a trying-to-be-objective researcher. In the last case, he had returned to Alabama for a third summer, not as an activist or as a journalist, but as a sociologist attempting to record and analyze the seemingly ambiguous status of many Jews in that southern state. Idenifying himself as a Jewish boy from Denver (which he was), he succeeded in eliciting many examples of the tensions a number of members of this insecure "third party" (read: white people, black people—and Jews) felt as they wrestled with what they knew was fair and just and what they feared would further alienate them from the (white) communities where they had long resided. He reported these findings in his honors project on the Jews of Selma.

Marshall, who seemed to clearly know where he stood, was troubled by the unwillingness he found among many of those he interviewed to stand up for the professed principles of "equality for all." He was growing even more troubled by what he saw as too much similar ambivalence among many who claimed to be liberals throughout this country. He said he needed to get away. At my suggestion and recommendation, he applied for and was admitted to the London School of Economics. From all reports, his time there was very unsettling for him—and as he became even more radicalized, it became so for those around him, not least the faculty.

Shortly after his arrival, Marshall became involved with a number of political action groups, was elected president of the Student Union, and led several demonstrations against the School's director, mainly, it was reported, because of the man's South African origins. During those protests a porter died of a heart attack and many blamed Marshall and his cohort.

I happened to be in London shortly thereafter and, one night, having dinner with three prominent members of the sociology faculty at the home of the anthropologist Percy Cohen, one of the other guests said, "I'd like to get my hands on the guy who sent that Bloom chap over here."

I smiled wanly, 'fessed up, and tried to defend Marshall as best I could. It was not easy because the more I had learned of the complexitiy of the circumstances, not least that there had been a considerable amount of ill-informed scapegoating, the more uncomfortable I felt.

When he returned to the States, Marshall seemed to be a different person. He flailed out at any and all, including his mentors, and this one in particular. As I recall, he first became involved with a radical group of black militants but soon found himself seen as too white to really understand their cause, and, as he told me, was "purged." The rejection was devastating to him. Badly shaken, hurt and confused, he decided to withdraw from the fray altogether.

Increasingly dependent on drugs and living in a commune not far from Northampton, he seemed to sink lower and lower into the depths of depression and despair. Many of us tried to persuade him to seek help but—at least in my case, each time we met, the tables seemed to turn and it was "you and your hypocritical friends" who were really in need of a re-do—and redemption. Not long after, Marshall Bloom committed suicide. It was November 1, 1969.

In my many years of teaching and working with students, I consider his death one of the greatest tragedies. And the fact that I seemed unable to help him, one of my greatest failures.

On any number of occasions, I tried to write something about Marshall but never found the words. What is finally related here hardly does justice to my feelings about Marshall, one of the key figures in the civil rights and communal living movement during that turbulent decade in which so many changes occurred in so many lives, including my own, forever to be known as "The Sixties."

III

The 1970s: Fully Booked

WHILE MY FOREIGN TRAVELING BEGAN with occasional academic excursions to unfamiliar places in the 1960s, over the next ten years it became almost routine. As the decade opened, Hedy and I were making plans for our first trip to East Asia and the Pacific.

It all started with an invitation to serve once again as a Fulbright professor—this time to go to Australia to deliver the inaugural lectures in the newly created Department of American Studies at the Flinders University of South Australia located in a suburb outside the very English city of Adelaide on the south coast of the country. Without hesitation I said "Yes." Soon after the appointment was finalized, I received a phone call from Jean Moretti, a program officer at the Council on the International Exchange of Scholars (CEIS), the body that handled senior Fulbright appointments. She asked if I might be willing to leave for Australia a month early and travel via Japan to teach for several weeks in what was called the Kyoto Summer Seminar in American Studies. I discussed this add-on with Hedy and like me, she was thrilled by such a prospect. Although we knew it would put a big dent in our bank account (CIES would be paying only for me), we decided we should beg, borrow, or steal the money and all four of us go. At the time we were sure it would be the trip of a lifetime. And it was, for many reasons. But we had no inkling that it was really just the beginning, one of many more overseas assignments we would enjoy over the next forty years.

Our first stop was Tokyo. Of course I knew better than to expect to see living examples of the buck-toothed, yellow-skinned, bespectacled

"Japs" that adorned the walls of schools and other public buildings during my childhood in World War II—crude and ugly propaganda caricatures instructing us to "KNOW THE ENEMY," were firmly implanted in my mind's eye. Still, I confess to thinking about those images when we were driven into the center of the city by someone sent out from the Fulbright Office to meet us. In fact we were totally unprepared for the people we met and for what we actually saw and experienced.

At first blush, though the faces were clearly Asian, everything else seemed quite familiar. Tokyo—at least the part to which we were brought—was a modern city with big department stores, bright lights and good subways. Most of the people, especially the young men, were wearing clothing that would have been fashionable in any American town. And yet it didn't take more than a day or two to see that not far beneath the Western facade was a truly different culture. We then realized that our education was so Eurocentric that we knew almost nothing about Japanese culture or character—nor, it would turn out, anything about the manners and mores of folks in other Asian lands.

Discussing this on our third or fourth night in town, we swore that we would rectify that failing in the days, weeks, months and years ahead. (In this I can report that we did make some progress on our own. At one point I even started taking Japanese lessons.)

We stayed near the American embassy in a hotel in Akasaka, Minato-ku, a quite cosmopolitan section of Tokyo, and visited some of the more touristy parts of the city, including the glitzy Ginza and the more traditional Asakusa, and some major shrines. We then moved on to the ancient city of Kyoto aboard the bullet train. En route we passed the only iconic representation of Japan that we knew: snow-capped Mount Fuji.

Waiting at the station to meet us was Akashi Norio, a young Japanese specialist in American history who had studied at the University of Wisconsin. Akashi-san, a junior member of the faculty of Doshisha University, had been asked to be our guide and my interpreter for the duration of our stay. When we met, he handed me his *meishi* (business card) and, knowing little about this tradition, I must have blanched when he stood there waiting for me to produce my own. Two days later I was given a packet of cards with my name, rank and college affiliation in Japanese on one side and in English on the other. I haven't traveled to Japan—or anyplace else—without such cards since then.

While in Kyoto I became fascinated by what I came to call the "double bow." The ethnographer in me began observing a number of Japanese who appeared to be strangers as they greeted each other. I noticed that, in most cases, once each had the other's proffered *meishi*, both would bow slightly and, holding the other's card, *seemed to be reading rank not name*. Then, depending on the result of the scan, adjusting the depth of a second bow. I learned to do it, too.

After we settled in at the Palace Side Hotel, opposite the old Imperial Palace grounds, Akashi-san invited us to join him and his wife at the parade celebrating the colorful *Gion Matsuri*, the Gion Festival, then in its tenth century of yearly festivities, first decreed in 970 as a way to honor the gods and seek propitiation against the ravages of plagues and other calamities.

It was an amazing spectacle. Tens of thousands of people lined the main avenues of the city to watch a seemingly endless parade of decorated floats. In the evening our hosts asked us to join them in the traditional walkabout through the side streets where local residents opened their homes, showing off their most prized possessions, and extending a warm welcome to all visitors, including *gaijins* (foreigners) such as the four of us. It was a most memorable introduction to the way in which the modern Japanese still retained their affection for and understanding of old practices.

I started teaching the next day. Hedy came with me. The kids, then ages ten and eight, stayed at the hotel. They played in their room or in the lobby where they quickly made friends with the desk staff, especially the concierge, a man they called Bright Eyes.

Bright Eyes became their language teacher and they learned to copy his phone answering technique. Back in the room in the evening, they would regale us with their mimicry. "*Moshi, moshi, anonay,*" each would say, pretending to answer the phone. Then, holding the imaginary instrument, they would nod to each other and say, "*Ah, so.*" Later they would learn the Japanese way of asking how you say something in Japanese. "*Nihon go-day do-no-yony ee-ee masu ka?*" they would say, making it sound like an American football cheer.

Of course, I was not in Kyoto to learn about and practice Japanese customs or mannerisms, but to try to explain to professors of literature and history and political science and sociology something about the nature of our society, in my case, that pertaining to discussions about race and ethnicity. This is how I described the experience:

> On the first day of the Kyoto Summer Seminar in American Studies, and, after a preliminary discussion with my students—actually all of them were fellow professors from Japan and Korea—I became quite aware that even for a group of self-identified "Americanists," neither pluralism nor inter-group relations were easy concepts to convey in a society that prided itself on its homogeneity. I spent much of the rest of the time in the course trying to introduce them to these ideas and to the meaning of prejudice and discrimination—and to the civil rights campaign—in the United States.
>
> Since those in the group were from very different fields I drew on various sources to illustrate my points. Often I would season my commentary by reading passages from the writings of novelists or reciting memorized poems—like Countee Cullen's "Incident"—to illustrate a point or two.

> > Once riding in old Baltimore
> > Heart filled, head filled with glee
> > I saw a Baltimorean
> > Keep looking straight at me.
> >
> > Now I was eight and very small,
> > And he was no whit bigger
> > And so I smiled, but he poked out
> > His tongue and called me "nigger."
> >
> > I saw the whole of Baltimore
> > From May until December:
> > Of all the things that happened there
> > That's all that I remember.

Even after changing, actually personalizing, my approach, I still found it was hard to get the class to have empathy with the little African-American child and the three stanzas that were at once literal and symbolic. But they tried.

Sometime during the last day of the first week I was in the middle of one of my very un-Japanese sorts of exercise when, suddenly, we were all startled to hear a deep bass voice singing "I'm comin', I'm comin', though my head is bending low; I hear those gentle voices callin' Ole Black Joe." The singer was my American colleague, an historian from Emory University in Georgia. I assumed he was trying to make a point in his course in southern history just on the other side of the paper screen that divides our temporary classrooms. A few minutes later I cringed as we all heard another resounding line. "Oh darkies, how my heart grows weary, yearnin' for the old folks at home."

Those in my class were fascinated and one asked, very politely, why I was wincing. I composed myself again and trying to use the incident to underscore what I had been trying to convey through Cullen's poem earlier. I asked if they could think of instances where they were subject to such prejudices. None could think of any.

But then, after a few moments, a young historian spoke about how Japanese-Americans must have felt after the attack on Pearl Harbor, when they were rounded up and relocated because they had been assumed to be disloyal to the United States and potential agents of Japan.

I used his remarks to introduce the concept of scapegoating. The word was hard to translate; its biblical origins quite meaningless in that setting. I groped for a way to explain how people blame others for their own problems and then steered the class into a rather stilted conversation about what it might mean to have to live with racism and to face categorical discrimination. Eventually I seemed to be reaching most of the group.[22]

Over the next two weeks, I spoke about and we all discussed many aspects of American patterns of immigration and integration and many problems that still confronted our very plural society.

Toward the end of the period, feeling on pretty safe grounds with folks with whom I had built up considerable rapport, I asked the

---

[22]"Countee Cullen in Kyoto," in *Guest Appearances*, 82–85.

members of the seminar to tell me something of the situation of minorities in Japan.

No one said a word.

I asked again, this time specifying my interest in their comments on the Ainu, the Koreans, and the Eta, the name I had learned for a large group of people also referred to in the American literature as "Japan's invisible race." Before I could say another thing, Akashi Norio tugged at my elbow and whispers. "You shouldn't use the word *eta*. It means dirty one. It is like saying 'nigger.' Just like in that poem!" Still speaking in hushed tones, he told me the correct expression for the group is not *Eta* but *Buraku-min*.

Chastened but still curious, I asked the class about the *Buraku-min*.

"Oh," said one English-speaker, "that is an old matter. Since the Meiji Period all Japanese have equality."

The others said nothing.

I let it pass—at least momentarily—and moved on.

"Then what about the Ainu?" I asked.

A history teacher spoke up. "Theirs is a sad story. Like American Indians, they were pretty much, well, exterminated. There are very few Ainu today so you can't really call them a minority group."

I was to learn that this was a sad truth. The Ainu, a Caucasian-like people who had lived for centuries in the northern part of Japan, especially on the island of Hokkaido, had indeed been wiped out in the northward expansion. (Today, in Sapporo, the capital of Hokkaido there is a fine museum to the lost people that reminds one of the anthropological museums in Vancouver and Victoria, tributes to the Kwakiutl, Tlingit, Haida, and Salish peoples. The difference is that many members of the latter groups are alive and intact in contrast to the tiny remnant of the Ainu people.)

I moved on, asking about the Koreans in Japan. Almost like a Greek chorus, four members of the seminar, all middle-aged English-speakers, said as one, "Oh, they're not Japanese!"

This, it turns out, was not just an ethnic distinction. Koreans constitute a large minority. Despite having been in the country for several generations, they are not accepted as Japanese.

Hesitantly, I maneuvered the discussion back to the subject of the *Buraku-min*. Some members of the group allowed that, despite all the claims to the contrary, the *Buraku-min* were a clearly recognizable, if not officially recognized, Japanese minority, especially noticeable in the cities of the eastern coast of Honshu, including Kyoto. They remained members of a marginal caste still experiencing discrimination owing to their ancestry as having been descended from those who did the dirty work of society, serving as slaughterers, butchers, tanners, gravediggers and collectors of the night soil (human waste).

They came to fascinate me the most.

I was actually to get to know some of the leaders of the Kyoto Branch of the Buraku Emancipation Movement. I learned about them from a young assistant professor from Nagasaki when he joined me in the cafeteria for a beer during a break in the seminar. He was eager to talk to me about the *Buraku-min*. (I will call him Sasaki Yoshio here.)

Soon after he sat down and we began to chat, another member of the seminar, a fellow social scientist my age—and one who had become so close a friend that he had taken the unprecedented step of inviting me and my wife and our children to his home for dinner a few nights before—joined us and began listening to our conversation about the *Buraku-min*.

I immediately felt some bad vibes emanating from the younger man. Still, I asked Sasaki to continue. He had just asked me if I would be interested in meeting some of the local members of the *Buraku* community. He said he knew some of them very well and would take me to meet them. The other man, Watanabe Hajime, who had been listening, asked if he might go along. The younger fellow hesitated. It was clear to me that he emphatically wanted to say no, but, after a pregnant pause, he agreed. He left to make another phone call and while he is gone Watanabe said, "This is going to be fascinating." He told me he didn't know any *Buraku* people but assured me that he did know something about them. Now it was I who was growing uneasy.

Sasaki returned and said everything was arranged. He would pick me up at my hotel at 11:00 a.m. on Saturday and would then swing by for Otani at 11:30.

On Saturday, my escort arrived early. Over a cup of tea, he told me how he came to know the *Buraku-min*.

"I am a Christian," he explained. "I came to Kyoto to study English at Doshisha (a church-related private university) and, while I was here I took part in activities sponsored by a minister of my church. I was very much concerned about continuing discrimination against the people called *Eta*, a sort of untouchable group, kept down by traditionalists who said they were dirty."

"In any case," he continued, "I joined with some social workers in their area and got more out of the good work than I expected." He went on to say that he met his future wife there and "despite objections, even from my Christian but-still-very-Japanese family, I married her."

I asked how she was received. Sasaki said it was very hard at first but when the first child arrived, they welcomed her into their home.

Sasaki was about to continue but realizing that we were already late, ended the conversation. We got in the car and drove over to pick up Professor Watanabe and then went into downtown Kyoto, into a neighborhood by the river. We moved very slowly through the Gion District's narrow but crowded streets, passing a famous theater, many curio shops, many more camera shops, every once and a while getting a glimpse of the hills above the city, a glimpse of a geisha en route to her club, a Buddhist acolyte en route to his temple and a bunch of uniformed giggly school girls heading home. It was a visual collage of compressed impressions—old, new, dowdy, bright, sacred and profane. Then we came to a less colorful and less cacophonous section. While poor by Japanese standards, the area was hardly a slum. It looked to me quite similar to many others I had visited or run through on early morning jogs around the city.

When we arrived at the right house, a man in his mid-thirties who spoke excellent English warmly greeted us. Several of his friends were there, too.

We were ushered into a western room, the kind found in many Japanese homes. It had an overstuffed sofa and a matching chair, each decorated with white, lacy antimacassars (the sort that was also found on the backs of Japanese taxi seats in those days), and a low coffee table. The only thing untoward was a large white banner on one wall. It had a bright red crown of thorns in which was imbedded a red star and beneath it some Japanese writing. I asked about it and was told it is the emblem of the Kyoto Branch of the Radical Socialist Buraku Emancipation movement. The leader told me that they had broken with the Christian social workers ("Too much do-gooder in their approach") and then with the Communists ("They only want to use us for their cause"). Before I left I was presented with a smaller version of the banner, used as a headband in demonstrations, and a red armband with the same symbol of political syncretism. (Both are still on display in my office, reminders of an extraordinary meeting.)

For me, it was the first of several meetings. That was not to be the case for Professor Watanabe.

After being invited to sit down, our host had asked if we would like something to drink, *"Beer-u,* soft-drink?" I asked for a beer. Sasaki said he'd like one, too. Watanabe had hesitated and then asked for Coca-Cola.

The drinks were served and the host raised his glass. *"Kom-pai"* he said and we all took our first sip. Except Watanabe. He brought the glass near his lips but never touched the rim. He smiled, rather sickly I thought, and put down the glass. The tension in the room was palpable. I had heard the word pollution often used to describe the "Eta" but I was now an eyewitness to truly insulting behavior. And I was not alone. Everyone was glaring at Watanabe. He was clearly embarrassed. But he never did drink from the glass.

After several minutes, with everyone acting as if Watanabe was somewhere else, we began to discuss the plight of the *Buraku-min.* As a student of and participant in our own civil rights movement, what was especially striking to me was that their local leader is echoing the sentiments of many of our own civil rights leaders. This was most apparent when I asked the host what the most important thing he had to do to help his people. Without hesitation he says, "Get them to hold their heads up." They, too, were being encouraged to address the tendency to internalize their disgrace and stop hating themselves.

After two hours we left, but not before I was invited to come back to see them at any time. *"Sayonara,"* pointedly said to me, was heartfelt. It was very clear that I was a welcome guest. Such was definitely not the case for Watanabe who was given a stiff, cold but courteous bow, which he reciprocated.

That evening, as planned long before the visit to the *Buraku* community, I went out to dinner with Watanabe Hajime. We sat cross-legged and shoeless on *tatami* mats in a neighborhood restaurant and made awkward small talk. As the kimono-clad waitress served us one delicacy after another, bowing, then serving, then pouring more *saki,* I felt myself forsaking the neutrality of one trained to respect cultural relativity and let myself go. I chided Watanabe about his blatantly discourteous behavior. He hung his head and expressed shame and embarrassment for what he clearly knew was offensive and hurtful.

"We were guests in another man's home...," I began. "A home," I wanted to say, "that, while smaller than yours, was just as neat and clean." But I never finish my sentence. Catching my drift, Watanabe did it for me.

"I know that was a very clean place and that the people there were well educated and very respectable, but...." Then he added something to the effect that there are things that are not easily overcome. He said, "You know, you're a sociologist. You call it socialization."

I sighed and we finished dinner in silence. The waitress bowed to us as we left the little room and moved down a narrow hallway toward the curtained entrance. There we took proffered shoehorns from another young woman and put on our shoes. Still we didn't speak. Watanabe drove me back to the hotel. I got out of the car and nodded to him. He nodded, too.

I didn't say goodbye. I didn't even say "*Domo arigato*" to thank him for dinner.

As I moved across the lobby, Countee Cullen's poignant words keep swirling around in my head. A variation on his "Incident" still haunts my memory of what was an eye-opening first of what would be many trips to Japan.

> I saw the whole of Kyoto
> That summer long ago.
> Of all the things that happened there,
> That was the cruelest blow.[23]

In addition to the time spent teaching and learning something about and attitudes toward those who were indeed minorities in Japan, we did manage to see many of the wonderful treasures of Kyoto: Kinkaku-ji, the Temple of the Golden Pavilion, Ginkaku-ji, the Temple of the Silver Pavilion, and a few other Buddhist temples (there are more than 1500 in the area), many Shinto shrines, and the grounds of the Imperial Palace. We also took the train from Kyoto up to Mount Hiei and, later, over to the city of Nara, with its famous deer park and gigantic Buddha, and we managed two trips to the most modern of sites, Expo 1970, the World's Fair taking place that very summer in nearby Osaka. Then after playing both teachers of our culture and students of Japan's, with a break of several weeks between assignments, we stopped off at two other Asian venues before heading for Australia.

---

[23]Ibid., 85–90.

We went first to Taipei in Taiwan and then to Hong Kong where we had good contacts who could serve as personal guides to each place. Both destinations also proved fascinating and eye-opening.

There were many highlights during our brief stay in Taipei but the ones best remembered were the trip to the National Museum, with its spectacular collection of art and artifacts mostly brought from the mainland when the Nationalists retreated to their Formosan refuge; an extended visit to a flea market where we saw puppies for sale the same way lobsters are sold in markets in Maine—and for the same purpose; and a dinner at Earl's Dumplings, where we were taken by my Smith College colleague, Steve Goldstein, who was in Taiwan on sabbatical leave. The last was memorable not only because of the gigantic size of Earl's pot stickers but also because of the shouts of waiters who were letting everyone know the size of the tips people were leaving, presumably a clever ploy to get cheapskates to shell out more in order to save face.

Hong Kong, the next stop on our itinerary, was like an enchanted island with its combination of very Chinese and very English styles and its extraordinary din of sounds, range of smells, and array of colors. Our guide there was a recent Smith graduate, Pearl Yau, who had been our children's piano teacher. Home for the summer between college and medical school at Stanford, Pearl accompanied us on the Star Ferry from Kowloon where her family lived over to the island of Hong Kong and up to the top of its famous peak. She took us to places not listed in the tour books and rarely seen by visitors. Most striking were the market stalls stocked with everything from pearls and jade to the latest in camera equipment to Chinese- and European-style clothing to every kind of condiment, all selling at amazingly low prices. As an extra treat, especially for Lies and Dan, before leaving Hong Kong we were invited to enjoy a day of cruising the waters around the crown colony on Pearl's father's company's yacht.

In the years that were to come, I would return to Japan, Taiwan and Hong Kong on numerous occasions, but my first impressions of all three places still linger vividly in my thoughts.

After a week in Hong Kong we flew south for our semester in Australia, stopping briefly in Darwin and then in Sydney, where we spent several days before flying over to Melbourne, where I had been invited to speak at a conference at La Trobe University.

Finally we arrived at our principal destination, Adelaide, and settled into a great apartment in the seaside suburb of Glenelg, arranged for us by our hosts at the spanking new—plate-glass as opposed to red brick—Flinders University of South Australia. There, in addition to my primary obligations and days spent teaching and seeing students on campus, we used our free time exploring the city of Adelaide and the area around it, not least the famous Barossa Valley wine country, and taking side trips to other places. This included an incredible day of skiing in deep snow on eucalyptus-lined trails on Mount Buller—it was, after all, Australian winter.

Over four succeeding weeks I delivered my four public lectures to a mixed audience of faculty members, students, and interested citizens of Adelaide. The series was a central part of the inaugural year of the first American Studies program in the Southern Hemisphere. (A decade later I would have the privilege of being the first to speak at the opening of the American Studies Center at the National Taiwanese University in Taipei and, in 1986, would do a similar thing at the opening of a new program at the Johns Hopkins University Center in Nanjing.) While at Flinders, I also offered a course and a seminar to undergraduates.

On the first day of class, I asked offhand if someone could tell me something about minorities in Australia. This was a time when what was clearly known as a "white Australia" immigration policy was very much the law of the land. I can still picture a young man raising his hand, then saying, "Well, sir, we actually have a number of colored people here."

"Do you mean the Aborigines?" I asked him.

"No, sir. In addition to those people, we have a number of Italians and Greeks."

Since that first trip I have been back in Australia many times, each time amazed to see how dramatically things were changing on the demographic front. Australia has become far more heterogeneous in culture and character than it was in the 1970s. In addition to those "colored" folks from southern Europe, it has a growing East and Southeast Asian population. In fact, Australia was one of the first countries to institutionalize the practice of multiculturalism, even to the extent of having a ministry for such pluralism and a well-funded TV channel devoted to presentations from the diverse communities. Sad to say, however, the native people—once characterized by a American friend who studied them as "tens times worse off than Native Americans who, themselves remain in dire straits"—are still suffering from discrimination in a variety of spheres of life.

Nearing completion of our first extended trip to Asia and the South Pacific, we briefly visited New Zealand, where I spoke at the University of Canterbury in Christchurch and then at the University of Auckland. We enjoyed the beautiful scenery and marked differences in topography and climate on the South and North islands and, going about on my sociological-autopilot, gained some insight into the distinctive differences betweem Australians and New Zealanders, two cohorts of people we had often lumped together in our stereotypes.

Reluctantly we left New Zealand's North Island for home, but not before making two more stopovers, the first in Fiji, the second in Honolulu—both places where multiculturalism, albeit sometimes strained, was a way of life long before it ever became an ideology.

There were two unexpected fringe benefits of the trip. First, meeting the Norwegian scholar and poet—and, at the time, one of the leading figures in American studies in Europe—Sigmund Skard, and then making the acquaintance of Leonard Robock, the American cultural attaché in Australia.

Skard, who was about sixty-five, had just retired from his position as head of the Department of Literature at the University of Oslo and was on a Carnegie-funded 'round the world tour of American Studies programs. His first stop was in Kyoto for the summer seminar in which I was teaching and that was where my family and I first came to know him. Sigmund's second stop was at LaTrobe University in Melbourne where we were both presenting papers. Then, like the four of us, he went on to Adelaide where, unbeknownst to me, he had been asked by the Australian historian, Paul Bourke, the head of the new Department of American Studies, to introduce me at the first of my lectures, making the event truly international.

At dinner at our apartment the night before he left Australia, Sigmund said that he would be seeing us the following year. I didn't understand. He then explained that he had just been in contact with Erik Jacobsen, the University of Copenhagen-based president of the Nordic Association for American Studies and had recommended me as a keynote speaker at the following year's annual meeting scheduled to be held in Kungalv, Sweden, near Gothenburg. Apparently Jacobsen and his committee accepted Sigmund's suggestion for a few months later I received a formal invitation.

Almost immediately we started planning another family trip, this time to Scandinavia. Our Norwegian friend, Sigmund, wrote to propose that we take a circular tour of his native land before joining him back in Oslo for the journey to Kungalv for the NAAS meeting. He said he would arrange it.

The next June we flew to Copenhagen and spent a few days there before taking the overnight ship to Oslo where we were met by Sigmund and began our pre-conference Norwegian tour going by train from Oslo to Bergen and on through the long Sognefjord by boat then, after disembarking, into the mountains and back to Oslo by train.

We stayed about a week at Kungalv and, after a very lively conference, enjoyed the Swedish Mid-Summer Festival and even got to sail on the Kattegat. Afterwards we took the train to Stockholm and the ferry to Helsinki, where our new host and guide was Per Amnell, a man I hadn't seen since 1953 when he was a graduate student in the School of Forestry at Syracuse and we were both ski instructors there. Per made sure we met his family, saw his home in the modern city of Tapiola, and arranged for us to travel by boat through a series of lakes and rivers to

Tampere and return to by train to Helsinki. All told, in addition to the main purpose of my visit, which was to exchange ideas with fellow Americanists from northern Europe, our Scandinavia sojourn turned out to be another series of exciting new adventures and, like the one the year before, and many to come in the years ahead, full of unexpected surprises. Here is one account of an amusing encounter that occurred in the very early days of the trip.

> After reading so much about it, we thought that Tivoli Gardens in Copenhagen with its variety of activities—concessions, concerts, rides and restaurants—was going to be one of the highlights of the trip, especially for the children. And it proved to be just that. We were there every night. One evening after the children persuaded us to stay at Tivoli very late in the evening, we finally leave. We start walking back toward our modest digs, a "mission hotel," located in the rough neighborhood by the docks. A woman hands me a flyer; I glance at it and discover it is a copy of *The Watchtower*. I read it hurriedly and then toss it in the nearest dustbin. Lies, our eleven-year-old daughter, asks me what it was.
>
> "A religious tract," I say.
> "What do you mean?" she asks.
> I try to explain.
> She says, "Aren't you interested?"
> "No, not particularly."
> "Why?"
> I don't respond.
> "Because we're Jewish?"
> Exasperated, I say "Yes, because we're Jewish."
> We walk on, turn the corner and enter the red-light district very near our hotel. A lady of the night steps outs and starts to hand me a business card.
> Before I can react, my daughter says, "No thanks, we're Jewish!"

As I have said many times, ways of sitting, posturing, arguing, playing honored guest, and learning to down (and hold) gallons of tea, beer, sherry, scotch, grapefruit juice, sake and jet-black coffee—and dealing with one's children—are some of the items that are often overlooked in briefing papers prepared for those about to embark on short-term academic tours in foreign climes or a year abroad. This was a prime example of such an omission!

The next summer I was a Martin Foundation fellow at the Hebrew University in Jerusalem. My family came with me to Israel. We stayed in a convent hospice in Ein Karem called Notre Dame de Sion. run by the Sisters of Our Lady of Zion. We became friends with the French- and Hebrew-speaking nuns, whose information about the intricacies of monastic life was both useful and illuminating. The other guests were a mix of Christian pilgrims, kibbutzniks, graduate students, and tourists. We loved being there and were touched by the integrity and incredible warmth of the sisters.

Among the few rules was one declaring no one should try to speak to the several contemplative nuns who were there. Another insisted there was to be no proselytizing of any kind on the premises. One day a group of Jehovah's Witnesses who were staying at the hospice began distributing leaflets and buttonholing other guests. Within an hour, they were politely but firmly asked to leave.

We enjoyed hanging out at the place, especially with our new friend, Canadian-born Sister Grace, but, of course, had other things to do while in Jerusalem, mainly on the campus of the Hebrew University.

When I wasn't at the university, we spent hours wandering through the Old City and made several trips to different parts of the country to visit ancient sites, small villages, and a number of kibbutzim, meeting both Jews and Arabs and trying to make sense of the complexities of that old/new society. I was particularly pleased that my family could now see some of the places I had visited on my previous trip, especially Yad Vashem and the Garden of the Righteous among the Nations, honoring those, like Tante Toos, who helped Jews during the Holocaust.

While in Jerusalem one evening, our daughter asked us if she might buy a silver Star of David and necklace like those she had seen in many shops and stalls around the city. We said of course she could, but after the kids had gone to bed, Hedy and I admitted to each other that we felt a bit uncomfortable about her getting it, if for rather different reasons. For Hedy it was a reminder of the yellow star with the Dutch word *Jood*

(Jew) she had had to wear on her outer garments as a little child before she was taken into hiding. For me, having spent years both studying ethnic identity and seeking to break down barriers between people, it was, like wearing a crucifix, not so much a stigma as a symbol of separation. As we spoke we realized that these were our problems not our daughter's. Lies bought her *Magen David* the next day.

We came home via Greece. This second trip to the country was, like my first one, educational in an unexpected way. This time it was more a reminder of what had happened when I served as a consultant to the navy the decade before, where stereotyping had played such a role in coloring my expectations.

For several years I had been in touch with a woman named Katrina Kipreos who had begun and directed a unique program called "Study in Greece" and had written about her approach, one of total immersion. Students, accepted for the program, most of them knowing no Greek and very little about the country, would be brought to one of the Saronic Islands, Agistri, for four or five weeks of living and working in a place where nobody spoke English. After that experience, Katrina would give each of the students a very limited amount of money and a batch of maps and send them off on a scavenger hunt that would take them as far away as Thessaloniki in the north and Crete in the south. Then, when they got back, having had to fend for themselves, she felt they would be ready to start a year of intensive study and to work on their individualized capstone projects on anything from Macedonian dances to winemaking to deciphering a myriad of frequently used hand gestures.

I was impressed with this creative approach to cultural study and was eager to meet this amazing Greek woman with such a fine command of English. I wrote to say that my wife and kids and I would be coming to Greece and would love to meet her. She was very pleased and said that we shouldn't even think about taking a taxi into Athens; she would be there to greet us at the airport. (The scene of our first encounter and the risk of mistaken identity popped back into my head very recently as I read Michael Frayn's comic novel, *Skios*.)

We landed on schedule, passed through immigration and customs and went out into the arrival hall and looked for Katrina. Every time I thought we spotted her, the person I was sure was she would then wave to someone else coming through the door. Finally, with only one very tall, very American-seeming blonde woman standing there, I said, "Well, I guess she was held up. Let's grab a taxi." At that point, the blonde came toward me, extended her hand in a most American fashion, and said, "Are you Peter Rose?" When I said I was, she said, "Great to meet you. I'm Kate Kipreos."

Kate *Butterworth* Kipreos, it turned out, was an American from the mid-west, who had initially come to Greece with her first husband. After a divorce, she stayed on and soon married a Greek surnamed Kipreos.

Not long after we returned to the States, Kate invited me to join her Board of Directors. The program flourished for many years with dozens of students, including some from Smith, recommended by an initially skeptical member of our classics department, Thalia Pandiri, who would become one of the program's most enthusiastic supporters.

Study in Greece closed when Greece was plunged into political turmoil (long before the economic crises of this decade) when many American parents were reluctant to have their college-age students run the risk of getting caught in some sort of upheaval. But Kate is still there—and we are still in touch.

One other noteworthy event occurred shortly after our first meeting with Kate Kipreos and after she took us to Piraeus to board an old liner called *Romantica* for a week-long cruise of the islands. On the first night on board our children were playing on the deck and overheard some adults speaking to their daughter Letitia. Pricking up her ears, Lies thought they were speaking Dutch and asked Hedy if it was true. It was. Later that day, I introduced myself to the family.

Over the next few days, I learned that the paterfamilias, Theo Bot, was a Dutch diplomat taking a family break between assignments in Vienna and Ottawa. I enjoyed sitting with him, exchanging stories about foreign assignments. At one point Ambassador Bot asked me what was the most interesting place I had visited or lived in for awhile. I immediately said Japan. He blanched a bit and said, "I've never been to Japan but I do know the Japanese."

He then explained that he and his family had been living in Indonesia when the Second World War broke out. Rounded up by the Japanese occupiers, they were sent to different prison camps. His was in Thailand near the Burmese border where he was one of the youngest of the seven thousand POWs forced to build the railway bridge immortalized in the David Lean film, *The Bridge over the River Kwai*. I asked if he had seen the movie. Bot said he had. Then he added, "It was much, much worse than portrayed there."

While he had nothing to do with our Scandinavian journey, our summer in Israel or any trips to Greece, Len Robock, the U.S. cultural attaché in Canberra at the time of my appointment in Australia, was truly the man most instrumental in my becoming a global lecturer.

Because the Fulbright program was the sponsor of my first trip to Australia, and the U.S. and Australian governments had contributed to the development of the program at Flinders, Len had come down to Adelaide from Canberra. We met again in the capital city which we visited before leaving for New Zealand.

While we were in Canberra, Len and his wife had invited us to dinner. During the course of the evening, he asked me if I had ever heard of the STAG program. I said it sounded rather sexist but, no, I didn't know it. Len explained that STAG stood for Short Term American Grantee, and that it was essentially a speaker's program run out of the offices of the U.S. Information Agency (USIA). Given my unexpectedly positive experience at the Pentagon a few years earlier, I asked him to tell me more. He told us that STAGs are often asked to do lecture tours in various parts of the world, usually on the basis of requests from university faculty members or directors of cultural programs, but they do not speak on behalf of our government nor are they expected to take a particular position. Assured that no one would have to clear my talks or preview what I might say, I decided to allow Len to put my name forward.

That conversation—ten thousand miles from home—proved catalytic.

Over the next 25 years I would make many trips back to Japan and also to China, to Southeast Asia, as far as Indonesia, back to Australia and New Zealand, to various parts of Europe, including Eastern Europe, to India and Iran, and to five countries in Africa, a number of them arranged thorough the speakers' bureau of USIA. The only years in which I never received an assignment were during the first term of the Reagan Administration, when, I would later learn, I had been blacklisted. This was at a time when the director of the agency wanted only speakers who would toe the government line. The policy proved to be an ideal example of a self-fulfilling prophecy, for it confirmed the suspicions of many that we STAGs, later called AMSPECS, or American specialists, were really CIA plants! The director's successor realized the folly of the plan and dropped it. I found myself being asked again to travel abroad and speak my own piece. And I did.

My three Fulbright appointments in England, Japan and Australia; early days as a STAG in Asia, starting in 1972; and my being a social scientist all led to another unexpected opportunity. In the middle of the decade I was asked to design and conduct the previously mentioned evaluation of the Senior Fulbright Program in East Asia and the Pacific. I accepted the job, took a semester of leave (while the government grant covered my salary), and conducted a study that involved many interviews on several trips back to the area and quite a number in this country. Each time I crossed the Pacific for interviews I followed a path that started in Korea and took me to the offices of randomly selected former Fulbright professors and the members of the respective binational commissions there and in Japan, Taiwan, Hong Kong, the Philippines, Singapore, Malaysia, Thailand, Australia and New Zealand. My full report, *Academic Sojourners*, based on many face-to-face meetings and supplemented by a mailed questionnaire, and a subsequent shorter version, "The Senior Fulbright-Hays Program in East Asia and the Pacific: Research and Recommendations," published in the journal *Exchange* in 1976, summarized the study, highlighted the complaints and suggestions of former Fulbright professors—including those Americans who went out to the same countries I visited, and made some specific recommendations.

My first trip was mainly for reconnaissance. I only spoke to a small number of administrators and alumni of the program in each of the countries, promising to return soon. It proved to be a very useful approach because, when I did go back, some of those I'd met in the first round said they hadn't been convinced they'd ever see me again and were now delighted to welcome me back. This was a strategy I would use a number of years later when I was studying refugee workers in Southeast Asia.

Before beginning fieldwork on the Fulbright evaluation, I was already alerted to certain concerns, though sometimes they were not immediately forthcoming from those I'd interviewed on my test run. While Australians and New Zealanders and many in the Philippines and in Taiwan were pretty straightforward about what they liked about the program and what they would change, those in the other countries, especially Japan and Korea, were very reluctant to criticize anything. Discussing this with a friend at the U.S. embassy in Tokyo, I learned that it wasn't considered appropriate to, as he put it, "bite the hand that is feeding you." I decided that I would have to change my approach. So, on the two succeeding visits—when the really intense interviewing took place—instead of asking what they thought was wrong with the program, I would say, "Suppose you were invited to become an evaluator of the Senior Fulbright Program for Japan (or Korea or Thailand...), what sorts of things would you recommend be considered?" It worked like a charm.

One other thing that was striking was the extent to which so many felt that their year in the States was one of the most important in their careers. It was not just the chance to work with colleagues in their fields and to get a sense of American university life but the opportunity to *see America.*

In those days, continent-hopping was far from the norm for the vast majority of academics from across the Pacific—or from here to there. I came to feel that the Fulbright program, at least the part that dealt with professorial exchanges, offered the best bang for the buck if we wanted others to understand this country while helping American professors get to know *their* overseas counterparts and *their* home societies.

In a parallel study, I asked a cross-section of Americans who had spent time in East Asia and the South Pacific about their own experiences as Fulbrighters. Not surprisingly, they were as enthusiastic about what they had done overseas as were those who had come here. They had some criticisms and some good suggestions for improving the program. One concern that was a bit unexpected came when I asked about recruiting some of their own colleagues to apply to the program. More than a few said that they could think of a number of people who would be great but, unless they could go to places that were in line with their research concerns, they would be reluctant to spend an entire sabbatical year or even a whole semester as a Fulbrighter.

Accordingly, one of my final recommendations to the Board of Foreign Scholarship was that its members consider adding a new category to those of Senior Fulbright Lecturer and Senior Fulbright Researcher, to be called something like "Academic Consultant" or "Short-Term Distinguished Fulbright Visitor." I explained that because it was often difficult to get the busiest and most in-demand professors to commit themselves to an extended stay in a place that might not have immediate relevance to their own particular work—such as getting a world-class historian who focused on China to go to Australia, even though he or she might be highly regarded there. I suggested that stays of four to six weeks might be a more attractive enticement. Such appointments would mean that participants would be anchored at a given institution long enough not just to give some lectures but also, as special guests, to enjoy ample opportunity to get to know their hosts and others on the campus, not least the students.

Although there was some interest in this idea, nothing was done about it. Not in the '70s or '80s or '90s. But early in the new century such a program was implemented. I first heard about it when I received a call from Washington inviting me to apply to the Fulbright Commission in Austria to be considered for an appointment as a Senior

Fulbright Specialist. (It sounded very much the sort of position I had recommended.) I did apply and was accepted and spent five weeks based at the University of Vienna in the fall of 2003, lecturing there and at three other institutions, including the Diplomatic Academy, and in several other parts of Austria. Three years later I held a similar position at the Roosevelt Academy, the international honors college of Utrecht University in the Netherlands. That time I stayed on site, offering lectures, co-teaching two courses, and holding office hours for students.

It may have been a result of my brief time teaching in Japan and my growing interest in that society, that I began watching—or re-watching—certain Japanese films. One that had a particularly strong impact on me was Akira Kurosawa's 1950 picture, *Rashomon*, the story of a murder and the recollections of a number of witnesses about what they thought had actually happened. While still in Japan, I began to think of an idea for a book on race relations in the United States that would be loosely based on the overall idea of *Rashomon*. I discussed the idea with Sheldon Meyer, vice president of Oxford University Press and the editor of my earlier book, *The Subject Is Race* (1968). He liked the concept and sent me a contract. I then recruited political scientist Stanley Rothman and sociologist William Julius Wilson to join me as co-editors and to help me persuade ten black and ten white writers to contribute to the volume. My idea was to assign them a sort of role-playing exercise, that is, to write their essays from a set perspective, often but not always based on something they had written about before or that reflected their own thinking. In the end we assembled a stellar group of commentators. Their contributions were then presented in four topical sections: "A Spectrum of Black Views," including those of the urban poor, the black bourgeoisie, black immigrants, integrationists, and black nationalists; "White Perspectives," comprising those of white southerners, the "silent majority," the Irish, the Jews, and other "white ethnics;" "Politicians, Public Servants, and the People," giving the views of black politicians, white politicians, welfare workers, policemen, teachers, and prison personnel and; "The Campus," covering white professors, white students, black professors, and black students. Our book, *Through Different Eyes*, with additional essays by Rothman and Wilson and my introduction, was published by Oxford in 1973.

Nineteen seventy-three was the same year that *Many People, One Nation* was published. It was my first book for junior high and high school students. Quite unlike anything I had done before, the volume was the result of discussions with editors in Random House's School Division with whom I had argued that something new and different ought to be available as ancillary material for American history courses taught to eighth and ninth graders. I envisioned such a book as a complement or perhaps a counter to the heavy emphasis on great men and great events in most texts being used at the time, books that mentioned "minorities" mainly as victims—if they mentioned them at all. The editors gave me a free rein and I immediately began an intensive search for a historian to take it on. Not being able to find a person well suited for the task, I did it myself and put together what would soon be advertised as "a text with stories, poems, essays, and songs about the many peoples of the United States."

Held together by my editorial cement, *Many Peoples, One Nation* is mainly an anthology of writings on the sociology and history of America's people with lots of stories, something that reflected my own approach to the subject, first spelled out in *They and We*. It is filled with excerpts from writers as diverse as Frederick Douglass, James Fenimore Cooper, Abraham Cahan, James T. Farrell, Shirley Jackson, Richard Wright, Bel Kaufmann, and Piri Thomas. The last story in the book is a truly Seussian take on race relations by none other than the creator of the genre, Theodore Suess Geisel (a.k.a. Dr. Suess). It is called "The Sneeches," and tells of the rivalry between those Sneeches who have stars on their bellies and those who don't but would give anything to have them—and do.

The book was widely adopted by many school districts as a principal text or used as a "reader." Most important to me, it seemed to have the impact on students that I'd hoped for.

Through an unusual set of circumstances, *Many Peoples, One Nation* would become a topic of conversation and, I thought, a possible model for a comparable book on far-away Malaysia.

It was several years after its publication when, while lecturing at the two universities in Kuala Lumpur, I had a most interesting and frustrating experience. I was invited by Tun (Lord) Sambanthan, then the Malaysian Minister of National Unity—which I had been told was "the second most important ministry in the country"—to meet with his colleagues and some senior civil servants to discuss models of integration and strategies for enhancing better understanding among the various ethnic groups in that very plural and very divided society. I agreed.

While my talk seemed to go well, with smiles and nods of seeming enthusiasm by the members of my elite audience, the discussion never left the ground. Rapidly dismissing almost everything I had said about what was going on in the U.S., Canada, and other multi-ethnic societies, including using the educational system to promote better understanding, it quickly degenerated into an argument between the Malay and Chinese officials. Those on one side told me that I had to understand that theirs was, after all, a Muslim country and suggested that the others, despite their wealth and influence, were really there on suffrance; those on the other side indicated that the Malays were a rather backward and ignorant lot, needing an affirmative action program for fellow Malays, although they were in the majority. Then one guy, adding injury to the insult, said, "They won't even eat pork!"

The Minister, of Indian background, seemed embarrassed. It was clear he could do little to mediate. He thanked me for my consultation and then, as we left the room, whispered to me that it would be a long, long time before Malaysia became one nation. I left thinking that the name of his ministry was an oxymoronic euphemism.

Recently, my good friend Hoon Eng Khoo, a Chinese Malaysian who lives in Singapore and is now involved in starting a new women's university in Malaysia, who knew the story of my odd encounter years ago, wrote to tell me that the Ministry of National Unity no longer exists.

Early in the tenure of the Smith's new president, Jill Ker Conway, she asked me to carry out studies and critiques of both the undergraduate and graduate programs in American studies and the relatively new Department of Afro-American Studies, two programs with which I had been affiliated from their beginnings. The second was far more difficult to start and sell to the faculty at large than the first. Indeed, it was quite a struggle as various colleagues admonished me and the other two promoters with such barbs as, "I thought you were integrationists but what you are promoting is tantamount to academic *apartheid*," "Will white students have to petition to take courses in the new department?" or "Next thing you know there will be a demand for Jewish studies and Hispanic studies."

We argued that until the English department recognized that the literature of black Americans is an integral part of American literature and the history department started looking more closely at the black experience, it was necessary to devote far more attention to this essential part of our society as a legitimate academic exercise. We said that of course any student would be welcome and that we would especially encourage white students to take courses in the proposed department. And we noted that faculty members of the department would have to meet the same criteria as in any other and would have all the rights, privileges and obligations, too. As for Jewish studies or Hispanic studies. Why not? (Soon we would have programs in both.) As for concern about politicization, we argued that that if black students wanted to have a black political organization, that was their—not the department's—affair. And if they had a black cultural center, so be it. It could be something akin to Hillel or St. Thomas More House, both found on many campuses. In the end, the faculty supported the establishment of the new Department of Afro-American Studies by a narrow margin. The Trustees supported the vote and it was established.

I agreed with President Conway that it was a good time to do some systematic assessment of the two programs, the first of which had been established about fifteen years earlier, the second much more recently.

At the time I was reluctant to take on the evaluation myself for it would mean, once again, taking time away from my teaching and several research projects. The president was very persuasive and I took on the jobs.

The results of my interviews with those who had taught or were teaching in the two programs and surveys of the opinions and suggestions of alumnae of the same led to a number of recommendations. The main one regarding Afro-American Studies was to have one or more tenured positions established to secure its position as a regular department in the college. For the undergraduate American Studies Program the top priority was to appoint a tenured faculty member to at least a three-year term as director and to offer at least two courses within the program to enhance the development of a corporate sense that seemed sorely lacking. Up to that point the headship of the program had been changing almost every year as individuals were persuaded to serve a stint as temporary directors.

I was pleased when the administration accepted both of my key ideas. I was surprised when the president then asked me to add to my work as the director of the graduate American Studies Diploma Program and assume the directorship of the undergraduate one as well. While the offer was appealing, I immediately turned it down. This was not because of a lack of interest in or commitment to the program but because I felt—and still feel—that it would not have been fitting for me to have made the recommendation I did, then take over the program, which could have been construed as fashioning the report in such a way as to feather my own nest.

Fortunately, the Department of Afro-American Studies continued to develop and to attract increasing numbers of highly talented faculty members, some of whom would soon receive tenure. After more than forty years it is still flourishing. While the rotating directorship of the undergraduate American Studies program continued for several more years, shortly after her arrival on campus in 1985, the new president, Mary Maples Dunn, appointed the gifted historian and fine administrator Daniel Horowitz to head the program. He would do so for many more years than the originally proposed term of three.

Because of all my foreign travel, I did far less writing in my own field in the 1970s than I had in the 1960s or would do over the next several decades. One publishing task I did take on, and one that was directly related to my own continuing involvement in American studies, was to edit and help to put into print a series of radio interviews with academics from fourteen different countries—Australia, France, Israel, Italy, Japan, Kenya, Korea, Mexico, The Netherlands, Norway, South Africa, Sweden, Switzerland, and the United Kingdom, broadcast over a number of months by the Voice of America. All of the participants were individuals I had met either here in the United States or on trips abroad. I did some of the interviewing myself in studios in this country and overseas, but most were conducted by VOA reporters following my guidelines.

The interviews were mainly focused on particular aspects of contemporary American life according to the participants' fields of specialization, their researches, and their personal experiences in this country. Those to whom we spoke were encouraged to be candid, with my guarantee that there would be no censoring of anything they said.

The topics they were asked about were divided into five general areas: social class and social mobility; child rearing and schooling; the character of higher education, college life, and student protest; racial and ethnic relations; and American literature and mass culture and the impact of both on their home societies.

Both the program and my book, *Views From Abroad* (1978), which had been based on the interviews, received highly favorable reactions and resulted in requests to the VOA to rebroadcast the series (which it did several times) and to initiate more such programs giving foreign perspectives on American society.

During the time that project was going on, I started doing more reading in other disciplines, especially trying to integrate what my colleagues in the humanities called literature with what the folks in mine called *the* literature, the latter referring to theory, data analyses and summaries. Increasingly in my teaching and later in my writing I stressed the interplay of history, sociology, oral narratives and documented stories and fiction related to race, immigration and social class. I often combined these fields using particularly revealing novels such as Abraham Cahan's *The Rise of David Levinsky*, Pietro di Donato's *Christ in Concrete*, Mario Puzo's *The Fortunate Pilgrim*, Jerre Mangione's *Mount Allegro*, Jade Snow Wong's *Fifth Chinese Daughter*, James T. Farrell's "Studs Lonigan" trilogy, Richard Wright's *Native Son* and James Baldwin's *Go Tell It on the Mountain*, and the play, *Dutchman*, by Leroi Jones (now Amiri Baraka). These became additional sources of data to the more standard documentary fare.

In 1977, invited to give the annual Engel Lecture at Smith, I discussed this in my presentation, "Nobody Knows the Troubles *I've* Seen: Some Reflections on the Insider-Outsider Debate." My lecture opened with a true story.

> Several years ago, with a light bulb flash of recognition, I realized that I was witnessing one of those events secretly dreaded by ethnographers. The natives were challenging the outsider's description of themselves.
>
> The challenge was not very dramatic or even very vocal. It consisted of whispers and the ultimate putdown, shrugs of dismissal. To those who belonged to the group in question, it was just one more piece of evidence to confirm the fact that acquaintance with something is very different from true understanding, that there is a wide chasm between *kennen* and *verstehen*. Outsiders might know a bit of another person's history and some cold facts; but, it appears, it is much more difficult for them to feel the undertones, to get the vibes.
>
> It wasn't Australian Aborigines or Bushmen of the Kalahari or Thai peasants being discussed, but some fellow Americans who, it turned out, were middle class Jews. Those who described them were students who had spent several weeks culling through the literature to present summary papers on the American Jewish community.
>
> What I experienced didn't really surprise me. As a sociologist who had studied and written about cultural prisms, I was sensitive to the differing perspectives of outsiders and insiders, of "them" and "us." But, somehow, I found myself troubled and rather uncomfortable.

The setting of my discomfort was a small seminar of fifteen junior and senior students who had come together to study four ethnic groups—Jews, Italians, Blacks and Puerto Ricans, as they related to their own "brothers and sisters" and to each other in one American city, New York. Together the students and I were embarking on an examination of the backgrounds and experiences of the four critical groups in an attempt to test the proposition put forth in the Preface of Nathan Glazer and Daniel Patrick Moynihan's 1963 book, *Beyond the Melting Pot*, that, "The melting did not happen. At least not in New York and, *mutatis mutandis*, in those parts of America that resembles New York."

During the first part of the semester the students were asked to decide on which of the four groups they wanted to concentrate. They were to develop whatever expertise they could in a short period of time. To assure adequate breath of coverage, not more than four were to be permitted to deal with a single one of the chosen minorities. For whatever reason, none of those whose first choice was New York's Jews was Jewish. It was the report of one of them that triggered the shrugs and sighs and unsaid message to me and several others in the class that, "They just don't get it."

At the time I let the looks pass. I wasn't even sure that everybody saw them or, if they did, understood what was happening. But I did, and so did the speaker. He shuddered a bit and pushed on with it, further confounding his credibility by innocuous but telling evidence of seeming insensitivity. For example, to make an important point about the Reconstructionist Movement in contemporary Jewish life, he began by saying that, "To most people, the Jewish church in America has but three divisions, Orthodox, Conservative, and Reform..." Apparently, he didn't realize that despite its functional similarity to other religious bodies, no Jew would ever describe his ecclesia as a church. (I doubt he would say "eccelsia" either!)

To help out a bit, I pointed out this fact of Jewish life to the smiles of my all-knowing fellow Jews in the room and to the blank stares of some of their classmates. Eventually we got back to the more general subject of Jewish settlement and mobility presented in the student reports. Discussion followed that day and on into subsequent meetings.

To my undeniable relief, several times the somewhat embarrassed presenters bested the too-smug insiders in arguments over points of fact. Feelings, they found, they could hardly touch.

Several weeks later we spent three hours on New York's Italians and debated the differing viewpoints of sociologists and historians who wrote about them. We discussed migration patterns, religious beliefs, and the nature of life for those often referred to as "birds of passage." We discussed the character of Little Italy and the role of family, church and workplace. We talked about stereotypes and reactions to them. It was a lively session.

As I left the seminar I asked myself why it was so different from the previous ones. Then it hit me. No shrugs this time. No sighs. No Italians either.

I was reminded of the several classes on "The Negro in America" I had taught not so long before when no black faces were in evidence and everyone enthusiastically discussed interpretations of what we now call "The Black Experience." Commenting on this to a colleague, he said, in utter seriousness, that it was easier to be objective in those days. Perhaps. Maybe our debates about the writing and researches of Campisi, Nelli, Lopreato, Pannunzio, Tomasi and the others were better than they might have been had one or more of the students been named Carbone or Marselli. Maybe there were advantages in being unchallenged assessors, playing the role of dispassionate observer. From things said during the preceding weeks, we had all become sensitive to the fact that there are obvious risks to including the subject of one's research in the discussion of it. About ten years ago, a Jules Feiffer cartoon made the point with righteous simplicity. His button-down, grey-flannelled liberal character states to his friend, "Civil Rights used to be so much more tolerable until the Negroes got into it."

And what about those Negroes?

In the third set of sessions we came to New York's blacks. This time two of the reporters were black, two were white. Though they had read the same material, general studies of blacks and specific studies of New York, including James Weldon Johnson's *Black Manhattan* and Gilbert Osofsky's *Harlem: The Making of a Ghetto*, it was clearly apparent that the latter two (the white students) constantly deferred to the former two (the black students). Moreover, whenever the black students presented their ideas, the white students tended to write them down with little or no challenge. Neither they nor the remaining blacks did the same when the white students gave their part of the report. On those few occasions when questions were asked about behavior or attitudes or social conditions, the tension was palpable. If a straightforward answer was given, everyone seemed relieved. If the speaker, almost invariably one of the black students, seemed annoyed, tensions mounted again. Part of the problem was that everyone was playing out their appropriate roles circa 1970, the black students playing the Insider's game and saying, in the words of the old Negro spiritual, "Nobody knows the troubles I've seen"—and nobody can.

Lastly came the Puerto Ricans. Again, with no representatives present and little general knowledge save for the "I-want-to-be-in Amer-i-ca" imagery portrayed in *West Side Story*, the students reverted to academic one-upmanship. We reviewed and debated what a number of scholars described. For example, considering the role of race in Puerto Rican society, one reporter began with the contention that, "There is a difference between people raised in a racially continuous society, one where there are people in all walks of life of varying shades, and those who grow up in a racially dichotomous one, where there are whites and non-whites, like ours."

"True, said another, "Clarence Senior makes the same point. But do you really think race is the main basis for difference?"

"I do," said the first speaker, "although I note that it is not such an important factor in the writing of Oscar Lewis. His use of the idea of the 'culture of poverty' would suggest that things are not very different on the island or here, at least for those who are poor. And he knows!"[24]

I ended my description of the events that led up to the lecture with that almost verbatim comment of the white southern Amherst student who wrote and spoke about Puerto Ricans, people he had admittedly never met, and about the late Oscar Lewis. It seemed fitting because it was Lewis himself who, perhaps more than anyone else, tried to get outsiders inside the experiences of others, who tried to convey the true meaning of culture "in their own words," who provided non-members with a vision of what it was like to be poor and Indian, Scottish, Mexican and Puerto Rican. As is well known to his fellow anthropologists and many others, even Lewis had difficulty convincing some that he was tell-

---

[24]*Nobody Knows the Troubles I've Seen: Some Reflections on the Insider-Outsider Debate* (Northampton: Smith College, 1978), 3–7.

ing it like it really was and even more difficulty convincing others that he had the right to attempt it.

The rest of my presentation dealt with this conundrum. In many ways it was an exercise in the sociology of knowledge but one with a highly-charged underlayer of very real political implications. I went on to discuss the various approaches social scientists had used to try to become outsiders within, including what I called the Walter Cronkite technique of being the keen, well-informed outside observer, taking in the whole scene while maintaining distance from it, and the Walter Mitty approach of becoming a participant observer. I then noted that in contrast to outsiders:

> Insiders are different. In general, they are not methodologists but members; they share not a set of professional tools but what many claim is a sort of privileged access to that which only they can say they know and feel. Their concern about themselves is not abstract but immediate; it is not intellectual but visceral; it is not objective but highly subjective. In the broadest sense, whether corporate executives, college professors, guest workers, Pakistani villagers, Blacks in Bedford-Stuyvesant, or small-town Jews, they are united by an interdependence of fate and a fellow-feeling that, most argue, cannot be penetrated. Monopolists of their own cultures, in the instance *they* are the "we" and everyone else is "they."[25]

To at least start to reconcile the seemingly unbridgeable gap between insiders and outsiders, I then proposed that social scientists begin to make much greater use of what I came to call "literary ethnographies," which might help them to gain insights into those parts of society with which they have so little knowledge and, however much sympathy, little true empathy. Citing some of the authors whose works I had selected for the high school text, *Many Peoples, One Nation*, and many, many more, including Countee Cullen's poem, *Incident*, I concluded my lecture with the following words:

> Reading real literature along with what we are wont to call *the* literature, looking at cultural material not conventionally considered as

---

[25]Ibid., 15–16.

"data" may have the latent function for social scientists of reconnecting us with our humanistic brothers and sisters. It does not mean abandoning the sociological perspective. That orientation still offers to provide the framework within which to understand what is being read, the larger picture of the systems in which people live and work and play and suffer, the context in which to indicate and test the variables that relate to human affairs everywhere.[26]

The latter part of the 1970s was also the period in which I got involved in designing and writing an introductory sociology textbook for high school students that, for a while, almost became the bane of my existence. It was a project that came about in a somewhat different way from *Many Peoples, One Nation*, although it, too, had its roots at the old Random House headquarters on Madison Avenue. This time the publisher was Ted Caris, a man who had become my editor at Random House before leaving sometime in the mid-1970s to become the president of Xerox College Books, a new organization that had recently purchased the venerable old Boston-based schoolbook publisher, Ginn and Company.

While he was still at Random House, Ted had tried to persuade me to join him in a new venture—writing "a different kind of college textbook in sociology." I demurred for several reasons. Perhaps foremost, it was because I liked the book that my late colleague and close friend, Ely Chinoy, had just published with Random House and had no interest in competing with him. Moreover, I felt that the market was flooded with introductory texts and I would have little new to say.

Ted accepted my argument; then he got another idea. He called and said, "What about a book for the growing market in high school sociology?" He explained that it would be a unique opportunity to introduce high schoolers to a subject being offered in an increasing number of schools in a book that would neither talk down to them nor overwhelm them with jargon. (Ted knew how much I abhorred "sociologese.")

The idea did whet my interest and I agreed to meet with several editors from Ginn. Within a short time, I had outlined the sort of book I

---

[26]Ibid., 27.

envisioned, submitted it and quickly received a contract which included a guarantee of considerable editorial support and the promise of a generous advance. I signed on. Not long into the project I started to have serious regrets.

With everything else I was trying to do—teach, do research, edit— and wanting to get back to more personal writing, I found I was having difficulty keeping so many balls in the air. After a year of struggling with only five or six chapters in various stages of draft, I called Ted and John Bremer, my editor at Ginn, to tell them I didn't think I could do the job, at least not in the tight timeframe to which we had agreed. I offered a counterproposal. I said I would find a writer and stay with the project, serving as a consulting editor as I had done with so many authors at Random House. The editors at Ginn were not keen on the idea and suggested that I take on a partner and share the writing. Always a lone writer—the only book project I had done with others was the edited volume, *Through Different Eyes*, I was very reluctant even to consider it. In the end, Ted and John agreed to my suggestion and I set about looking for a good writer who was also a good sociologist. Suddenly, I had an idea. Perhaps my Smith College colleague, Mickey Glazer, whose book, *The Research Adventure*, I had brought to Random House and then edited, might be the right person.

I approached Mickey with the idea. He was intrigued and said he'd think it over. A few days later he said he was interested but not along the lines of the proposed arrangement. He said he would only do it as a co-author, with each of us sharing the same amount of responsibility for the writing. Stimulated by his enthusiasm, I acquiesced. The publisher was pleased and quite willing to draw up new contracts specifying a fifty-fifty split in workload and royalties.

It wasn't too long before Mickey would also feel the pressure of other work and proposed that his wife, Penina, a former high school history teacher and at the time an assistant professor at nearby Hampshire College, join us as a third member of the team. He and she would work together on his share of the work. I agreed and within another year, against all the odds, we had a completed manuscript that was "turned over"—as they say in the trade—to the publisher and, after careful review, accepted. It was now Ginn's to publish and market. Then came a terrible blow.

We received a terse notice that Ginn, long known for its science and math textbooks, decided it didn't want to publish in the social sciences after all. We were terribly disappointed after having worked so hard to write a challenging textbook and very angry, feeling we'd been led down the garden path ("Surely somebody must have known what was coming.") and very concerned about having to return the substantial advances we had received. Ted Caris heard about our frustrations and assured us that because we had met all the terms of our contract, the manuscript was ours to take elsewhere and the advances we had received in good faith did not need to be repaid though it was hoped that any publisher that wanted to do the book would be willing to reimburse Ginn.

Although we were still reeling from the sudden news that Ginn had cut the legs out from under the project on which we had devoted so much time and energy, some of our concerns were assuaged as we set out to find a new publisher. What happened next astonished us. Somehow the word of the completed manuscript had gotten around at the very time many publishing houses had decided that the growing field of sociology as a high school elective, like economics and psychology, was ripe for new books. We had a hot property on our hands and found ourselves in an auction situation with four major companies competing for our book. In the end we signed on with Prentice-Hall, making as part of the deal, an agreement to hire Paula Franklin, the former Random House editor and freelancer with whom I had worked on *Many Peoples, One Nation*, to work with us as we polished the text.

The first edition of the book, *Sociology: Understanding Society*, along with a teacher's manual, was published in 1978. It proved to be a huge success, obtaining statewide adoptions in several places and system-wide approval in many others. New editions were released in 1982 and 1989. In the end there was not only the satisfaction of seeing our efforts materialize in classrooms across the country after all the *Sturm und Drang* of creating, writing and producing it; but also a nice pot of gold at the end of the rainbow.

In addition to learning how different writing for high school readers is, we also learned a great deal about how much the high-stakes publishers of such books were willing to gamble. This was evident not just in the care taken in the editorial and design processes to make books most appealing, but also in the incredible (to us) outlays for marketing. While we never compromised on the content and lost some adoptions in the South because we were accused of being secular humanists, presumably for describing religion as a social institution, we did find it invigorating to go to conventions of social studies teachers to talk about our book. It proved to be a most rewarding experience—in more ways than one.

Late in the fall of 1970, right after returning from our sojourn to Japan and Australia, Hedy and I purchased a modest little rectangular cottage in South Wellfleet on Cape Cod. A former architect's studio all of 672 square feet (48 feet long and 14 feet wide), it was named "The Shoebox." It was a place we would live in for nearly twenty summers, and where I would do a considerable amount of writing. At the end of each of those summers we would start thinking of how, someday, we would buy or build a larger place. It finally happened in the early 1990s. With our income augmented by royalties from several of my books, including the high school text, we took the plunge, bought a piece of land on an island off Wellfleet, and built our dream house on a knoll not far from The Shoebox. I had wanted to name the knoll "McGraw-Hill" (the publishing house that had taken over publication of *They and We* for its fourth and fifth editions), call the modern building itself "Random House," and its main room, a large, airy space with cathedral ceilings and loads of sunlight, "Prentice Hall." Hedy thought it all too gauche and suggested something better, like "Nooitgedagt," Dutch for "Never thought it possible!" or "Unbelievable!" And that is what we called it.

For me, one of the most unusual experiences of the very busy 1970s came at decade's end when, along with nine others, I was asked to join the team charged with reviewing the accreditation of Yale University. I immediately thought that this could be an opportunity to learn more about a place where I had briefly served as a visiting professor a decade earlier but still knew very little about, especially regarding two concerns that I had. The first was to learn something of the experience of "going co-ed" (women had been admitted to Yale for the first time but only a few years before, we at Smith were still wrestling with the question of admitting men); the second was to find out how junior faculty felt in a place where almost no one—at least at that time—rose up from the ranks and received tenure. (I knew from colleagues that Yale's president, A. Bartlett Giamatti, had been the last one in the English department to have done so, and that was something like eleven years before we got there.)

As in all such accreditation reviews, each committee member, led by a chairman—who in our case was Dennis O'Brien, then president of Bucknell and later to become president of the University of Rochester, and the only Yalie among us—was given a set of briefing papers and copies of the self-study done under the aegis of the provost's office. We had been asked by the accrediting body to look especially at the social sciences, the sciences, and the professional schools, especially, their programs in music and drama. (It was apparently felt that the humanities needed little review.)

Shortly after arriving in New Haven, we had meetings with the provost, the dean of Yale College, and then with Bart Giamatti. We were then assigned by Dennis O'Brien to three teams, each to do the major investigating of the three areas of top concern. I chaired the team on the social sciences. The other two members were an economist from a nearby college and a social psychologist from a university on the West Coast. Because of my special interests in the issues of co-education and the plight of untenured professors, it was arranged for me to have lunch each day in one of the residential colleges and to meet with both students and junior faculty members. What I learned was as interesting to me as what we found regarding the sectors of the university under the greatest scrutiny.

With regard to coeducation, I was amazed at how smoothly the process seemed to be going. In contrast to what I had heard about the situation at several other former men's colleges, the women at Yale said they did not feel like second-class citizens or intruders in that traditionally male bastion. (Later I was to learn that all was not quite so rosy as pictured, although I was not far off in my assessment of Yale compared to other colleges undergoing the same transformation.)

Also contrary to my expectations, junior faculty members at Yale had few anxieties about their status and few illusions about their real chances of joining the permanent faculty. Unlike the situation at Smith and many similar institutions where not getting tenure (and it frequently happened in those days) was seen as tantamount to failure, those at Yale, holding little hope of staying on, told me that, like their students, they were enjoying their time at Yale, and knew that having taught there and getting good recommendations from their senior colleagues was a great stepping-stone-experience. What they lacked, at least in my view and, I would imagine, that of others who had spent years in smaller colleges, was a sense of corporate loyalty.

As to our group's mission at Yale, I have to report that we did recommend reaccreditation across the board but with two key suggestions, one coming from our science subcommittee. Impressed by the quality of the facilities, programs and research projects, they felt that the university should do more to recognize its science programs and to publicize them outside the Yale campus. Said one, "They've got great science here, but its luster is hidden under a bushel basket." The other suggestion came from those focused on the professional schools. While impressed by their quality and renown, they worried that the programs were too remote from what was still the core of Yale University, that is, the undergraduate college, and were not really serving that primary community. (Interestingly, it wasn't too long afterward that Robert Brustein left the Yale Repertory Theater and his position of dean of the Yale Drama School for Harvard where he joined the faculty and became the founding director of the American Repertory Theater affiliated with the university.)

With regard to the social sciences, our report was mixed. We found, as others had, Yale could proudly tout its Department of Government as one of the very best in the country. The economics department was also most highly rated. But, alas, this was not the case for sociology. The assessment was less consistent. For one thing, a number of students complained that the best of the sociologists always seemed to identify themselves with a secondary affiliation—whether in the law school or the medical school or with a program such as American studies. The junior faculty had their own concerns unrelated to the lack of hope for mobility within the department but tied to more basic matters involving the nature of the field and the way they felt it was being represented.

Changes at Yale and at many universities, and indeed the country at large in the 1970s, were often quite significant. Many grew out of persisting provocations by militant blacks and radical whites demanding structural changes in society and greater demographic representation in student bodies, faculties, and administrations. But they were nothing compared to what was going on in other countries, especially toward the end of the decade. The worst case was the revolution in Iran, the ransacking of the U.S. embassy, and the taking of forty-four American hostages. It all took place just eight months after I had been in the country to lecture at the university in Teheran, to speak in several other cities, and to visit colleagues, the beginning of a tour that would take me to Athens, then to Kenya, Malawi, South Africa and Lesotho.

I flew into Teheran on a cold winter day and was given a tour of the city, beautifully situated beneath high mountains—when you can see them. The pollution was as bad as I had ever experienced. Even more depressing, when I asked about getting together with certain professors with whom I had been in contact I was told by the American cultural attaché, that they were being held by the Shah's five thousand-man secret police force, Savak.

This was my welcome to Iran. And, with a few exceptions my stay in the country never improved. While my lectures were well received in a formal way, it was hard to get a real sense of audience concerns. I did manage to have some intense political discussions with several faculty members and also a number of Americans living there. All talked mainly about the tight controls of the then-current rulers and of the difficulty of challenging the regime. What is interesting is that I can't remember anything being said about any sort of immanent threat from Islamic fundamentalists.

While I was there the weather was terrible. Snow and slush every day prevented me from taking side trips to Ahvaz and Isfahan, site of ancient Persepolis and one of the oldest Jewish communities in the world. On top of those disappointments my departure from Iran was delayed. On the bus to the airport back in the States, I'd accidentally dropped the health certificate that showed that I'd had all the shots, including for yellow fever, required to enter Kenya. The document had been found, and Hedy was immediately contacted. She called to tell me that she had been advised to get it to a special office in Washington by overnight express mail so someone at the State Department could forward it to me the next day in the diplomatic pouch. It didn't come. Not the next day nor the next nor the one after that. I kept extending my stay and revising my schedule.

An Iranian at the university, hearing of my plight, said I should bite the bullet and get the shots again at the Pasteur Clinic. Very reluctantly I went there with him. One look at the clinic and he was as shocked as I. It was chaotic, dirty and unkempt. I decided to wait again. The next night while having dinner with an embassy official, Gordon Winkler, I mentioned my problem. He said he had a solution but first asked, "Are you really sure you had the shots?" I convinced him that it was so. He then called the head of the American medical unit, explained my situation and asked if he would write out an affidavit testifying to the fact that I had had the shots. The medical chief agreed and we rushed over to his office where he drew up a letter certifying that I was properly inoculated. On the way out, Winkler said, "I've got another idea, let's make it look really official."

We drove over to the American embassy and were admitted to the visa section by the marine guards. After entering the room where all the official business was conducted, my new savior put a bunch of imposing looking stamps on the document.

I left the next day.

After a brief stopover in Athens, I took the night flight to Nairobi. I felt quite comfortable with my very authentic-looking letter but, to my surprise, nobody even looked at it!

The time in Kenya was frenetic: meeting people, speaking at two universities, taking a day off to go on a mini-safari in a nearby game park within ten miles of the city limits, where we spotted a pride of very skinny lions, papa, mama and five cubs, and saw hundreds, perhaps thousands of other magnificent animals ranging from antelopes and rhinos to packs of hyenas and vultures feasting on the carcasses of hapless victims lying on the bone-dry earth.

On my last day in Nairobi I was interviewed on Radio Kenya. I was mainly asked about the plight of African Americans and to compare the situation in the States with that in South Africa, especially in regard to feelings of national identity. That evening I had an encounter relating to the latter subject. I described it several years later:

> I was sitting on the veranda of the Stanley Hotel. Three black men with Afros wearing dashikis walked in and sat down. They didn't look African to me (no Africans I knew there wore Afros, and few wore West African dashikis in the East African place). My suspicions were confirmed when I heard very clear American accents. After a few minutes, they, doubtlessly sizing me up and realizing that I was out of place, too, started up a conversation.

> "Hey, Bro," said one, "Where you from?"
> "Massachusetts. And you guys?"
> "*Brooklyn, New York, U.S.A.*"

> We joined forces and talked over our beers for several hours. They told me that they had come to Africa searching for their roots— and found how very American they really were.[27]

---

[27]Adapted from "Peripatetic Academic," *Cornell Alumni Quarterly,* September 1987, 11–14, later reprinted in the title essay in *Guest Appearances,* 97–98.

From Nairobi I flew to Blantyre in Malawi where I was supposed to spend a few days speaking at the university on the topic of campus politics and new challenges in academia and meeting with various academic groups. It was not to be. After I cleared immigration, a man from the American Embassy approached me and asked if I was Professor Rose. I said I was. He introduced himself. "I'm Bill Pfender. Welcome to Malawi." Then, he said, "I'm sorry to tell you that I have bad news."

I immediately thought something had happened back home and asked about it.

"No," he said, "it's here. You can't speak here. You can't even stay here."

"Why not?" I asked.

"The president won't allow it."

"The president of what?"

"Dr. Banda, the president of the country!"

"Come on, how does he know me?"

"He knows everything through his very effective secret police. They must have found out the topic of your talks and immediately seen you as a threat."

"Why?"

"Because one doesn't talk about university upheaval in a one-party state!"

Since all the flights had gone and it was too late to depart that night, Pfender sought and obtained permission for me to stay with him and his wife. Armed guards escorted us to his home and several sat outside all night long.

It was an interesting evening with talk about politics in Malawi and other parts of southern Africa and a promise on my host's part that he would get me back there someday soon. Before going to bed, he asked me where I wanted to spend my time (the six days I was to have been in Malawi) and before my next venue, Lesotho. Without thinking about it for more than a few seconds, I said, "South Africa—and I would like to try to meet with some of the anti-apartheid leaders."

Unbeknownst to me, early the next morning Pfender called Brook Spector, a fellow Foreign Service officer who was at the American embassy in Pretoria, to see what he could do to arrange for me to see some of those activists. It turned out that Spector was able to set up a number of appointments.

So, before going to Lesotho and the satellite campus of the BSL (Botswana, Swaziland, and Lesotho) University, I spent almost a week based in Johannesburg. There I did manage to see and interview a number of outspoken whites, including members of the Liberal Party, the editor of the Raven Press, and Christian Frederick Beyers Naudé, a Stellenbosch-trained pastor and one of the founders of the racist *Broederbond* (Afrikaans for the word Brotherhood) who had broken completely with the organization and the vast majority of his diehard white supremacist fellow Afrikaners. I also met Fatima Meer, an outspoken, charismatic leader of the Indian community. She took me to a tent village of hundreds of Indians who, under some new rule to increase separation, had been moved out of Durban and were living at the time on a soccer pitch.

I couldn't get to meet any of the black representatives of the African National Congress I had wanted to see but I did get together with a small group of black academics in a meeting arranged by Brook Spector and several more at a dinner arranged for me by a person in the cultural section of the U.S. embassy in Pretoria. I left for Lesotho with loads of notes, a foreboding sense that things would get much worse before they got better, and a promise from a number of new acquaintants there that they would bring me back.

With the help of several American foreign service officers serving in southern Africa, especially Bill Pfender who, as good as his word, arranged the trip, I returned to Malawi to speak a year later. (In my list of topics sent in advance, I never mentioned universities in turmoil!)

I also got back to South Africa. That time it was mainly to lecture. My main subject was race relations in the United States and I was invited to speak at the universities of Witwatersrand, Durban, Natal, and Capetown and the University of the Western Cape, at the Center for

Race Relations in Cape Town, at several seminaries, including one for blacks only in Pietermeritzburg, and two cultural centers. Other than Beyers Naudé, however, I was unable to meet with any of those I'd spoken to on my first trip. All were either under a "banning order"—a sort of house arrest, in prison along with Nelson Mandela on Robben Island, or had left the country.

IV

The 1980s: Flood Tides

FROM THE 1930S, EXILES AND REFUGEES, and those who worked with them, were a part of my life.

My parents were very much involved in finding homes for those dispossessed by the mounting menace of Nazi Germany. A number of refugees stayed with us for several days, and four lived with us for an extended time. Max and Alma Einstein from Hannover, Germany, were the first to become members of our family. They were my parents' ages. Walter Leipziger from Leipzig (a name I thought was pretty neat) was much younger. He stayed with us for about a year before entering the U.S. Army. Then, after the Battle of Britain, Michael Weingott, his sister and his mother were brought to the United States from London. His brother, who was in the Royal Air Force, and his father, a member of the Home Guard, remained in the U.K. His mother and sister stayed with other families but Michael, a year and a half older than me, lived with us. For four years I, an only child, had a foster brother. Michael was with us until a few months after June 6, 1944, D-Day, when the three Weingotts-in-exile were able to return to London.

Right after the war, my parents signed the affidavits needed to bring Lilli Hug to the United States. Lilli was a nurse from Saint Gallen who served in the Swiss Red Cross working in prisoner of war camps in Europe during the war. She lived with us for a year and, among other things, urged me to go to school in Wengen, the home of her former boyfriend, a ski instructor there, and tried to teach me some rudimentary *Schwyzerdütsch*. I can still say *"Grëuzi," "Uf Widerluege," "Genau,"* and "*Chuchichaeschtli*." The last was what Lilli called the place where I was to put the dishes she washed and I dried after dinner. Later I learned that being able to pronounce it correctly meant that you were really hip to Swiss German.

A few years later, in the summer of 1953, I met Hedy. She and her sister, Betsy, had come to this country in 1947 through the good offices of the Joint Distribution Committee (one of the agencies I would later study). Her sponsors were her mother's brother, Alfred Schwarz, and his wife, Anna, both originally from Vienna. They had escaped in 1939 and 1940, respectively, and were among the lucky few who'd managed to obtain visas to get to the United States just before this country entered the war. They would become her new parents—and my in-laws.

Having parents involved in the rescue of refugees; having Max, Alma, Walter, and Michael all living in our home during the war; meeting Hedy and her adoptive parents; interviewing a number people who had also come to America in flight from Hitler in the late 1930s and had been placed in small towns by the Hebrew Immigrant Aid Society when gathering material for my doctoral study of small-town Jews and their neighbors, may all have contributed to my interest in the dispossessed. But what might seem odd today is that it wasn't until the end of the wars in Indochina that I began to do research or write specifically about refugees. What triggered my new interest in doing so was a concern about what happened to the intellectuals in South Vietnam after the fall of Saigon.

As I have written elsewhere, I must have been pretty naïve for, once I started digging into the subject, I quickly learned that France got the intellectuals and we got the generals! Perhaps unfairly, the plight of the latter was not something of interest to me. But in the course of starting my inquiry I became intrigued by what determined how refugees were protected and cared for and how certain ones were selected, admitted, and resettled.

Perhaps the first revelation was learning that the United States never had an explicit policy toward people fleeing their homelands and seeking sanctuary in this country until 1952 when the McCarren-Walter

Act defined refugees mainly as "those fleeing communism." Later, much later, in 1980, refugees were redefined according to United Nations protocols, in almost the same language referring to "those with a well-founded fear of persecution." This lack of prior recognition explains why so few of the many hundreds of thousands of targeted victims who might otherwise have been saved could never enter this country during the dark years of the Nazi period. Only those who received visas under the tight quota restrictions of the 1924 immigration law were ever admitted.

My early exploration of the situation, circa 1980, revealed that the rescue and resettlement of refugees was still a complex collection of moral, political and legal concerns, commitments and highly politicized strategies. One of the best books on the subject was written by Gil Loescher and John Scanlan, published in 1986. It was aptly called *Calculated Kindness*.

It was around the time Loescher and Scanlan were starting their project that I, too, was turning to studying the making and implementing of U.S. refugee policy, a subject that would occupy much of my research and travel throughout the 1980s. With a small grant from the Weatherhead Foundation and then a larger one from the Rockefeller Foundation, I set about to learn as much as I could about the history of U.S. refugee policy and to meet those in governmental agencies, nongovernmental organizations (NGOs, also called voluntary agencies or VOLAGS), and private advocates involved in its operation. I also looked at those who were opposed, including certain members of Congress and certain organizations such as FAIR (Federation of Americans for Immigration Reform) which I decided should be called UnFAIR.

The first part of the research involved going to Geneva and to New York for meetings with the officials of the United Nations High Commission for Refugees (UNHCR) as well as many staff members, and interviews with various authorities in the departments of State, Justice, and Health and Human Services in Washington, all of whom played critical roles in policy about and services for refugees. I then met briefly with the heads of the thirteen major VOLAGs, eleven of them faith-based and two, nonsectarian—returning later to interview each of them after conducting extensive fieldwork in Southeast Asia and in this country where refugees were being resettled.

Among the colorful baker's dozen of agency leaders was Charles "Carel" Sternberg, the head of the International Rescue Committee (IRC), who started his career as a publicist for Twentieth Century Fox in Prague and came to the United States in the 1940s as a refugee from the Nazis. (Suspicious of me at first, once he knew I was serious and would stay the course, Carel became the key gatekeeper in getting me in to meet his colleagues, providing letters to open the generally guarded entries to refugee camps and, later, opening IRC files to me.) Another particularly memorable executive director was Gaynor Jacobson of the Hebrew Immigrant Aid Society, the oldest of all the immigrant and refugee agencies. Gaynor turned out to be a man my father had known as a young social worker in Rochester and who later spent years helping the dispossessed in Europe during and after the Second World War. He had developed a special relationship with the king of Morocco to save many Jews who had taken refuge there during the war. Then there was John McCarthy, a Jimmy Cagney look- and sound- alike—with both a law degree and a Ph.D. who headed the largest agency of them all, the Migration and Refugee Service of the United States Conference of Catholic Bishops. Dale DeHaan, who some described as a guy who looked and dressed like the stereotypical foreign correspondent, had cut his teeth as a committee aid to senators John F. Kennedy of Massachusetts and Philip Hart of his home state of Michigan and later became the Deputy High Commissioner for Refugees at tge U. N. When I first met DeHaan he was the executive director of the World Council of Churches Refugee Service. Ingrid Walters came up through the ranks: she was a displaced person in a German camp where she was first assisted by the agency she would eventually head, Lutheran Immigration and Refugee Service. Jan Papanek started at the top. When I first met him he was a ninety year old. A former diplomat from an aristocratic family, he had served as a member of the first Czech legation to Washington, Czech ambassador to the United Nations, and the founding head of the American Fund for

Czechoslovak Refugees. (When I asked Papanek the question I posed to all of the agency heads—"When did you first start working with refugees?"—he leaned on his silver-headed walking stick, stared off into space for a few seconds and replied "Let's see, it was during the war. Nineteen seventeen. I was a sublieutenant in the Austro-Hungarian army.")

After completing a series of meetings with the six individuals mentioned here and the other agency directors, one of whom, Le Xuan Khoa, was a very learned Vietnamese professor-in-exile who headed the Indochinese Resource Action Center, I wrote in my notes:

> Observing, interacting with, and talking to these leaders at meetings, overseas or in their offices in Washington, D.C. or on Park Avenue South or upper Broadway in New York City, theatrical metaphors kept coming to mind. They seemed an intrepid if highly idiosyncratic troop who, though frequently expected to act together are not really ensemble players. Each is a veteran actor, each a star. Some are quite vain; others more self-effacing; but all seem quite sure of themselves. I thought of them as "The Vicars of the Volags."[28]

Going into the field, I made one rather short trip followed by two much lengthier ones to Southeast Asia to visit refugee camps, all under the titular authority of the UNHCR, and to observe the rescue, relief, and resettlement activities being conducted by American officials in the "countries of first asylum": Thailand, Malaysia, Singapore, Indonesia, the Philippines, Hong Kong, Macau, and even, ironically, communist China. (Many boats heading across the South China Sea for Hong Kong or Macau were blown ashore and ended up on the Chinese coast. For a variety of political reasons, the authorities there were most cooperative and allowed the U.S. consulate in Guangzhou to process the refugees.)

In each of those places I spent long hours interviewing and following the activities of the resident REFCORD (the refugee coordinator attached to every American embassy) and his or her counterpart, the JVAR (Joint Voluntary Agency Representative), the

---

[28]See "The Vicars of the Volags, *Tempest-Tost* (New York and Oxford: Oxford University Press, 1997), pp. 151–168.

in-country representative of one of the American VOLAGs such as the International Rescue Committee, the Catholic Migration and Refugee Service, Lutheran Immigration Refugee Services, even the American Fund for Czechoslovakian Refugees, which had a contract with the State Department to do the screening, selection, and recommendation of eligibility for refugee status—but not the approval of petitioners—from Vietnam, Laos and Cambodia. Approval was the exclusive purview of the INS (Immigration and Naturalization Service).

To see their work at ground level, I spent time in fifteen different camps, including the largest in the area, Khao-I-Dang, and several others on the Thai-Cambodian border, up north near Laos, in the southern panhandle of Thailand and the transit center, Lumpini, located right on elegant Wireless Road, "Embassy Row," in Bangkok, as well as those in other countries mentioned earlier.

Among the many things I learned, perhaps the first was most useful—how to talk to those in close-knit systems doing very specialized work. While to be sure many academics use arcane language, only during my brief time at the Pentagon fifteen years before had I ever been exposed to such intense insider lingo. (I remember leaning over to ask the admiral on my left what the badge CNCATLAIRFLT on his pocket meant. "Commander in Chief, Atlantic Air Fleet," he coolly replied. I also remember gulping, then smiling wanly.) Perhaps my greatest early triumph after the first of my trips to Southeast Asia on the refugee project was learning the bureaucratic jargon of the moment and being sure I knew what I was talking about.

Here is an excerpt from notes I made after a discussion I had with Lionel Rosenblatt, then the liaison with the American Embassy on refugee matters in Thailand and later to become head of the organization known as Refugees International.

> Had a reincarnated George Orwell gone to Southeast Asia to observe the refugee relief and resettlement operation in 1980, he might have thought that "newspeak" was already the order of the day. The paths to the clinics, food distribution points, registration desks, transit camps—indeed, to the United States or any other "third country"—

were signposted with acronyms most confusing to the uninitiated. To trace the resettlement process from the time a boat is spotted or a muddy border cross to Anytown, USA, as I first did in the fall of 1980, first required the decoding of these neologisms and then learning where each of the organizations represented by the shorthand expressions fit into the complex system.

After a few intensive weeks in the field I found I could speak like a pro and knew, more or less, what I was talking about. Here I was checking to see if I understood how the processing of refugee worked.

"So, after the UNHCR gives permission, you have your people from the JVA, who, I understand, are mostly ex-pats working under contract to the IRC, do the prescreening to prepare the biodata for ACVA in the States and for the INS officers out here. If they are accepted, ICEM will handle the medical checks and prepare to move them, Cats I and II being given top priority, right"

Lionel smiled, and then said, "Well you forgot that they have to have a Visa Falcon before they are INSed. And if they're rejected, we have to internationalize them. Otherwise you've got it down pat."[29]

What I had said in the argot of the in-group was that after the representative of the United Nations High Commission for Refugees—the nonoperational overseer, funding source and legally responsible body— gave permission, caseworkers from the Joint Voluntary Agency, one of the American refugee organizations contracted by the Department of State (in this case, the International Rescue Committee) which employed many Americans—some of them already overseas, including a number of former Peace Corps volunteers—would begin processing the potentially resettleable refugees. They would prepare background information for the American Council of Voluntary Agencies, a consortium that coordinated sponsorship and facilitated resettlement as well as for the Immigration and Naturalization Service, the organization responsible for passing on eligibility for entry into the United States. When people were ready to move to the United States— or to another country for those wanting or, more often, having to go elsewhere, the Intergovernmental Committee for European Migration

---

[29]Originally published in "Links in a Chain: Observations of the American Refugee Program in Southeast Asia," *Migration Today*, 19:3, 1980, 7–23.

(later to be renamed the Intergovernmental Committee for Migration) would give medical examinations and make arrangements for transportation from the camp to the point of resettlement. Priority was given to spouses, parents, and children of the applicant (Category I) or former employees of the United States government (Category II). There were two other categories: III, for those of high risk such as former South Vietnamese soldiers and employees of the deposed government; and IV, a sort of residual rubric under which married siblings and other relatives were placed.

I was told that I had gotten things pretty straight but should not have forgotten that a security check—the graphic euphemism, "Visa Falcon"—was always required before the Immigration and Naturalization Service officer could even consider the case. And, should he or she find a person ineligible—a rare occurrence—the application would be rejected and the case turned back to the UN High Commissioner's in-country representatives for placement elsewhere. "Internationalization" was the term used to describe a search for a welcoming host country.

I was learning. I was to learn and see much more and to conclude that the operation was not a prelude to an Orwellian nightmare but a superhuman response to the trauma of those caught up in the aftermath of an excruciatingly protracted war. Out of what might well be called ordered chaos, nearly one million refugees from the former Indochina were able to come to the United States and most have done amazingly well as new Americans.

I now think that much of their particular success was related to two phenomena. The first was the convergence of a belief, shared by those long labeled "hawks" and those called "doves," that Americans owed those people something. The former argued that we had promised to save them from the communists but failed; the latter said that we had destroyed Vietnam. And both agreed that it was America's responsibility to help them. The second clearly observable factor in the overall success of the resettlement program was the dedication of those who facilitated the rescue and resettlement of the refugees.

There was much to report about my experiences in the camps and offices in Southeast Asia and about the refugees I followed back to the United States. A number of my commentaries and summaries of various aspects of the research were published in various journals and magazines. Several of those, mainly about the advocates, caretakers, gatekeepers, guides and go-betweens I met during the fieldwork phases of the study appear in *Tempest-Tost*, a book published by Oxford University Press some fifteen years later, in 1997.

Not only about refugees from Southeast Asia, *Tempest-Tost* is divided into three sections—views, reviews, and interviews. It includes an essay written at the request of Nathan Glazer for his book, *Clamor at the Gates: The New American Immigration* (1985) after he had seen some of my reports on the Indochinese refugee program. He asked me to include material from the study but to broaden the scope considerably and write about Asian Americans in general. I called my contribution to his book "From Pariahs to Paragons." It began:

> Chinese exchange students. Japanese salesmen. Korean greengrocers. Recent immigrants from Hong Kong and the Philippines. Thousands upon thousands of refugees from Vietnam, Laos, and Cambodia. Asians are everywhere. Some say they are taking over but, more often than not, the comment is made only in mock horror.
>
> Although "takeover" is a far from accurate image, in recent years the United States has become the magnet for any number of people from Asia. While many have come to study or to ply their wares, many more have come to stay. Between 1970 and 1980 the number of persons who specified Asia or Pacific Island ancestry to United States census takers increased 146 percent, making it the fastest growing segment of the population. Since 1980 the pace has accelerated considerably, augmented by several large waves of Indochinese refugees. In the years ahead, the Asian cohort will continue to grow because of high birth rates and the effects of chain migration (i.e. once citizenship is attained by an individual, his relatives move up the priority list for entrance to the U.S., and many do come.
>
> A hundred years ago the prospect of such a "yellow tide" would have—indeed had—evoked hysterical outcries against imminent inundation, urgent calls for measures to stay the flow, and ruthless attacks

on those who were already here. Not today. While some still feel that there are too many immigrants—including Asian immigrants—are being allowed to enter the United States, concerns about threats to our way of life, when expressed, are far more apt to be directed against those crossing the Rio Grande than those crossing the Pacific.

The images of those who used to be called "Orientals" have changed dramatically. No longer viewed as kowtowing inferiors or as inscrutable heathens, Mongolian scabs or untrustworthy neighbors, loyal only to their motherlands, they are now seen by many as members of "model minorities." The pariahs have become paragons, lauded for their ingenuity and industry and for embodying the truest fulfillment of the American Dream.

Already noteworthy in fields of science, medicine and the arts, Asians are increasingly found at the top of honor rolls, high on lists of academic prize winners and scholarship recipients and prominent in student rosters of elite universities. They are also beginning to swell the ranks of law schools and to seek careers in politics, areas where, in the past, they were rarely to be found.

Often compared to Jews, many Asian Americans do seem to share certain values, modes of acculturation and patterns of mobility with those once called "Orientals" themselves. The characteristics are familiar: a deep sense of ethnic identification and group loyalty; a high level of filial respect; a heavy emphasis on proper demeanor and the seriousness of life; a firm belief in the importance of education; a tendency toward extrinsic assimilation (taking on the trappings of dominant groups—speech, dress, musical tastes—while often remaining socially separate), and an overriding attitude that one must advance as far as possible not just for oneself but so that parents can enjoy the Chinese, Japanese, Korean, Vietnamese or Indian equivalent of what in Yiddish is known as *nachas fun die kinder*, that is, personal pride in the accomplishments of the children.

Of course, there are un-Jewish Asian Americans (and un-Jewish Jews) who do not toe the mark, who reject traditional mores, who disobey their parents, who do not want to delay their own gratifications. There are those who start work in the backrooms of restaurants and laundries, in factories and sweatshops and do not advance up the economic ladder. Some simply drop out. Some join gangs. But most do stay the course. Demographic studies show that, along with Jews, Asians are the most upwardly mobile people in the country. As an aggregate they have caught up to and are even surpassing the Joneses and Smiths—and the Cohens and Levines.

William Petersen, the demographer most closely associated with the use of the term "model minority," indicates that their comparative rate of progress is remarkable. He points out that what the Chinese and Japanese had to endure might well have resulted in a pattern of poor education, low income, high crime rates and unstable families. Instead, Petersen notes, "they broke through the barriers of prejudice and, by such key indices as education and income, surpassed the average levels of native-born whites.[30]

I went on to note an interesting quandary that confronted some Asian American social scientists who felt that too little attention was being paid to those who did not find it so easy to move from the margins of this society to its mainstream.

Of late there has been a tendency to gloss over the inglorious history of anti-Asian attitudes and practices, to look at demographic attributes rather than underlying psychodynamic phenomena and to ignore continuing divisions between those now moving into and through the system and those left behind. The latter is reflected in what some call the occupational dichotomy between managers and workers. It is evident in other places, too. Nonetheless, what is most striking is that many Asian Americans writing about the dilemmas of being both a part of and apart from this society returned again and again to the model minority motif themselves! They often ended their assessments by conceding that, after all, the "myth" is still more real than not.

The sociologist Harry Kitano has said "the judgment of Japanese Americans as the 'model American minority' is made from a strictly majority point of view. Japanese Americans are good because they conform—they don't make waves—they work hard and are quiet and docile." Kitano suggest that, "Ideally, members of the ethnic community should share in any evaluation of the efficacy of their adjustment." In view of this obligation, he concludes:

> In spite of different definitions of what constitutes success and philosophical discussions that may show Japanese as short of being an "ideal" group, they have achieved a niche in America society. They have been effective in social organization, in socialization, in controlling deviant behavior, and in

---

[30]"From Pariahs to Paragons," in *Clamor at the Gates: The New American Immigration*, Nathan Glazer, ed., (San Francisco: Institute for Contemporary Studies Press, 1985), 181–212.

coming to grips with success in American terms. When we look back at the past prejudice and discrimination faced by Japanese we find that even their most optimistic dreams have been surpassed.

Insider Kitano's words echo what outsider Petersen has written. "As extraordinary as have been the positive achievements, the lack of a countervailing negative record is even more astounding.[31]

The term "model minority," popularized by William Petersen in an article in the *New York Times Magazine*, was further elaborated in his book, *Japanese Americans,* one of the volumes in my Random House series, published in 1971. My own thoughts about it, which I've just quoted were written a decade later. While Asians from East, Southeast and South Asia continued to come to the United States in increasing numbers and do quite well as new Americans, over the years the growing presence of the other migrants, especially Latinos, was raising echoes of old fashioned xenophobic nativism. In the years ahead, most of the resurgence of anti-immigrant sentiment would be focused not on a new "Yellow Peril" but on "the invasion from Mexico." But tensions were also mounting between both cohorts of newcomers and the minority group with the deepest roots in this country, African Americans. As I would write in *Tempest-Tost* "The tempests that stir passion and fear, altruism and resentment are not only off-shore."[32] Those thoughts were already on my mind when I turned my attention back to the U.S. in mid-1980s, especially while completing work on a new collection of essays, *Mainstream and Margins,* a volume that included a piece I called "Blacks and Jews: The Strained Alliance" that sought to put both affinities and tensions in an historical context.[33]

Just as Jews and other European immigrants had moved into this society, often into neighborhoods where blacks were living in northern cities, then moved past them and on up the socioeconomic ladder, there

---

[31]Ibid, pp. 183–184.

[32]*Tempest-Tost: Race, Immigration and the Dilemmas of Diversity* (New York and Oxford: Oxford University Press, 1997), xii.

[33]*Mainstream and Margins* (New Brunswick, New Jersey: Transaction Books, 1993).

now were Asians, and in some cities like Miami and Los Angeles, Latinos, repeating the pattern and, once again, many inner-city blacks were being left behind. I would look more closely into this leapfrog phenomenon, too, but not for another decade.

While much of my attention was focused on refugees and American minorities, yet another interest was whetted during the early 1980s.

The year before I began the fieldwork on the refugee project, I hosted a sociologist named Hans Adriaansens who had come to Smith as a fellow of the American Council of Learned Societies on whose selection board I had served for three years in the previous decade. While on the board, I complained that most of those foreign scholars to whom we awarded year-long grants all seemed to want to go to the same places— Harvard, Princeton, Yale, or Berkeley—but rarely to any of the smaller colleges, like Amherst, Williams or Smith. Perhaps because he remembered what I had said before I left the board or because he really thought it would be a good fit, Dick Downer of the ACLS called me a few months later. He said the committee had just given a grant to a Dutch sociologist whose research proposal involved doing a study of voluntary organizations in a small community. If I gave him the green light, Downer would urge Professor Adriaansens to consider Smith. He came, he saw, and quite unexpectedly he had a career-changing experience. He became a devotee of the idea of the liberal arts and would in time become the founder of two university colleges attached to Utrecht University in the Netherlands and a leader in the movement to change undergraduate education across the continent of Europe.

His "reeducation" began to germinate when Hans and I took daily runs through the trails in the woods adjacent to the campus. We would discuss many things but, aside from his keen desire to learn as much American slang as possible—involving sudden halts for him to take out a notebook and write down something I said—our talks often tended to get back to the nature of the liberal arts. On one of those runs we talked about someday bringing Smith College to the Netherlands. Ten years ago I wrote about the scheme that had been hatched in Northampton way back in 1980:

If one believes that imitation is the best form of flattery, then the members of the Smith College community should feel very flattered. Over the last fifteen years two new English-language international honors colleges—University College Utrecht (UCU) and the Roosevelt Academy (RA)—have been established and are flourishing in the Netherlands. Smith served as the catalyst and model for both. The two colleges are a part of the venerable old University of Utrecht, founded in 1636.

University College Utrecht is located halfway and an easy bike ride between the center of the medieval city where some of the original university buildings are located and the very modern suburban campus in an area known as the Uithof. Created on the site of a former army post, like most American colleges, UCU is self-contained, integrating academic and residential buildings and facilities for dining and student services around a series of quads. Its 400 Dutch and 250 foreign students all live on campus, though some take courses, mainly in lab sciences, in the Uithof area. There is a core faculty, mainly those who chair one of the four main units—Humanities, Sciences, Social Sciences, and one that offers orientation courses such as Dutch history and language for international students—and a number of tutors. Other instructors come over from the main sectors of the university or from other Dutch or foreign universities.

UCU was the first institution of higher learning in the Netherlands and one of the first on the European continent to offer a Bachelor of Arts degree.

Instead of the pillared design that characterizes almost all European universities, in which graduates of classical high schools go immediately into narrowly specialized disciplines such as literature, law, economics, or medicine, the plan was to have incoming students take courses across the curriculum and then, in the second year, to start moving toward a concentration. The more pyramidal scheme proved to be a prototype of what is now widely known as the Bologna Protocol, an agreement by most European countries to move in the direction of the vast array of degree programs with a BA/MA sequence. At UCU, the designers of the program opted for a three-year BA similar to what is found in most universities in the United Kingdom.

In almost all other respects, not only is the UCU a near-replication of the American liberal arts system, but also its academic structure and curriculum, including original course designs and much of their content Smith-based. This was no accident.

I then described the story of Hans Adriaansens's conversion experience in much greater detail and how, almost single-handedly, he built the two colleges and what they were—and are—like.

The main building at University College Utrecht soon became known, in good Smith tradition, as College Hall. The army barracks, some having been turned into classrooms, were given loftier names like Locke and Pascal and Fermi; the mess hall became the dining complex, and several halls of residence were added. Students started arriving before the construction was completed and before the paint was dry. They had the feeling that they were pioneers. And they were.

The UCU exceeded even Hans'—and my—wildest expectations. Within a few years it gained a reputation as a premier institution of higher learning in the Netherlands, garnering more prizes per capita than any other, and placing its graduates in master's and doctoral programs throughout the continent, in the U.K. and in the U.S.

With so much accomplished, it was time to move on. Unlike the center of the country, where there are many great universities including Utrecht, Leiden, Delft, and the Universiteit van Amsterdam; the southern province of Zeeland never had one. Hans, now a highly regarded academic innovator, had a new idea: to build a liberal arts college as the core of a new university. He decided to do this in his—and the Roosevelt family's—hometown of Middelburg in the southern province of Zeeland....

A few years later the Roosevelt Academy, the second Dutch liberal arts honors college linked to Utrecht University opened its doors. Instead of having an enclosed quadrangle, the campus of the RA is the city of Middelburg, known for its unique fifteenth-century Flemish-style *Stadhuis*, the former city hall. That stately building on one side of a town square and marketplace is now the administrative hub of the new college and locale of one of the handsomest lecture halls in the country. Nearby buildings were taken over to provide classrooms and halls of residence.

Today, like its sister institution, UCU, the RA attracts students from all over the Netherlands and many other countries in Europe as well as from Africa, Asia and North America.[34]

---

[34]"Smith in the Netherlands: A Trans-Atlantic Connection," *Grecourt Gate News*, December 14, 2007.

I should note that I was honored to have been asked to give the commencement address to the first graduating class at the University College of Utrecht University. The ceremony was held in the Dom, the old cathedral in central Utrecht. Dressed in my bright red Cornell doctoral robe, I marched through the corridors and into the sanctuary along with the members of the UCU faculty members attired in their very Calvinist black robes and white bibs. I felt a bit like a cardinal in a flock of magpies. Then, when it was my turn to take the podium, knowing of Hans' fondness for sailing, I used nautical metaphors to speak of the institution's origins, from the laying of the keel to its launching and the critical role its helmsman played in managing to sail out through some pretty rocky shoals.

Several years later, when Hans was the dean of UCU's sister international honors college, the Roosevelt Academy, Hedy was invited to give a special convocation address. It was on the sixtieth anniversary of the outbreak of War War II and she was asked to speak of her personal experience during the early 1940s in her native city of Amsterdam. Knowing the pre-announced subject of her talk, in addition to RA faculty members, staff, and students, a number of people came from all over the Netherlands to hear her. (The procession across the city of Middlebury to where Hedy would speak is featured on the cover of this book.)

One time, during the year Hans Adriaansens was at Smith, he went with me to Harvard to visit our son, Dan, who was in his first year there. Hans was eager to return to the campus where he had spent a year as a graduate student, learning from and later writing about the sociologist, Talcott Parsons. Two years later I was in residence there myself. Starting in the academic year 1983–84 I was a fellow at the Kennedy School of Government, where I tried to pull together much of the data I had gathered in the study of refugee policy. In 1984–85, serving as a visiting professor at Harvard, I offered a course on a related subject. I called it "The Dependency of the Dispossessed."

Among the material distributed for that class were a few paragraphs I had written previously on the meaning of "trust." They were provided to help set the stage for one of the key issues we would be discussing.

"Trust" is an interesting word. It has a number of connotations, some of which suggest a particular kind of symbiotic relationship between two or more parties. In popular parlance, for example, the word is frequently used to mean reliance on or faith in others. But there is another common way in which it is rendered, expressing an obligation or responsibility imposed on one in whom authority is placed—as "in a position of trust." In the first of the two definitions the emphasis might be said to be on the "weaker" party, the one in need of guidance or assistance or protection. In the second it is on the "stronger" one, the person or group on whom the dependent ones are expected or required to place their confidence. The relationship between refugees and those who care for them illustrates a classic case of such dependency.

Wherever they may find themselves, refugees—weakened by the circumstances of their uprooting, suffering from chaotic and often anomic conditions in camps or other temporary quarters, frequently disoriented, confused, and alienated in the most literal sense of the term—are almost invariably dependent upon others for their immediate and, in many cases, long-term survival. Sometimes those others are strangers, true Samaritans. Sometimes they are kith and kin, co-religionists or compatriots, political allies, or personal friends. Compassion and empathy with the plight of the dispossessed may mitigate but can never entirely eliminate the nature of the dependency between the victims and those on whom they must rely for care, safety and succor...

We know why refugees must put their trust in others. They have to. But why do those others risk their lives—or, in the case of refugee workers, spend their lives aiding the uprooted. We are only beginning to understand this as the attention of increasing numbers of researchers begin to consider the psychology of altruism in specific regard to refugees as well as the sociology of exile and the politics of rescue.[35]

Enrolled in the class were Harvard undergraduates and graduate students from the Kennedy School and from the Fletcher School of Law and Diplomacy at nearby Tufts University. From the start I wanted the students to interact with key players in the process of refugee rescue,

---

[35]These thoughts were later expanded and presented in a paper at a seminar, "Trust and the Refugee Experience" sponsored by the United Nations University in Helsinki, Finland in June, 1992. They also formed the core of a much longer essay, "In Whom They Trust," published in *Tempest-Tost*, 135–50.

relief and resettlement, so, using what was left of my Rockefeller grant, I invited ten people to speak to the class. Among several guests who came were Hai Ba Pho, a Vietnamese refugee teaching political science at the University of Massachusetts, Lowell, and Eve Burton, a former Hampshire College student of mine who had come over to Smith to take my course on U.S. refugee policy and got hooked. Later I would supervise her thesis and help her get to Southeast Asia where she would spend a year working for Save the Children in one of the worst camps I visited. It was in Songkhla, Thailand, very near the Malaysian border.

I asked both Hai and Eve to talk about their experiences: he as a refugee, she as a refugee worker. It was one of the most interesting sessions of a very exciting semester, not least because I had also asked each to begin by speaking in Vietnamese, which I knew no one else there could understand. That Hai Ba Pho spoke the language was hardly a surprise, but that Eve could do it was an eye- (and ear-) opener to all, including Hai. Then both reverted to English, explaining what they had been saying. My purpose in asking them to do this was to show how it was possible to become a particularly skillful observer—as Eve had done. This was something I had witnessed first hand in many camps in Southeast Asia when conducting my research and had seen many young refugee workers attempting to master the language and get a grasp of the cultures of those they were trying so hard to assist.

Perhaps most moving to me was the time when, on one of my trips to Thailand, without telling Eve, I flew from Bangkok down to Hat Yai, the nearest city to Songkhla, to see her. After getting past the UNHCR gates and establishing my *bona fides* (I always carried letters from the REFCORD and the JVAR), I made a beeline for the hut where I'd heard she would be giving an English lesson. I will never forget the look on her face when she first glanced up, saw me, did a double-take, then, hardly missing a beat, said to her students, her words translated by a young Vietnamese man, "I am your teacher. There is my teacher." Forty heads swung around to gaze upon this bearded stranger with a camera.

Eve returned to finish her thesis, "A Vietnamese Odyssey," about the resettlement process, but not before arranging to sponsor three refugees she'd met to come to the States. Her parents and Hedy and I were pleased to help in this endeavor. One of the three is still living in our community.

Eve spent some years working on refugee issues for the U.S. government, then went to law school, served as counsel to the International Rescue Committee's project on women refugees, and is now a highly regarded First Amendment specialist. She was a great model for my Harvard students, several of whom decided on the basis of the seminar and, perhaps particularly because of her story, to enter the field of immigration and refugee work themselves.

During my two years at Harvard three unrelated events were to shape much of what I would be doing the rest of that decade and well into the next one. The first was a meeting with Kitty Dukakis.

While I was in the Boston area, I decided to interview Governor Michael Dukakis' wife who was very much involved in the resettlement of refugees, especially Cambodians. Knowing little about Mrs. Dukakis, I was curious to know why she was focusing so much attention on the general problem and on that particular group. I managed to make an appointment and went to see her in her office, very close to her husband's in the State House on Beacon Hill. Her secretary told me I had twenty minutes. Our session lasted almost two hours as we discussed many of my concerns about how U.S. refugee policy in general was being handled and her own about domestic resettlement. She told me about her experience traveling with Elie Wiesel and others to the Cambodian border and her more direct involvement with programs in Boston and Lowell and other Massachusetts cities. I told her about my research overseas and back in the States, including right there in Boston.

Before leaving, I asked Kitty (she had said, "Call me Kitty") why, of all the refugee groups in the world, she had focused so much on the Cambodians. The Governor's wife looked at me a bit incredulously and said, "Don't you think every Jew should be concerned about genocide?"

That was not the end of our relationship but the beginning. Shortly after that meeting in the State House, I received an invitation from the governor—doubtless prompted by his wife, to join his Governor's Council on Immigration and Refugee Policy. There I met many key figures representing key agencies, NGOs, church groups, and political organizations, and the Cambodian American, Dan Lamm, point man for all refugee programs in the Commonwealth. In time, Dan, Kitty, several other refugee workers and I would join together to form an organization focused on citizenship for new Americans. In special deference to Kitty and my grandparents, I named it "The Medina Project." (The Arabic word, *medina*, used in several languages, means town. *Goldene Medina*, was what many Yiddish speakers who came to New York—indeed, to America—called their place of refuge during the waves of the great Atlantic migration of the late nineteenth and early twentieth century.)

In the late 1980s a number of those involved in resettlement, including a number of representatives of refugee committees in Massachusetts, came to Smith College for a day-long discussion on issues relating to adaptation and integration. It was in many ways a follow-up to a much bigger symposium held at Smith in 1983. That conference, called "Working with Refugees," brought together over one hundred people I had met and interviewed in Washington, New York, Boston, New Orleans and cities up and down the west coast, in Geneva, Switzerland, and in all the countries ringing the former Indochina in Southeast Asia. The participants in that conference included the U.N. Deputy High Commissioner for Refugees, representatives from the Departments of State, Justice, and Health and Human Services, the heads of almost all the VOLAGs, social workers, a number of foot soldiers who served literally in the trenches of the refugee camps. Several political scientists attended, along with lawyers and sociologists who were specialists in the field, including Norman and Naomi Zuckerman, authors of *The Guarded Gate,* and Gil Loescher and John Scanlan, who wrote *Calculated Kindness.* After the meeting, I put together the proceedings in a little book published by the Center for Migration Studies. It, too, was called *Working With Refugees.*[36]

---

[36] *Working with Refugees* (Center for Migration Studies, 1986).

The conference and the book were both dedicated to the memory of Simon S. Shargo, a remarkable man who was born in Nikoliev in the Ukraine, trained as an agronomist, worked as a local official for Herbert Hoover's American Relief Administration's mission in the Crimea, twice became a refugee himself (first fleeing from the Soviet Union to Berlin and later moving from there to Paris, then Lisbon, then to Geneva) and then spent a lifetime caring for the victims of political persecution. For more than fifty years he was a high official in the European offices of the American Jewish Joint Distribution Committee, an agency devoted to relief, rescue, and reconstruction. (It was the "Joint" that facilitated my wife and her sister's move to the United States after World War II.) Late in his life, Simon Shargo moved to Northampton to be near his daughter, Nelly Hoyt, a colleague of mine in the history department with whom I had twice led seminars on the experience of exile.

Simon helped me plan the "Working with Refugees" conference but sadly he died the summer before it took place. In a moving gesture, Bob DeVecchi, then president of the International Rescue Committee, paid special tribute to Simon, reminding us all—as we gathered to discuss the experiences of refugees after the fall of Saigon, that there had been those like Simon Shargo who were working with—and for—refugees for decades before the war in Vietnam and that many more would be required to do so in the years ahead, sometimes giving their lives to the cause. The last proved to be a most prescient remark.

One of the attendees at the gathering was attorney Arthur Helton, founder and director of the Forced Migration Project of the Open Society Institute and program director of peace and conflict studies at the Council on Foreign Relations, and one of the best advocates refugees ever had. In the summer of 2003 he would accompany the United Nations special representative Sergio Vieira de Mello to Iraq to evaluate conditions in that war-torn country. Both men would be killed on August 19, 2003, in the bombing at the Canal Hotel in Bagdad. In fact, the only survivor of those in the room where they died was another participant in our conference, political scientist Gilburt Loescher. Gil lost both of his legs in the explosion. Now living in Oxford, England, Gil is still actively pursuing his own research on refugee rights.

In the early 1980s I became involved in another new project. As one always interested in reaching out to those outside the groves of academe, it offered a unique opportunity. It all began when a young anthropologist in our department, Tom Riley, came back from visiting his parents at their summer home in Kennebunkport, Maine, and told me about a program called "Salt." The woman who ran it was trying to launch a college-level, junior-year- or junior-semester-in-Maine to train liberal arts students, particular those studying sociology, ethnography and folklore in field research, WPA-type journalism, and documentary photography. Knowing my interests and my oft-stated view that journalists needed to learn to think more sociologically and social scientists needed to learn how to write clear English free from insider jargon, Tom thought I might be a useful adviser to Pamela Wood, the founding director of Salt, and mentioned me to her. She contacted me almost immediately and shortly thereafter we met and quickly found ourselves to be on the same wave length.

At that first meeting I learned about the history of the program—and Pam Wood's history, too.

Originally from Oklahoma, she had met and married her husband, John, from Minnesota, when both were undergraduates at Harvard in the 1950s. After graduation they decided that they wanted to become journalists. They spent a few years in Minneapolis, worked for a short time on a small-town newspaper in California, then moved to Chile where they published an English language paper for several years, leaving a short time before the bloody coup in which President Salvador Allende was killed. Returning to the States, the Woods saw an advertisement from a publisher seeking a partner for a weekly paper in Kennebunk, Maine. They applied, were accepted and headed east to relaunch their careers. Sadly, it was a short-lived dream.

Soon after they arrived in Maine, it was discovered that John had incurable cancer. With John unable to work and short of money, Pam took a job in the English department of the local high school. She was assigned to work with those she said were considered the least able students, "the ones many thought were hopeless." Instead of buying into the prejudices of her new colleagues, she sought ways of reaching her students, most memorably by starting a mimeographed magazine about their lives. She urged those in her classes to gather material by talking to—actually interviewing—family members, friends, former teachers, shopkeepers, fishermen, and others. As the project developed, Pam said they needed a name for their journal. Someone came up with "Salt," and it stuck. I remember Pam explaining that the kids said they liked it because it spoke to their seaside environment and the salt air.

This was the late 1970s and there was still a good deal of government money available for innovative projects in education. After John died, Pam applied for and received a small grant. She left the high school, put a deposit on a boatyard in Kennebunkport and set out to do two things simultaneously: renew the purpose of the place by teaching boatbuilding and other carpentry skills to young people, and continue to develop her magazine. She was not very successful with the first and the second seemed to need new direction. It was then that she thought of moving from an oral history program geared to high school students to one for those in college or university.

It was shortly thereafter that I entered the picture and after a number of stumbles, we managed to launch a program that not only continues to this day in a building on Congress Street in Portland but also has a highly regarded graduate component. Directed today by a former student, Donna Galluzo, the Salt Institute for Documentary Studies offers three tracks of professional training: one in writing, one in photography and a third in radio.

I served for many years as the chair of Salt's educational committee and for many more as a member of the board of trustees, going every few months to Kennebunkport, then to Cape Porpoise, then to Portland—towns where the ever-moving, ever-growing institute was located. I have many memories of my days with Salt but one is especially vivid.

A little while after Pam and I had our initial meetings. I had some ideas about what was needed in developing an academic program for Salt, at least in terms of faculty and core courses. But to add a bit of prestige to our preliminary plan, I asked Pam how she would feel about using a bit of her grant money to put together a star-studded committee made up of those rated among the very best anthropologists, folklorists, journalists, and documentary photographers in the country to plan our curriculum and then serve as our senior advisers. She liked the suggestion and we invited a truly stellar group to join us at a retreat of sorts in Cape Porpoise, the new venue of the program located in a little fishing village near Kennybunkport and the boatyard. Each person we asked responded almost immediately and in the affirmative. We set a date and they all came to join us for a three-day session. It turned out to be a big mistake.

Within a day after our star-studded group assembled, I realized that I had created a hydra-headed monster. Each one had a different idea about not just what we should do to make the place over, but how to remake it in his or her image, the other fields being ancillary. The sessions grew testier as Pam and I looked at each other with knowing glances. Even before the meeting broke up, we realized we had to start over.

After bidding our guests farewell, we went to a local lobster shack, had dinner and a few beers and talked for several hours recounting the pretentiousness of our "consultants" and their transparent attempts to upstage one another in discussing what we should do next.

In the end we decided to go back to the original idea of what the program should be, and invited a not-so-well known group of people in the same fields who were more sympathetic to our eclectic approach to join us as advisers. We made our final preparations and by the following fall Pam was ready to launch the college-level program.

While having its ups and downs, Salt kept taking at least two steps forward for every one that faltered and, in a few years, it had become a smooth running operation led by Pam and a fine professional staff, including one full-time and a number of part-time faculty members, a very active academic committee, and a supportive board of trustees. Over the years many graduates of the program, having been strongly influenced by their time at Salt, would follow career paths in documentary studies, anthropology, folklore, photography and journalism, an ongoing tribute to Pam Wood's imagination and leadership.

While still at Harvard in the spring of 1984, I was invited by the *Christian Science Monitor* to write a review of a forthcoming book by Thomas Sowell, *The Economics and Politics of Race*. (I say forthcoming because, like other major newspapers, the *Monitor* usually sent bound galleys to reviewers in hopes that they would turn in their copy in time to print it on or very near the day of publication.)

I had written a few reviews for newspapers before but most of my reviewing up to that time had been for journals in sociology and history. I found it truly refreshing and exciting to see my efforts in print where they could be most relevant instead of having to wait six months or a year to see them—sometimes after a reviewed book had already been remaindered!

That early review for the *CSM* was followed by several more, mostly on issues of race or refugee policy. While this was understandable, given my professional interests, I soon became frustrated. Now a part of the *CSM* stable, I told my editor that I read books on other subjects as well. To my delight he got the dig and I began getting requests to write reviews of books on all sorts of subjects, including volumes of narrative nonfiction, like Peter Matthiessen's *Men's Lives* and John McPhee's *Rising from the Plains*; historical studies, including David Wyman's *The Abandonment of the Jews*, Michael Marrus's, *The Holocaust and History*, Robert Hughes's *The Fatal Shore*, Frances Fitzgerald's *Cities on a Hill*, and Daniel Boorstin's *Hidden History*; and biographical accounts, including Nien Chiang's *Life and Death in Shanghai*, Gao Yuan's *Born Red*, and Pin Yathay's *Stay Alive, My Son*. There were also books to read and write about on contemporary politics, including three concerning the fall of Ferdinand Marcos; David Grossman's *The Yellow Wind*, a poignant account of the tensions between Israelis and Palestinians; Benny Morris's *The Birth of the Palestinian Problem, 1947–1949*, and a volume edited by Edward Said and Christopher Hitchens, *Blaming the Victims*, on the same general topic, and Guenter Lewy's more general study, *Peace and Revolution*. I reviewed several novels, including Peter Matthiessen's

Killing Mr. Watson and Ward Just's *The Translator*. A special treat, owing to my early fascination and the magazine's significant impact on my life course, was being assigned to write an essay on C.D.B. Brian's *The National Geographic: 100 Years of Adventure and Discovery*.

All told, by the end of the decade I had written well over twenty reviews for the *Monitor*. Owing to the shake-up at the paper, the resignation of editor-in-chief Katherine Fanning and her entire editorial staff (which had my complete sympathy), I stopped reviewing for the paper. But then, ten years later, with Kay Fanning's encouragement, I returned to the stable and ended up writing thirty more reviews before the paper ceased to publish a print edition. My last review for the *Monitor* was, perhaps prophetic. It was on Jane Jacobs' pessimistic book published in 2004, *Dark Age Ahead*.

Firmly hooked on the challenge of book reviewing for the general public, during my years away from the *Monitor*, I reviewed for *New York Newsday* and became a regular commentator for *Congress Monthly*, the magazine of the American Jewish Congress, and continued to be for many years until it, too, fell on hard times with the scandals related to the AJC's principal financial manager, the notorious ponzi-schemer Bernard Madoff.

Helping to develop new educational programs and book reviewing for a variety of journals weren't the only new tasks I took up in earnest in the 1980s. It was also a time when, quite by accident, I became a travel journalist. It all began with a friend's challenge: to write and submit an article to the *New York Times* on my and my family's passion for adventure (well, soft adventure) travel. I decided to do it and wrote a long piece I wanted to call "Challenging Days and Star-Studded Nights." To my delight, the *Times* did accept it and, on Sunday, July 5, 1986, it was published on the front page of the travel section. They changed the title to "Adventure Tours for Kindred Spirits." Here are some excerpts from that self-explanatory essay which I would later reprint under my own preferred title in *Guest Appearances* (2003).

"Enjoy unspoiled wilderness." "Sail away from it all." "Rock and roll through a sandstone chasm." "Go with the flow." "Have the adventure of a lifetime." Such phrases advertise carefree vacations on foot, afloat, and on a bicycle. Further copy promises that outfitters with such intriguing names as Backroads, High Desert Adventures, Tailwinds and Yankee Packet Company will supply everything from board and bedding to a cohort of kindred spirits. They also promise to provide crews to serve as guides and gofers, plus high adventure and breathtaking scenery.

Ever a skeptic, even I have found that there can be truth in advertising.

Over the past thirty years I have taken part in a number of three-day to two-week packaged expeditions. With members of my family, I have cruised Penobscot Bay aboard the schooner *Stephen Taber* and the Caribbean on the brigantine *Belle Blonde*. We have also sailed "Downeast" from New York City to Camden, Maine, on the ketch *Angelique*, rafted the Grand Canyon from Lees Ferry to Lake Mead, paddled Oregon's "Wild and Scenic Rogue River," and been inn-to-inn bicycle wanderers in Vermont.

On my own I have gone windjamming through the Hawaiian islands and the San Juans, floated and bounced through Cataract Canyon in Utah, kayaked the Klamath River in California, done some social climbing with the Ryder/Walker hiking company in Switzerland, and taken numerous bike tours, including those that looped through the wine country in Napa and Mendocino counties, went up and over the Continental Divide in Colorado from Santa Fe to Taos and then around the Sangre de Cristo Mountains in New Mexico, down the coast of Oregon and around the Big Island in Hawaii.

There was a sameness about these excursions. I mean this in an analytical not a pejorative sense. They were all appealingly advertised, well planned and well orchestrated.

To all outward appearances the organizers of such expeditions and their crews seem quite sensitive to the problem of bringing strangers together to travel and live in close quarters. The clients have varied motives for joining such adventures. Some are energetic but lonely singles looking for companionship, and some are retirees who like to do interesting and different things each year.

Others are people like me who, while preferring to do things on their own, also like many activities that take considerable planning and organization for which they have little time.

For those in each of these categories—and others—the full-service guided tours fill several needs at once. They promise their clients (or "guests," as the outfitters prefer to describe them) packaged experiences with challenging days, star-studded nights and ample conveniences for their care and feeding. And they assure them that the groups will be small and congenial.

Many years ago a favorite student put a "Peanuts" poster in my office. It says, I LOVE MANKIND, IT'S PEOPLE I CANT STAND. It seemed an appropriate joke-shibboleth for a sociologist.

The fact is that this sociologist really likes people but I admit to thinking of Linus's epigram the first time my wife and I signed on for one of these trips. I wondered if we would be herded and regimented and expected to sing old college songs around a beachside campfire, play charades and be sociable even when we wanted to be left alone. My fears were hardly eased the first night when, together with fellow shipmates on the squared fantail of the 68-foot schooner *Stephen Taber*, Mike Anderson, the skipper, tried to get us all to know each other. It was a bit unsettling and I wondered how we would survive the voyage.

In fact, we managed very well. And we later learned that many of those with whom we sailed had had the same apprehensions.

Weather-wise the trip was a disaster, with rain and fog for six days. We were grouped together in the tiny galley and smaller day-cabin much more than even the most gregarious of our group would have wanted or dreamed possible. But we got along, and it turned out to be a great vacation. In fact, the next season we took a second weeklong trip on the *Taber*—and the weather was perfect!

The skipper's briefing on the *Taber* proved to be standard procedure. There is always that first awkward encounter on such trips. Names are called out, hands are shaken, and everyone is told something about rules, routes and daily routines. Afterward the entire group has dinner together.

The meal is a kind of rite of passage. Conversations tend to center around the fleshing out of cryptic words of identification made at the earlier meeting.

"Sam Jones. I'm a teacher from Indiana and this is my wife, Sally. We grew up on the Connecticut shore and miss the salt air. We try to do something by the sea, Atlantic, Pacific, you name it, every summer."

"George and I are retired. We just love to hike; in fact, we've just come back from the Italian Dolomites. Rugged but fantastic."

Personal anecdotes get related, especially about other vacations, and reputations get established.

Regardless of the type of trip, the next morning is always a time of high excitement and, for many, trepidation. What will it be like if the wind really picks up? How will I deal with the rapids and holes in the river" What does it mean to do 50 miles over "fairly hilly" terrain? How will I look to the others?

For some, the last question becomes especially crucial now that everyone knows who's who—and might remember how, the night before, during the nervous banter of that first supper, they had boasted of talents and experiences about which they now wished they'd kept quiet.

It is a time of testing and of stoking up.

Finally, pushing away from a table stacked with plates that had held three-egg omelets, bacon, pancakes, sweet rolls and toast, the time of reckoning is upon the group. Gear is stowed and sails are hoisted; camp is struck and rafts are loaded; boots are tightened and packs are shouldered; tires are checked and helmets buckled on. What all have been waiting for is now reality. There is no turning back.

The first full day—getting one's sea legs, sensing the power of white water, climbing the first long hills—is exhilarating and fatiguing. There is so much to take in; so much to sort out.

After several hours of sailing or rafting or paddling or riding or hiking there is a break for lunch. Tour organizers do not skimp on meals. My amazement at the amount of food available—sandwich makings, homemade breads, salads of all sorts, cookies and fruit—is only topped by my amazement at the amount consumed.

After a leisurely rest, the entourage is off again. Aboard ship one can continue to relax and enjoy the sun; on the river or the road there is still work to be done for there are, quite literally, miles to go before it would be time to rest.

Once at the mooring or campsite or lodge, the guests' workday is pretty much done. They may help to lower and furl sails, unload rafts, gather firewood, set up tents, or move bikes under tarps, but by and large it is a quiet time for reflecting on the day's accomplishments—and waiting for the next meal.

Whether on a water or land trip, by the second evening the sociologist in me notes how we move into the next stage of group dynamics: establishing a sort of quasi-community. By the end of that first full day, the guests, now more secure in what they are about, begin to sort each other out, gravitating more to one person or couple or group, avoiding others in a polite but noticeable way. This pattern becomes clearer the next morning when individuals and couples gather for breakfast. They hesitate, waiting for a seat next to somebody or away from somebody else.

The eggheads always seem to find each other; so do the jokesters, the oldsters, the drinkers, the yuppies, and the diehards. The last bunch often includes the sort of people who own their own boats, sail, hike, kayak and bike a good deal, and come on these trips not because of the uniqueness of the activity but for the convenience of the provisioning. Ever talking about equipment, weather conditions, distances covered, and energy expended, they are often seen by the others as purists.

Those who view them as such seem to have little idea that real purists would define them as phonies for taking part in such ersatz expeditions.

By the third day things have shaken down and a kind of rhythm has been worked out. It is the same on board as on the river or road. Those with similar backgrounds and interests stick together; so do the skilled and the not so skilled.

In addition to the formation of cliques, another sort of bonding invariably takes place. It is most noticeable on sailing trips where the working passengers (they do help to raise and lower sails, weigh the anchor and stand watch) quickly come to identify themselves with the boats they are on. This becomes especially apparent on "shore leave" when all are given a chance to wander the main streets of little coastal villages. There they exchange greetings and compare notes with those from other boats (who, like themselves, already feel they are a cut above the regular tourists they see). They then hurry back to the harbor for the yawl boat that will ferry them back to their mother ship.

On biking and hiking and kayaking tours, without the floating base of a windjammer on which all are literally living together for long stretches, such a feeling of identification is more symbolic than real but the loyalties of the participants upon meeting those in another group is very much the same. Doubtlessly, the tee shirts and caps with company logos that everybody buys and wears enhance the sense of solidarity.

All told, the social systems established early on a given trip generally remain intact. Not only do people tend to maintain the attachments they form the first two days, but the intensity of their relationships grows—up to a point. Whether the trip is four, five, six days or two weeks long, it seems to reach its zenith sometime toward the end of the last full day.

On the final evening *gemütlichkeit* fills the air as the members of the subgroups begin to set aside their differences and join together.

Often there is a party to which everyone contributes something— beer and wine, talent (guitar playing is still very much in), contributions for a collective tip, and tales of misadventures with other groups that "were never, ever, as congenial as this one."

The last morning is usually much like the others; the routine still holds. But when the long trip back to base gets under way, an interesting thing happens. People who have just spent as much as a week or two together begin to draw back into their own worlds.

As the gangplank is lowered for the last time, as the rafts are deflated and stored in the outfitter's trucks, as the kayaks or bikes are racked on the trailers, as the vans are loaded for the bus station or airport, hands are shaken, hugs are exchanged, words of "Keep in touch" are expressed, but too often the gestures are perfunctory. The guests are going their different ways. Suddenly it all seems quite ephemeral.

What is forgotten first—and there are some exceptions—are the people with whom one shared a most intense experience. What linger are memories of long days at sea under full sail, of the high excitement and potential danger of rafting through huge rapids that the boatmen called "the best in the river." Remembered too are such rare moments of Walter Mittyish transcendence as when, after a week of pedaling nearly 350 miles in high country, it seemed possible to climb any mountain.[37]

Around when the *Times* story went to press, I was off on one of the most circuitous of excursions—actually circuitous in several meanings of the term. It would be of several months in length. I first flew from Hartford to New Mexico to bicycle and write about pedaling for five days with the group called Backroads, starting from Santa Fe and going up and over the mountains to the north, through Chimayo, then Bobcat Pass, then down to and through Eagles Nest and Red River, and on the last day looping back, pedaling the nearly one-hundred-mile final sprint back along the Rio Grande to Santa Fe.

---

[37]"Adventure Tours for Kindred Spirits," *New York Times Travel Section*, July 5, 1986.

At the end of the trip, quickly exchanging my biking helmet for my mortarboard, I flew to San Francisco and on to Beijing for several weeks of lecturing there and at universities on another circular tour, this time from the capital city to Tianjin, then back to Beijing and on to Xi'an, Nanjing, and Shanghai, all under the aegis of the Chinese Academy of Social Sciences where I was called both a fellow and a "foreign expert." While in China on that trip, perhaps because it was only a few years after the thaw in relations with the United States, I was treated like a visiting potentate. Wherever I went I was feted, wined, dined, and often presented with a rather large, crude copy of the famous Tang Dynasty horse. I confess to having given most of these away because they were so big and cumbersome and hard to carry. But I did keep other, smaller gifts and many, many fond memories. Most vivid of all were the striking contradictions I saw in what was still a very poor country, a land still trying to recover from the Cultural Revolution while clearly about to make some new leap forward into or perhaps over the Industrial Revolution that seemed to have passed it by. Many told me that what I was seeing then in the middle of the 1980s was what Japan looked like in the 1950s. That may have been so but one thing that struck me as being very different from Japan was that I was in a country that, while dominated by the Han Chinese, had some seventy other ethnic groups and at least acknowledged this at its Central University for Nationalities in Beijing and in several other places where I spoke, including an institution in Xi'an, a city with a very large Muslim population.

That trip to the Middle Kingdom—my second that year, and my experiences with newfound friends, especially my wonderful interpreter, Hu Yafei, gave me many ideas about intergroup relations in that country but also fodder for travel pieces that I would use in the future. The best known was a sort of bird watcher's guide to American tourists in China, "Avis Americanus."[38] Another that mentioned my time in China was a story about how I got to see many cities on my own.

---

[38]"A Field Guide to a Species Seen in the People's Republic of China," *Hampshire Life,* January 22, 1988.

For me there is nothing better than getting up at the crack of dawn, slipping out of the hotel in the middle of a strange city, making a turn left or right, and then jogging off on a new adventure. I do it all the time, in the U.S. and abroad.

Over the past ten years I have run around the Charles River Basin in Boston, San Francisco's Embarcadero, Chicago's Loop, Vancouver's Stanley Park, Sydney Harbor and the Ringstrasse in Vienna. I have run down dusty roads in suburban Nairobi, through back alleys in Hong Kong, in and out of little villages above Lake Como, down bustling avenues in Beijing, by the canals of Venice and the klongs of Bangkok, and along the banks of the Liffey, the Thames, the Seine, the Amstel and the Rhine.

Such running around the world has a special quality to it. It is a kind of inversion of the oxymoron "same difference" we used to use when we were cool teenagers. The different sameness of what I do to keep in shape and to see new places before starting a day's work is a most satisfying fringe benefit of my itinerant life style. Research projects, meetings, and lectures keep me on the move.

While I have occasion to meet many people and to visit many interesting places on my trips, it is on early morning jogs and weekend wanderings that I can especially feel the wondrous unity and amazing diversity of the family of man. Time and again I am struck by continuities and connections with those whose habitats provide me with "field sites" for comparative study.

It is when I am quite literally on the road that much of what I study, write and teach about, namely, culture and character, becomes most personally meaningful.

Most of the people I've encountered in my off-the-tourist-route outings are warm and friendly. In places unused to the likes of me, they are sometimes confused by my half-dressed presence as I suddenly appear from around a cobble-stoned corner or over the brow of a brick-laid hill. I have often seen the proverbial "double take" as early risers look at me, stop, and look again in cities as diverse as Madrid, Melbourne, Mexico City, New Delhi, Dubrovnik, Suva in the Fijian Islands, and Sendai in Japan. Sometimes they do more.

I was once stopped by an elderly street cleaner on a corner in the center of Graz, Austria. Shaking her finger, she lectured me in German for at least five minutes, explaining that, "One must not cross the road against the light," even though it was 5:30 a.m. and there was no traffic anywhere in sight.

"Rules," she said, "are rules. And here, in Austria, they are obeyed."

Not, apparently, in Italy. There, by contrast, taking morning jogs on various trips to Rome as well as Florence, I have been laughed at by passersby as I waited for a light to change in the first rush of traffic of the day. Some even asked me what I was waiting for!

Like a Pied Piper, I've been followed by groups of Chinese children along Shanghai's Bund and down by the beach at Penang, Malaysia. I've been cheered by Swedes who called, "Hup, hup, hup" as I ran along Stockholm's quay and by New Zealanders as I headed into the sheep-covered hills above Christchurch.

My obsession has rarely gotten me into serious trouble. On the contrary, it has often opened doors. I've found that occasional stops to talk or to try to communicate with the local people can pay off in a variety of ways.

I remember a morning in Xian in the People's Republic of China. I ran from the grounds of my big, Soviet-style hotel, off to the right, toward the center of town. There, in a giant plaza, were hundreds of people in groups ranging from six or eight to forty or fifty, all doing their exercises.

Few paid much attention to me as I loped by; but I was most curious about them.

I ran for another mile or so, and then retraced my route. As I returned to the area of all the activity, I stopped nearby and watched. At one point a young man came up to me and, in school-book English, said, "You jog, sir."

"Yes," I said.

"I do not jog. I exercise with this," he said, showing me his wooden sword.

I asked him to tell me what he did with it. He beckoned me to follow him. We walked past several clusters of older people doing a kind of stylized shadowboxing to a waiting group of young men. My new friend nodded to me then joined the others. They started an elaborate routine of thrusts and parries, all accompanied by carefully choreographed foot movements.

While participating in the swordplay, the young Chinese who brought me there did not look at me—but I did notice him turn slightly and smile shyly when, after ten minutes or so, I waved to him and took my leave.[39]

[39]From "A Jogger's Guide to World Travel," *Christian Science Monitor*, June 10, 1988, 20. Reprinted in *Destinations: Uncommon Trips, Treks and Voyages*, (Sonia Thomas, ed.), Boston: Christian Science Publishing Society, 1990, 80–83.

From Shanghai I flew to Hong Kong to visit old friends and former students and then continued my circling, this time to Milan. By the time I got to Italy, I had gone two-thirds of the way around the world—the first of five such orbits I would make in the 1980s and 1990s. With perfect timing I met Hedy near the Milan train station. She had flown in from Boston the same morning. Reunited, we spent the night in Milan and the next day were driven to the little town of Bellagio where I was a resident scholar at the Rockefeller's famous retreat for six weeks.

It was shortly after our arrival in Bellagio that I first saw my *Times* story in print. It had been brought to me by one of the program officers at the Rockefeller Foundation who'd picked it up before leaving the States, and seen the little blurb at the bottom of the piece that said I was currently a fellow in Bellagio. He was intrigued to see that one of their scholars was also an adventurer.

I was in Bellagio to do more writing about my refugee project, but, as is often the case, working and living with a fascinating group of fellows proved to be the highlight of the experience. Our immediate neighbors were Malcolm Bradbury, the British novelist; Bob Putnam, the Harvard political scientist who would become a household name with his book, *Bowling Alone*; Charles Hamilton, civil rights lawyer and co-author with Stokely Carmichael, of the book, *Black Power*; Rosellen Brown, who had just published her first novel, *Civil Wars* and the British Africanist Michael Crowther. At the main villa and in other residences were fellows from the United States and the U.K. and around the world. For solitude, each scholar was given a study—sometimes attached to the living quarters, more often in another place—but we also had ample opportunities for the exchange of ideas, interesting seminars, fabulous meals, and, for those so inclined, wonderful material for imaginative scribblers.

Asked to give reports on our experience there, I decided that if my new friend, Malcolm Bradbury, could write his in the form of a novel, I would try to fashion a short story. Unlike my oft-reprinted *Times* piece on adventure travel, my little tale of academic excitement and intrigue, "Saluti da Bellagio," submitted in very rough form to the Foundation, never appeared in print. In fact, although I kept reworking it on and off for the rest of year, I finally gave up and filed it away. When I dug it out recently, I decided that, while it did offer some sense of what I was observing and thinking when Hedy and I were in Bellagio more than twenty-five years ago, it was still not ready for prime-time.

I never told Malcolm what I was doing regarding my report, but he and I had several lively and hilarious discussions of our experiences being on lecture tours arranged by the British Council and the United States Information Agency, respectively. I marveled at how accurately he had captured the flavor of such trips, especially in places that were still behind the Iron Curtain, in his book, *Rates of Exchange* (1983). His character, like me (and obviously like him) confronted the contradictions of welcoming but wary hosts, enthusiastic but careful-to-be-not-too enthusiastic audiences, and escorts (a.k.a. minders) privately expressing an eagerness to learn about the outside world while publicly, almost robotically, praising their own. But that was nothing compared to what Malcolm would do in his terrific spoof, *Why Come to Slaka? A Guidebook and a Phrasebook Translated into English by Dr. F. Plitplov* (1986), which I now appreciate not only as a veteran global don and still not-completely-jaded promoter of intercultural understanding but as a travel journalist.

Why Come to Slaka? is a comprehensive guidebook, with introductions by a high government official and a learned professor to a mythical Slavic nation, Statii Pre'letanii Slakam, Slaka, for short, a country ruled by the Party and run by loyal apparatchiks and their flunkies. For those who don't understand the Slakan language, Bradbury provides a useful glossary of his own, made-up, Slavic-sounding terms. *Why Come To Slaka?* begins with these gushing words of welcome addressed to English-speaking would-be *touristi*.

> Slaka!!!
> Where in the heart that does not high upleap at the very merest name of your immemorable city! Slaka!!! City of flours and gipsy musick, of grat buildungs and fine arts, we toast you in your own brandy spirtus!! Slaka!!! Grate city at the international crossroads, where for centuries people of the most varos parts have liked to come

together for congress. Slaka!!! Butsling metropole of traders and entrepeners, where one time a year exhibitionists of world-wide fame foregather in your great halls of conference in most festivating mood....Slaka!!! duel of the crown of our favoured country, where the best heritages of old times and the contemporary charms of socialistical cooperaton meld to composite a life-style both antiquated and progressive.[40]

An exaggeration to be sure, but from what I have experienced, it still typifies the sort of hype tourist bureaus around the world put out to entice people to come. And, although our English is better, we Americans are among the biggest local boosters of them all.

Not long after our stay in Bellagio, we were back in Italy. I had been invited to give another series of lectures at the University of Rome, this time on U.S. refugee policy. Sadly, the day after we arrived in the city, we received word that my mother, who lived in Tucson, Arizona, had had a stroke and died. As we made hurried plans to fly there the next day, our daughter, Lies, who was living in Rome at the time, gave us a special gift to put on her grandmother's casket. It was Women's Day in Rome and Lies had been marching in the campaign for women's rights just before she heard the news. She brought us some mimosa, the symbol of the movement. We smuggled the sprigs back into the States and, at the simple burial ceremony surrounded by as an small rainbow coalition of her friends—white, black, Latino and Native American, Hedy and I honored her with that special tribute.

My mother is buried next to my father under what was then a small and is now a tall and handsome pine tree in the shadow of the Catalina Mountains.

Many times I have tried to put my thoughts about both of my parents into words but never found the right rhythm or style. I'm still working on it.

In the busy decade that was coming to an end, I was also privileged to spend time at Oxford University, the first of three stints as a fellow at

---

[40]Malcolm Bradbury, *Why Come to Slaka?* (London: Arrow Books, Ltd., 1987), 11–12.

the Refugee Studies Centre based at Queen Elizabeth House, the home of its international programs. The colorful anthropologist and authority on what some call "The Aid Game," Centre director, Barbara Harrell-Bond, initially invited me there. During the first two trips, which took place during Smith's extended inter-term periods lasting around three weeks, I stayed at the Old Parsonage, a wonderful building that had been converted into a modestly priced warm, friendly B&B, very near to Queen Elizabeth House. (It is now a very expensive and very upscale boutique hotel.)

The third time I was in Oxford for a much longer stay. On that occasion I held the fancy title of Rhodes Trust Visiting Professor in Refugee Studies and was a fellow of St. Catherine's College. Because St. Catherine's had no facilities for housing visiting fellows, on the basis of my previous work, I applied for and was accepted as a resident fellow of the Oxford Centre for Hebrew and Jewish Studies. I lived in its wonderful manse in the village of Yarnton, a few miles north of Oxford and commuted into town on their mini-bus.

As a sociologist and, especially, as an ethnographer, I found my triple appointment quite enlightening, particularly in the fact that I kept shifting among three different cultural worlds. The first, the Refugee Studies Centre, was concerned with understanding and trying to deal with both the internally displaced and officially recognized refugees. It attracted both researchers and activists from all over the world. The second, St. Catherine's, offered a snapshot of old Oxford. This was not so much in its physical character which, from the very modern architecture of one of the university's newest colleges to its airy Scandinavian-style interior, was very different from the ones familiar to all who think of Oxford. Rather it was in the demeanor of a number of its clearly distinguished but terribly self-absorbed and self-important permanent fellows. I had little contact with the students but my sessions with faculty members seemed a living caricature of the one-upmanship of British academics, especially around and after mealtime. I found it stimulating at first, but it soon became tiresome and I spent less and less time at the college. My third affiliation was unexpectedly the most engaging. In a place committed to combining historical and contemporary study almost single handedly created then led by Sir David Patterson, it was a treat to exchange ideas with fellow fellows, some of whom were the last people I would have expected to find there. Indeed, it turned out that my closest colleague, who was also staying in Yarnton, was a Japanese professor of Yiddish literature who was an authority on the writings of Isaac Bashevis Singer. (He and I often spoke of a rather odd book, *The Japanese and the Jews*, by Isaiah Ben-Dasan published in 1981, the first of a number that sought to show the similarities between the two "tribal peoples," which both of us thought was quite a stretch— and quite a sketch.)

While in Oxford on those several trips, I gave a number of talks about my own research, exchanged ideas with others and actually managed to do some more writing.

Back from Oxford, I also managed to briefly play a new role: adviser to two documentary film companies, Florentine Films and Camerini-Robinson. The first assignment involved consulting on *Rebuilding the Temple*. The film turned out to be a masterful portrait of the resettlement of Cambodian refugees in Massachusetts, mainly in Lowell and in the Pioneer Valley, where Northampton is located. Working with producers Larry Hott and Claudia Levin was an education in itself as I learned about how good documentaries are made. (I even had a bit part in the film as a talking head. My only on-screen appearance!)

The other documentary was even more challenging, being a multi-year project depicting the human side of the not-so-blank faces of the "bad guys" in the immigration service bureaucracy then responsible for deciding on petitions for refugee status in the United States. *Well-Founded Fear,* the title chosen by producers Michael Camerini and Shari Robinson, focused on the Immigration and Naturalization Service. (The expression comes from the law defining the principal reason for granting asylum in the United States: "a well-founded fear of persecution in one's home country," something I would continue to write about.)

I can't leave the busy 1980s—and so many comments about various forms of written expression, from book reviewing to travel journalism to both straightforward and offbeat research reports—without relating my one other attempt to write in a new form myself.

Knowing my fondness for making up silly poems and my proclivity for sounding off about certain public figures, my colleague, philosophy professor Murray Kiteley, urged me to put some of the things I was always jabbering about into clerihews. I said, "I'll try." Then I had to look up what clerihews were. (I found out that the form, named for the English writer Edmund Clerihew Bentley, was invented in the 1920s. These are "short comic verses, typically in two rhyming couplets with lines of unequal length and referring to a famous person.")

I wrote a bunch of them in response to Murray's challenge. Here are four. The first was about a trip made by Prince Philip to East Asia and his racist aside, which, like Mitt Romney's big gaffe in the 2012 presidential election alleging that forty-seven percent of the population was on the take, was recorded and rebroadcast over and over.

> Prince Philip thought the mike was off
> When hosts he did quite roy'ly scoff.
> "Slitty eyes, indeed!" as one thought they.
> To see such faux pas every day.

The next was about the death of Mao Zedong.

> Mao Zedong is now at peace,
> His long, long road did finally cease.
> He lies displayed in old Beijing.
> Now isn't that a curious thing?

Then there were some thoughts of mine about the man who was president of the United States throughout most of the decade.

> Reagan is the chief of state.
> He alone controls our fate.
> Brings good programs to a halt.
> And all I think is "Oy gevalt!"

Finally, I wrote about the retirement of "the most respected man in America." I called it "Oxymoronic Walter."

> With verve he ruled the waves of air.
> He was avuncular and fair.
> Now he rides the waves at sea.
> A moving anchor, Cronkite, he.

V

The 1990s: Transitions

EARLY IN THE NEW DECADE I SERVED A TERM AS PRESIDENT of the Eastern Sociological Society. Given my own research interests and a desire to urge American sociologists to return to an area in which such early luminaries in our field as Florian Znaniecki and W. I. Thomas, co-authors of the five-volume study, *The Polish Peasant in Europe and America* (1918–1920), had worked, I chose immigration as the theme of the annual meeting. The Program Committee and I made sure that each day we would offer at least four sessions on some aspect of that main topic, along with the standard subjects of such gatherings.

It is a tradition of the ESS to have the president invite someone to introduce him or her prior to the delivery of the presidential address. In preparation for my own presentation, I was pleased that my first choice, Robin M. Williams, Jr., agreed to do the deed. There was a not-so-latent function in my desire to have him there: I wanted to use the occasion to honor him, a man who not only had chaired my doctoral committee but also had been a moving force in the establishment of the organization and had served as its president himself and as president of the American Sociological Association. He was also the founding editor of the ESS journal, *Sociological Forum*. Casting about for a special way to honor him, I hit upon the idea of getting fellow former students as well as colleagues of Robin's at Cornell and other places to provide seed money to establish a lectureship in his name.

On the big night, after Robin introduced me but before I gave my address, sounding a bit like Yogi Berra, I announced, "Before I speak, I

would like to say something." I said that, as my last official act before giving my talk and then turning over the reins to my successor, I would use
the president's prerogative to change the agenda and say a few things
about the man who had just introduced me. The audience's puzzle-
ment—and Robin's—was resolved when I then presented him with a
huge framed proclamation of the establishment of the Williams Lectureship and announced that each year a committee of the society would select a distinguished sociologist to deliver lectures at various institutions
and then, at the end of the year, a final one at the annual meeting. Robin,
a rather self-effacing man, was both embarrassed and pleased.

I then turned to my presidential address, "Exile, Ethnicity, and the
Politics of Rescue." I began by asking those assembled to use their
imaginations.

> Think of the heartrending photograph of the thin, wan refugee
> mother and her dull-eyed, dying baby, a "mere apostrophe of an in-
> fant," as Thomas Keneally has described it.
>
> That image of "the Madonna of the Refugee Camp" is often used
> by journalists, by publicists for relief and resettlement agencies like
> UNICEF and CARE and the International Rescue Committee, and by
> officials of the United Nations High Commission for Refugees to
> bring to public attention the private suffering of the vast numbers of
> human beings caught up in the cross-currents of revolution and war.
> In the 1970s and 1980s the woman and child of the poignant pieta
> tended to have Asian or African faces. They might as well have been
> Afghani or Salvadoran. Today they are Hutu and Haitian, Albanian
> and Bosnian, Burmese Muslims in Pakistan, and Shiite Iraqis in
> Saudi Arabia.
>
> The specific ethnicity of the emblematic figure may be and usu-
> ally is directly relevant to why they are where they are, but in a tran-
> scendental sense, it is less significant than their collective condition.
> With silent eloquence each singular representation communicates the
> general pathos of being uprooted and displaced, estranged and afraid.
>
> Here I am concerned with all that that image represents, that spe-
> cial category of migrants—currently estimated to be between fifteen
> and twenty million—known as refugees. They are victims of racial, re-
> ligious, or political persecution who seek asylum in safe havens across
> the borders of their native lands.

> While the term refugee has only recently entered the vernacular, the seeker of sanctuary, driven out by forces beyond his or her ability or control, is as old a figure in the human drama as communal life itself.[41]

I went on to give examples of dispossession from ancient to modern times, emphasizing the fact that, whether those experiencing such upheaval are expellees or escapees, the social consequences are usually quite different for them from those of voluntary migrants. The former are dominated by centrifugal forces that are most often political or religious or nationalistic; the latter by centripetal ones that are almost invariably economic. I then turned to the state of affairs at the time. My prepared remarks dove-tailed rather neatly with many of the papers presented and discussed in the special sessions that had been held over the preceding three days and the talk generated the sort of after-buzz one always hopes for.

While that ESS meeting was a chance not only to address issues that I had long felt were being neglected by sociologists, and to pay tribute to Robin Williams, it turned out to be a sort of personal milestone. For a variety of reasons after the sessions were over I started removing myself from active involvement in professional academic organizations, the ESS and two others: the Society of Social Problems where I once served a term as vice president and the American Sociological Association where I had been a member of the executive council for three years. I was approaching sixty-five, the traditional age of retirement, and wanted to be free of many organizational commitments—though I was far from wanting to abandon my first love, teaching, or my research. I simply wanted more time for other things: to devote time to the American Studies Diploma Program at Smith and to finding sociologists, political scientists and historians to join me in contributing to a special issue of the *Annals of the American Academy of Political and Social Science*, which I had been invited to organize and edit. I choose as my *Annals* theme,

---

[41]The address was later published as "Tempest Tost: Exile, Ethnicity, and the Politics of Rescue," *Sociological Forum*, March, 1993, 5–24; five years later it became the title essay of my book, *Tempest-Tost* (New York and Oxford: Oxford University Press, 1997).

"Interminority Affairs in the U.S.: The Challenge of Pluralism." My own essay, "'Of Every Hue and Caste:' Race, Immigration and Perceptions of Pluralism," proved to be something of a reflection of my concerns about the general subject as developed over the forty preceding years.

The article is too long to reprint here but excerpts from the last few pages offer a summary of some of those thoughts on the subject at the time.

> A decade ago [1981], Milton M. Gordon, the sociologist who had written so insightfully about cultural and structural assimilation, seemed to reconceptualize the old idea of pluralism, suggesting that there were, in fact, two kinds, one "liberal"—which sounds to this writer at least, rather conservative—and the other "corporate."
>
> "Those who favor the liberal form," Gordon argued, ..."emphasize in their arguments the ethical and philosophical values of the idea of individual meritocracy and the notion that current generations should not be expected to pay for the sins of their fathers—or, at least, those who lived here before them, whether genetically related or not. They also point to the possibility that measures such as forced busing and affirmative action will create a white backlash and serve as continuing major irritants in the relationships between racial and ethnic groups. Those who favor policies which fall, logically, under the rubric of corporate pluralism emphasize the moral and philosophical position which posits group rights as well as individual rights, and the need for major compensatory measures to make up for massive dimensions of racial discrimination in the past." Gordon predicted that deciding which approach to pluralism to adopt, or which path to follow, would become an issue not only for scholars of American culture but for the society as a whole. Resolving this "new American dilemma," as he referred to the problem, "will have much to do with determining the nature, shape, and destiny of racial and ethnic relations in America in the twenty-first century...."
>
> It ought not be at all surprising that those who have become successful, particularly but not exclusively, the old white ethnics, favor what Gordon calls the liberal approach and see the other less in terms of enhancing the richness of the society—as many of their own parents and mentors have argued—than as the vehicle for its disintegration. On the other hand, it is equally understandable that those who are still on the outside—and who have suffered discrimination gener-

ally greater than that ever conferred upon the others—want to use collective action to satisfy a design for acceptance on their own terms. It is something that another pluralist of the "Hyphen-Connects School," W. E. B. DuBois, said in 1903....

DuBois' famous statement that "one ever feels his twoness,—an American, a Negro"—ends with a desire: "He simply wishes to make it possible for a man to be both a Negro and an American, without being cursed and spit upon."

Horace Kallen once said that "men may change their clothes, their politics, their wives, their religions, their philosophies to a greater or lesser extent: they cannot change their grandfathers. Jews or Poles or Anglo-Saxons, in order to cease being Jews or Poles or Anglo-Saxons would have to cease to be." The same sentiment is now again being expressed not only by newcomers but also by many spokespersons for those old, very old Americans—from Africa.

Few engaged in the new movement for group recognition want to tear down the foundations of society, but they do favor altering the structures to truly be more inclusive. But their opponents, often using the most extreme examples, claim that the would-be multiculturalists are, in fact, polarizing particularists or subversive separatists. They further argue that the corporate tactics are alienating members of their own groups from still-needed allies while accelerating the balkanization of the United States into a fractured mosaic. If it continues, it is argued, only cohort membership will be the *sine qua non* of identity and power.

While concerned about the "centricities" of those who are making the strongest demands, there seems to be an underlying motif in the expressions of many who worry about "the cult of ethnicity." Their most strident language is often used in objection to the rise of Black Chauvinism and, as Arthur Schlesinger, Jr., puts it, "the guilt trips laid on by champions of cultures based on despotism, superstition, tribalism, and fanaticism, especially the Afrocentrists."

It should be noted that, even for opponents of multiculturalism, somehow the demands of Native Americans to recapture their old ways, the assertions of those from Japan and China and India to have their presence acknowledged and to be granted special recognition, even certain cultural proclivities of Mexican Americans once viewed, as were those of Italian Americans and French Canadians, as being too peasant-like, seem more tolerable to many white Americans—including a number of old fashioned liberals—than the claims of blacks.

The old argument that "the Negro has no culture of his own" is now transmuted into statements that he has no culture worth resurrecting or reasserting: not the African heritage; not that of the Diaspora, which, of course, would have to include so much of the music, literature, and icons of the popular culture now regarded here and throughout the world as quintessentially American. The persistence of what George Frederickson has called the peculiarly American arrogance of race continues to diminish the significance of Afro-American culture and the significance of those who want to celebrate their own contributions to a society that claims to be one that appreciates those "of every hue and caste."

There are many parallels between what was going on in the waning days of the last century and what is happening today. But whereas the main fault line in the society, north and south, had long been between whites and non-whites, the ground is now shifting. In the future, the sharpest divisions may well be between blacks and non-blacks.[42]

In 2005 I would revisit these matters. In an essay, "The Persistence of (an) Ethnicity," picking up on a theme of the Dutch Americanist, Rob Kroes, author of *The Persistence of Ethnicity* (1995). In my essay I noted how prescient Gordon had been about the role of corporate pluralism and how my own predictions regarding black and other Americans had fared.

Once the essays for the special issue of the *Annals* were edited and the manuscript had been turned over to the publisher, I was ready to start traveling once again.

One of my first trips abroad in the decade of the Nineties was very special. I had been invited back to the Netherlands to receive the Medal of the University of Amsterdam. It was presented to me by the president of the university, Jean-Karl Gevers, at a luncheon attended by several very close Dutch friends. Later that day I delivered a public lecture related to the award. I spoke of my continuing interest in race and

---

[42]"Of Every Hue and Caste: Race, Immigration and Perceptions of Pluralism," *The Annals*, 530, November 1993, 187–202. The essay appeared in a special issue of the journal edited by the author, *Interminority Affairs in the U.S.: Pluralism at the Crossroads* (Annals of the American Academy of Poetical and Social Science and Sage Publications, 1993).

ethnicity and immigration policy in the United States and my growing concern about the reception of migrants and refugees in Europe, particularly in Holland. (It would be another decade before the bare bones of my argument were later developed more fully in an essay, "Minus-Sum Games in a Land of Guilty Memories.")

While in Amsterdam I received an invitation from Jonathan Imber, editor of the journal *Society*, to join with others to offer our views of a *Time* magazine forum on "The Rift between Blacks and Jews" and a Paul Berman article in the *New Yorker* on "The Other and the Almost the Same." I read them both and wrote back to Imber saying I would be willing to send him my thoughts on the issue. I called my response, "Blaming the Jews" and, among other points, noted that:

> While it is doubtful that Louis Farrakhan or Khalid Abdul Muhammad or Leonard Jeffries of the City University of New York or others who have been widely quoted for their diatribes against "Jewish interests" and, not infrequently, Jews themselves, ever read the writings of the German sociologist, George Simmel, but, like so many others who need scapegoats to advance their own causes, they clearly understand the concept of "the third element." Third elements not only greatly complicate social relationships and provide "opportunities for transition, conciliation and the abandonment of absolute contrast," as Simmel put it, they also offer a vehicle for considerable manipulations of the other parties, even by the weakest member. What the black demagogues are seeking to do—and to gain—is what many others have tried before....
>
> Without using the word "triadic," Berman notes that the relationship between blacks and Jews (and other whites) in the United States, at least in the twentieth century, has been precisely that. In his essay, he removes Jewish Americans from the rubric "white"—but he does not put the "non-white" Jews and blacks together in a single category (of, say, "minorities"). While members of both groups are literally as well as sociologically speaking "minorities," they have very different backgrounds and cultures and have had very different experiences in America.[43]

---

[43]"Blaming the Jews," *Social Science and Modern Society*, 31:6, September-October, 1994, 35–36.

Pointing to my general agreement with Berman's assessment of the two communities, mentioning the fact that "those who used to be called Negroes did share a sense of biblical affinity for they long identified themselves with the time 'When Israel was in Egypt's Land' and with the call to 'Let my people go!'" I argued that members of neither group really knew very much about the other. I went on to say that for many years on the occasions when African Americans did meet or interact with real live Jews, they did not encounter Moses but rather merchants and doctors and others, none of whom seemed to have much connection to their spiritual icons. I noted that, while it may well be true that, as many blacks claim, they could not tell who was Jewish merely by looking ("white folks are white folks"), many would still allow that, although they didn't know many Jews personally, they knew about them, and they knew they were different from those in the dominant sector, the white Christian community. I continued:

> Those differences couched in varied ways—some religious, some political, but mostly economic, are well fixed in the folklore of the Old South where, as Harry Golden once said, "the Jewish store is as commonplace as the Confederate monument that stands in the town square."
>
> Black storytellers long acknowledged the Jewish presences, limited though it was in their very regional *Weltanschauung*. A common opener in a joke was: "One day a Negro, a white man, and a Jew..." And the distinction was not limited to the South as James Baldwin, writing about his own childhood in Harlem pointed out. "The grocer was a Jew and being in debt to him was very much like being in debt to the company store...we bought our clothes from a Jew and, sometimes, our second hand shoes." Baldwin's image was that of thousands of others who grew up in similar circumstances. It is not hard to see how easily it could be asserted that what Jews accomplished could only be done by contrivance and connivance at the expense of those in the weakest power positions, like the blacks....
>
> Withal, there is little doubt that what many blacks are thinking about Jews today is, in large measure, a narrowly focused reflection of a deeply rooted, triple sense of powerlessness, dependency and envy. It implies being left behind, the persistence of discrimination, an in-

creasing sense of isolation, and a growing feeling of desperation. Jews have made it and those Jim Sleeper has called "the closest of strangers" have not.

Many African-American leaders, such as Martin Luther King, Jr. acknowledged the critical role Jews played in the struggle for civil rights, but even there, some speak of their paternalist attitudes. Others want to confront all of these issues in constructive ways, not least by trying to engage in dialogues with still sympathetic—if not always empathetic—outsiders, especially Jews. Their goal is to re-form alliances based on mutual respect and common commitments. But many others seem too willing to accede to demagoguery and demonology, blaming the Jews for all their problems, or, if not that, remaining still when they hear of or personally witness expressions of either. They and the members of what is in fact their own highly stratified and quite diverse community, and the now-wary Jews, are not the only players, of course.

What is striking is how few voices have been raised to counter the campaigns of vilification. The lack of strong opposition to Jew-baiting by certain blacks in much of the white community is most unfortunate but hardly surprising. But to see such a lack of public reaction as agreement with the extreme expressions of hate is to grossly misread the situation. If there is any Machiavellian plan underlying the statements of Farrakhan and his minions holding Jews responsible for every conceivable wrong within society and, most specifically, the current condition of black Americans in order to win white support, the effort will prove futile, even counterproductive. Those few white Christians most apt to resonate to the rhetoric of African American anti-Semites about Jewish control are likely to be most vehemently anti-Black as well.

Thus, aside from instilling pride by increasing group chauvinism—and group narcissism—at the expense of further alienation of those (mainly Jews) who have been most helpful in the past, it is highly doubtful that the net effect of the tactics being used on the streets and on the campuses will serve either the purpose of *divide et impera* (one of the ploys outlined by Simmel) or help to overcome the real problems faced by African Americans, especially those in the seething caldrons of the urban ghettos. Most likely they will simply deepen the divisions between blacks and others—"white" as well as Jewish.[44]

---

[44]Ibid., 37–40.

The paper was finished and sent off to the editor shortly after we returned from the Netherlands. That trip proved to be one of the few times Hedy and I would travel together in the 1990s.

When our kids were small, we often traveled as a family. But once the children were in school, much of what I did meant going alone. Hedy's own professional work—teaching at Smith, then at Hampshire College in nearby Amherst, and then at Wesleyan University in Middletown, Connecticut, curtailed our plans to resume the old pattern. The Wesleyan job, which began in 1988, also made for an even more significant change in our lives.

Middletown is only a little over an hour from Northampton, but the nature of Hedy's double appointment as director of the educational studies program and teacher of both undergraduate and graduate students, the demands of her role as Wesleyan's representative to the state education-certification authority and to many education associations, and the fact that her elderly Westport-based mother was ailing, meant that it was best if she spent Monday to Friday based in Connecticut and her weekends back home with me. At first it was a difficult adjustment—much more for me, I'm sure, than for Hedy.

For Hedy, Wesleyan offered a challenging experience and, I know, a liberating one. But, despite the fact that I often had gone away on my own to lecture or do research any number of times, I found her being away from me a bit daunting.

I had always admired how she had managed to care for the children and me, keeping home and hearth together while working part- and sometimes full-time. A 1958 Cornell graduate, she went back to school to get a master's degree in comparative education at Smith in the 1970s, and a doctorate—with a dissertation on law and the civil rights of teachers—from the University of Massachusetts in the mid-1980s, and a certificate in mediation a few years later. But preoccupied with my own research and teaching and writing, I realized only long after the fact how little I had done to help ease the burden.

While Hedy was working full-time at Wesleyan, I continued to teach at Smith, direct the Diploma Program, and keep busy with new writing and editing challenges.

In July 1984, as indicated earlier, I reviewed economist Thomas Sowell's, just-published, *The Economics and Politics of Race* for the *Christian Science Monitor*. I had known Tom only slightly when he taught at nearby Amherst College but knew and admired his earlier book, *Ethnic America: A History* (1981)—more so, in fact, than the newer one. We never directly had exchanged ideas about the subject that interested us both but did begin a long-distance correspondence from Northampton to Palo Alto, where he had settled down as a Senior Fellow at the Hoover Institution at Stanford University.

Tom and I were then and still are ideologically very different. Many call him a conservative. I think he sees himself more as an iconoclastic libertarian. I am neither. Still, our exchanges over the years led him to recommend me as a visiting fellow at the Hoover Institution, that well known bastion of conservative thinking.

With a leave coming up in the spring of 1996, I finally took him up on his offer to help bring me to Stanford. I was intrigued first because I thought it would be a great opportunity to interact with and argue with Tom. A second reason I was eager to go there was that I had just learned that almost all of the case records of the Indochinese refugees interviewed and resettled by the International Rescue Committee had just been given to the Hoover Institution. The IRC was one of the principal agencies I was writing about. Third, I knew that the archives of the Hoover Institution were originally created to house the papers of Herbert Hoover, especially those relating to his monumental work in saving millions of Belgians from starvation during the First World War, and later doing the same for people in the Crimea. I was interested in learning more about Hoover's American Relief Administration which in many ways signaled the beginning of the institutionalization of voluntarism in the field of refugee assistance. Later I would write about that, too.[45] Finally, the

---

[45]"Getting to Know Herbert Hoover, Enigmatic Humanitarian," *Social Science and Modern Society*, 47: 6 (2011): 529–33.

Hoover Institution would give me a good place to finish work on a book that included contemporary examples of such behavior.

The semester at Stanford was most productive. My one regret was that I met with Tom Sowell only once. (I later learned from members of the Hoover staff that he generally worked at home and rarely came over to mingle or schmooze with anybody, let alone visiting scholars.)

During that first extended visit to Stanford I got to know some of the senior fellows and often listened in on conversations of a number of others in the Common Room. Several of the latter were recent members of Ronald Reagan's inner-circle, George Schultz, Ed Meese, and Martin Anderson, a devotee of Ayn Rand. Those sessions themselves were most educational, providing opportunities for this ethnographer to try to gain insight into the cultural bases for the political propensities of these "locals." But there were even fewer kindred spirits thereabouts than I had expected, though one senior fellow, John Bunzel, a political sociologist and former president of San Jose State University, did take me under his wing. Once, discussing the political climate at the Hoover Institution, John told me that, when asked by a Stanford newspaper reporter if there were any liberals at the Hoover, he answered, "Oh yes, quite a number. We *both* meet every day near the water cooler."

Before leaving Palo Alto at the end of that sabbatical semester, I wrote in my acknowledgements for *Tempest-Tost*:

> The pulling together of all the pieces and the fine-tuning of the manuscript was done at Stanford University, where I have been a visiting scholar at the Hoover Institution. I came here in early February 1996, to complete the essay "In Whom They Trust," to finish the editing of the rest of the manuscript, and to dig into the Institution's superb archives in preparation for my next project: a study of the early days of the International Rescue Committee. The institution's library is a treasure trove of papers on many refugees and refugee workers, including Herbert Hoover himself...and the several major agencies in which I am interested.
>
> After several months of working here and interacting with my new colleagues, I, an old-fashioned liberal, must report that I sometimes feel like a refugee tossed on a strange shore myself. But like

the best of the refugee workers I met in dusty camps in Southeast Asia and Central Europe and in resettlement centers throughout this country, my hosts provided me with solace and comfort and asked for nothing in return—not even a change in my political orientation.[46]

Hedy couldn't go with me for that semester in 1996 but she has accompanied me back to Palo Alto every winter since 2006. We are now more or less permanent visiting scholars. I go there to work on various projects; she has been focusing her own research on the years immediately before and then during the Nazi-occupation of the Netherlands, especially from 1942 to 1945, when she was an *onderduiker*, a hider. Having also worked in the war archives in Amsterdam and in other documentary centers, Hedy has found the Hoover Institution's library and archives to contain one of the richest collection of Dutch and German newspapers, journals, broadsides, posters and books on her subject anywhere.

The year before my first appointment at Stanford, the head of Smith's board of trustees, Kate Webster, invited me to join three other faculty members to serve on a presidential search committee to find a replacement for retiring Mary Maples Dunn. Although I was the senior member of the faculty and had been on most of the major elected committees, and was, I suppose, a logical choice, I was reluctant to join the group. I feared being nothing more than window dressing for what I assumed was a rigged operation. Kate and a former student of mine, Joyce Moran, who would chair the committee, convinced me that the faculty members on the committee would be full participants at every stage, and I signed on. And the chairpersons were true to their words.

On the committee were three other faculty colleagues, eight members of the board (five women who were alumnae, and three others —all men), and two recent graduates, one of whom had been the president of the student government, the other the president of the senior class the year before. Together we would spend many weekends and often weekdays over the next six months reviewing CVs and letters of recommendation, winnowing down the long list to a short one,

---

[46] *Tempest-Tost*, xii.

.

conducting what now seems like hundreds of interviews in several cities but mostly in Boston, then narrowing the search down to four finalists. In early December 1995, after a final round of interviews, we unanimously selected Ruth J. Simmons, then the acting provost of Princeton, as our choice to become the ninth president of the College. The next day our entire group trooped down to New York City where we presented the case for our definitive choice to the full board of trustees. Immediately after we spoke our piece, we on the faculty were thanked for our work and excused. The board would discuss and then vote on our recommendation behind closed doors.

Just before leaving I asked Kate Webster to call me at the president's house where I was scheduled to be that evening and let me know the outcome. About five hours later, while I was having dinner with a visiting lecturer, someone came into the dining room to tell me that I had a phone call. I rushed to the little room off the main entrance hall and took the receiver. It was Kate. "White smoke," was all she said.

When it was announced that Ruth Simmons would be coming to Smith, there was much talk about her being the Jackie Robinson of academia, for she was about to become the first African American to head the college or, indeed, any Ivy League university. It would take but a few months on the campus for that sobriquet to be replaced by one that described her as a first-rate administrator and very hot property. Almost from the start of her tenure at Smith she was being wooed to run much bigger universities. In her sixth year she accepted the proffered presidency of Brown University where she served in that capacity until the spring of 2012. But while she was with us, we felt very lucky to have Ruth Simmons as our leader.

Speaking at her last meeting with the faculty I remember saying something to the effect that "she's going to Brown and we're all blue." And I meant it. In my dual role as the senior member of the faculty and a member of the search committee seven years earlier I had been asked to undertake several tasks relating to the appointment of Ruth Simmons. The first was to speak on behalf of the committee when we introduced her to the Smith community, and nine months later, to say something at the dinner the night before the inauguration and then to welcome her on behalf of the faculty at the event itself. I was also invited to sit on a new committee to figure out some special way to mark the beginning of the new era under President Simmons. Let me briefly reprise those events.

Board of trustees chair Kate Webster, President Mary Maples Dunn and I—and Ruth Simmons—stood on the stage in a packed Sage Hall, the auditorium of the music building. The three of us each spoke very briefly, then gave Ruth the floor. It was a wonderful moment and, as I stood there, I thought to myself, "We did well!"

The following September at a gala dinner on the eve of the inauguration, when it was my turn to speak I, often choosing to put my words into verse on such occasions, decided to describe the search process in rhyme.

> Ten years ago I wrote a rhyme
> To honor Mary Dunn
> And now another I will add
> For Ruth, who clearly won
>
> The contest for succession at
> The school we know so well.
> It wasn't such an on'rous task
> It only seemed like—well,
>
> Like trying to find a needle
> In a haystack made of names
> Affixed to résumés proclaiming
> Matchless skills and hard-earned fames
>
> Of deeds achieved in ivied halls
> And other such venues,
> To dazzle even jaundiced eyes
> When asked about their views
>
> Of how to run a complex place
> And raise the needed money,
> And handle faculty and staff,
> And students and alum-nee,

And be in town and far away
At home and College Hall
Administrator, scholar, friend
A leader for us all.

From hundreds we reduced the pile
While searching for the few
To make the list of those to see,
Then cut that one down, too.

In cities far we interviewed
And probed and snooped and tried
To make the list still shorter yet
Before the snow first flied.

We cut it to a short-short list:
 "A," "B," and "C"—and Ruth,
With different strengths to offer us,
But when we tell the truth,

Penultimately, it was clear,
For each of us to see,
When time did come to make the choice
The group was only three.

Actually t'was only two.
Well hardly that
We all soon knew.
The final one was you know who!

In case anyone is curious, the poem for Mary Dunn mentioned in
the first stanza was far shorter, just four lines. I recited in May of 1996
at her own last faculty meeting as president of Smith.

"No man an island," said John Donne
"Nor women either," Mary Dunn
You see at Smith we quote the two
He's Donne. She's Dunn. I'm done, too.

At Ruth Simmons' inauguration, my remarks were just as brief.
From the podium of the huge indoor track and tennis facility, I looked
out at the thousands of students, staff members, faculty, alumnae,

friends of the new president, and 125 robed delegates from universities from all over the world, then, speaking on behalf of my faculty colleagues, turned to the newly installed president and said, "Ruth, I am delighted to stand here today to welcome you to Northampton, to Smith, and to the ranks of our sometimes curmudgeonly, often cantankerous, usually creative, and always committed Smith College professoriate."

My last inauguration-related task was to work with colleagues to decide on some way of marking the significance of the event in a lasting way. In meetings the spring before the big event, we had decided that a series of monthly lectures showcasing the catholicity of our faculty would be a special way of welcoming the new president. We invited all members of the community to submit recommendations for possible candidates. Many did. In the end, we chose eight—starting with the dean and provost, John Connolly, a philosopher. His talk was actually given the afternoon before the inauguration. It was called "The Academy's Freedom, The Academy's Burden." Others that followed were by psychologist Jill de Villiers; Andrea Hairston of the theater department; Lester Little, European historian; Elliot Offner, artist, sculptor, and printer to the College; Suzan Edwards, astronomer; Marie Banerjee, professor of Russian, and political scientist Philip Green.

Once the series was over, I worked with Elliot Offner as he designed and I edited a book containing all the lectures and introductions and a special contribution written by Ruth herself, a response of sorts to what she had heard. The title of our series had been "Professorial Passions," and that was the name we kept for our edited volume.[47]

At the end of the extremely well-attended lecture series several of us suggested to Ruth that in the future, following a European tradition, all professors appointed to endowed chairs should be invited to present inaugural lectures. Since then almost every such person has. And almost every one of the talks have reflected the speaker's own professorial passion. I look forward to the day when the college publishes groups of those lectures together in a series of new volumes like the one that honored Ruth Simmons.

---

[47] *Professorial Passions* (Northampton: Smith College, 1998).

The year we published *Professorial Passions*, 1998, was a landmark for me. I turned sixty-five. Unbeknownst to me, Hedy had planned a fabulous birthday party in The Gamut, the downstairs lounge of the Mendenhall Center for the Performing Arts on the Smith campus. When we walked in I noticed that the place had been transformed. There was a dance floor in the corner, a roaring fire in the huge fireplace, a bar, tables laden with food, and, best of all, nearly a hundred of our friends and members of our small family. Lies came up from Connecticut and Dan, his wife and our two grandsons had come all the way from California. My favorite local jazz ensemble, "The Propellers," provided the entertainment.

Later I saw the card that Hedy had sent out inviting people to come to the birthday bash. On the front was a picture of me taken on the steps of the main lodge at Bradley Brook Camp when I was about six years old. A caption beneath it read, "Now we are 6..." Then, when you turned the page there is another digit added, "5."

I could never match that but on Hedy's seventieth birthday, February 8, 2006, I surprised her with a dinner party at a restaurant to which I had invited around twenty of our closest friends. I, too, sent out an invitation. Mine said, "Not a Dutch Treat, but a treat for a Dutch wife, mother, grandmother, and friend" with information about the venue and strict instructions not to call the house but to RSVP to my office number. Hedy was as surprised and as pleased as I had been with her party for me.

I've never found it easy to sit still, and during the late 1990s my travel writing began to take on a life of its own. Some of it centered on the places visited; some—the kind I preferred doing—was more ethnographic, recording the customs and behavior of groups of people. "Waikiki Watch" is a good example of my segue from being mostly an academic writer to using my sociological perspective in a new way. I wrote the piece while on one of several trips to Honolulu and the East-West Center during that decade.

For me, a social scientist with an insatiable curiosity, every trip away from home is a busman's holiday, a chance to do "field work." For example, on a recent trip to Honolulu for a conference, I was having breakfast in a chain restaurant. It was about 7:30 in the morning and, as I was sipping a second cup of coffee and reading the *Advertiser*, the morning paper, a family of four sat down next to me. Aside from the fact that they had very reddened skins, they resembled many of those I had seen three days before boarding American Airlines flight #73 in Chicago.

On the spot I decided to play hooky from my meeting. The objects of my attention didn't know it, but they were soon the subject of my ethnographic fancy. I could feel the adrenaline surge as I took out my pad and jotted some notes.

> Four people. From Iowa, Indiana, Illinois?
>
> Woman (Mother) about 40. Grant Wood face.
> Somewhat plump. Wearing white shorts,
> Bright red tank top and floppy hat over
> straw-blond shaggy hair.
> Big bracelet. Kicking flip-flops on and off.
>
> Man (Father). Same age as M. Big man but
> not athletic. Balding. Belly covered by yellow tank
> shirt with big black letters "HAWAII." Also wearing
> shorts and thongs. Blue cap on chair. Also says
> "HAWAII."
>
> Two kids.
>
> Boy 10-11. Looks like father but
> skinny. Wearing pale blue T-shirt with picture
> of a wiggling hand—thumb and little fingers
> extended—and the inscription "Hang Loose."
> Bathing suit. Heavy high top sneakers. Untied.
> Cranky.
>
> Girl 6-7, looks like Mother. Seems to
> be in bathing-suit, big pink sweatshirt
> covering everything. Very subdued.

They ate in silence. I drank more coffee and plotted my strategy. I decided to stay with them at least until 8:00 p.m. when I would have to shed my own shorts, T-shirt (mine said "Primo Beer") and sandals for less comfortable garb and return to the symposium for an obligatory evening session.

The family left the restaurant at 8:15 and walked eastward along the main drag.

The Waikiki strip was beginning to stir. While most of the clothing stores were still closed, the places that sell groceries, magazines, souvenirs and beach supplies were already busy. I crossed to observe the family from a greater distance and watched them pass one cross street then turn left on Ulunui, walking slowly up to Kuhio Avenue.

The family ignored the aloha-shirted clones that walked by (some redder, some tanner), but they did seem genuinely curious about the representatives of the other main cohort of strollers, the Japanese tourists, noticeable immediately not so much by physiognomy (after all, many Hawaiians are of Japanese background) but by bearing, manner and dress. Many of the men were wearing designer T-shirts, white trousers or white shorts and new white running shoes. The women were similarly dressed. Almost all carried 35mm cameras. Many held video cameras, too.

The family I was following conferred, then turned left and walked along Kuhio to the recently refurbished hotel, a building with a Chinese facade. (My notes say: Curious place. Dragons. Chinese roof. Busy modern lobby.) They went into the hotel, crossed the lobby, and waited for the elevator. I got in with them and took the car to the floor above the one where they got off. Then I went back down to the lobby and waited. I was beginning to feel like a gumshoe in a 1940s movie, especially when the only seat I could find was behind a potted palm!

I had to wait a half-hour before the family reappeared. Each member was laden with beach paraphernalia, including newly purchased straw mats, (Sign in ABC store: "Get your mats here. Only 99 cents each.") hotel towels stuffed into big canvas bag and their digital cameras. They walked past the Outrigger East, down Kanekapole, and back onto the Avenue where they joined the throngs moving back and forth along Kuhio. They stopped rather abruptly and, kicking off their sandals, strode across the sand and plunked themselves down as if staking a claim. They spread their gear, took out suntan lotion and a few magazines, and settled in for what seemed to be a long stay.

It was. Two hours and twenty-three minutes to be exact.

Father, who, without his shirt and covered with oil, looked like a beached whale, slept most of the time. Mother never relaxed. She sat a stoic vigil, fussed with her hair, reapplied Coppertone, poked her arm every once in a while as if to see if she was sufficiently "done," and most of the time watched her boy race in and out of the water with a bogie board. Eventually he latched on to a group of teenagers he'd stopped to observe. They were local kids, with long, weathered flower-patterned shorts.

Little Sister didn't seem to know what to do. She kept coming over to her mother and, stamping her foot, saying something. I imagined it was "When are we going back?" or "Will you come into the water with me?" She was not pleased with the responses. Her mother seemed reluctant to placate her, or to play with her.

Father made the decision to leave. Quite suddenly, without warning, he sat bolt upright, shook his head and beckoned to his son, still in the water but no longer alone, to come in, "NOW!"

They gathered their things quickly and retraced the path to the Miramar. I followed and, once at the hotel, waited again. This time I maintained my watch outside and across the street, lurking behind a lamppost.

About 45 minutes after they went in, Father and Son came out, but not the others. Never imagining they might split up, I thought fast, then made a decision. I followed the guys. They went to McDonald's. From the back of the room, I was relieved to see them approach a table with a tray laden with more food than even Father could put away. Somebody else was coming to lunch!

As if on cue, mother and daughter arrived, neither looking very happy.

They all wolfed down their Big Macs and fries, sipped their shakes more slowly, then walked out into the brilliant sunshine, turned the corner, trudged another few blocks, crossed the street, and joined a small group at a bus stop.

"Oh boy," I thought to myself, "an adventure at last."

TheBus (that's its name, "TheBus") came. They got on. I followed. They moved to the rear. I stayed in front. TheBus was heading to the Ala Moana Shopping Center. So, it turned out, were we.

Getting off at the Center, they—and I—then spent the next two hours in a grander version of the average American all-purpose suburban mall. They went in and out of 14 shops (I counted!), sometimes staying together, sometimes going their own ways.

At 4:10 p.m. Father organized his troops. The two smaller ones were really dragging, but Mother was somehow buoyed, her upbeat mood doubtlessly enhanced by the purchase of the brightly colored muumuu which she now wore. I noticed that she also was wearing a pair of new white Japanese-style zories with big yellow plastic flowers over the toe straps. She kept looking down at here feet in delight as the four of them made their ways to the busy bus rank behind the parking lot.

Twice, while they were walking, Father glanced back as if he thought they were being followed. The second time it happened I tightened up and thought that I'd best leave well enough alone. Turning on my heel, I walked back toward the stairway. I wrestled with my desire to pack it in, to abandon my mission and go swimming. But duty to my cause won out. I turned around and started back toward the bus stop. The place was empty. Undaunted, I ran into the street, hailed a taxi, told the driver to take me to the Princess Kailulani Hotel which, I knew was quite near to their hotel.

Nearing the center of Waikiki, we passed TheBus. I glanced up and there, just behind the door, stood Mother, splendid in her new muumuu.

I got out of the cab and sauntered nonchalantly by the side of the Hyatt Regency, window shopping along the way, but watching, too. I glimpsed the muumuu again, but it was heading away from ground zero. Puzzled, I pursued it. Five minutes later I realized I was following the wrong muumuu-clad mom.

I went back to their hotel and stood outside, eating a macadamia nut ice cream cone and hoping they would come out—or back—soon.

I waited quite a while. When, for the second time, I was ready to give up, they appeared in the doorway. All were dressed up, Father and Little Sister both in bright Aloha shirts. The little girl also wore a hibiscus in her hair and some puka shell beads around her neck. Both were pretty upbeat. The boy wore the same untied basketball shoes and a T-shirt similar to the one he had worn at breakfast, but his bathing suit was replaced with Hawaiian-style surfing shorts. (In notebook I wrote: Real cool! And I meant it.)

Mother, who seemed fresher, younger, and much redder (her face was glowing), was wearing her new muumuu and flip-flops and, like Little Sister, had a flower in her hair.

This time I let them pass. I bent over to adjust my sandal and, as they went by, Father looked right at me. He had a quizzical expression.

Since it was 6:45, very close to my predetermined cut-off time, I decided it was really time to pack it in. After all, I told myself, I already had a head full of ideas and a book of notes about how some ordinary tourists behave by day in Waikiki.

We were close to a corner. The family, very near to me, stopped for a red light. I turned away but remained close enough to hear Father loudly whisper to his wife, "You see that guy there?"

Silence.

"The one with the beard and sunglasses." He tossed his head in my direction. "I bet we've seen him five times today."

"What d'ya mean?" his wife asked. "Do you think he's following us?"

"Na. Why should anybody follow us? He's probably a tourist like us. I bet he also went to the beach, wandered around, had a burger, went shopping, rested a while. I bet you we see that guy tomorrow when we take the tour around the island."

The light change and they crossed.

I let them go.[48]

Not long after returning to the campus from my first spontaneous exercise in tracking tourists, I found myself again being pulled in several directions at once. I reconnected with colleagues at the *Christian Science Monitor* and starting reviewing for them again. I began to do much more travel writing, now mainly for web-based magazines. And I contributed occasional stories to the *Daily Hampshire Gazette's* local weekend supplement, *Hampshire Life*. I wrote a number of "First Person" pieces for *Hampshire Life*, but only one was about Northampton itself. Well, sort of.

The story was ostensibly about Eureka, California, five days of it spent on a sort of "fam" (for familiarization) trip with a group of professional travel journalists who all belonged to IFWTWA, the International Food, Wine, and Travel Writers Association. I should note that on such junkets, frequently arranged by the media staffs of local or area visitor bureaus, folks at the hotels and restaurants and shops put on their best bibs and tuckers (whatever those are) in hopes that all the writers will

---

[48]"Waikiki Watch" in the author's collection of essays, *With Few Reservations* (iUniverse, 2010), 187–192.

say nice things to promote their places and products. As I'm always a bit uncomfortable with such arrangements, I generally want to decide well in advance on what I'll focus. Often my decision is based on previous trips to the area or something I've heard about from friends or read about in places *other than travel magazines.* While I often check out what fellow travel writers mention as highlights in advance of a trip, I rarely pay particular attention to PR copy or the orientation packets that are frequently thrust upon us. Of course sometimes I wing it, assuming that, somehow, I will find a theme later that isn't too hackneyed.

Going to Eureka didn't present such a problem. I had a mission—and a storyline. Shortly before getting the invitation to join the IFWTWA group, I had read a book by John Villani called *The 100 Best Small Art Towns in America.* Eureka, California, was ranked as number one. He listed our town, Northampton, Massachusetts, number two.

Villani had spent several years roving from coast to coast and border to border to help others "discover creative communities, fresh air, and affordable living." He gathered information and recorded impressions on locations, lifestyles, arts and crafts, general ambiance, and special amenities. Then, after reviewing all his data, he made his informed—if admittedly subjective—ratings.

My first reaction on reading the book was delight in learning that the place where we had been living for nearly forty years had gotten such a high ranking. (Villani rated his home base of Taos, New Mexico, number three.) But then a gnawing sense of disappointment set in. Why, I asked myself, was Northampton, the "Paradise of America," *merely* the penultimate small art town in America? What was it that made that western place the Hertz of art towns to our eastern Avis? We flew to San Francisco and then drove up to Eureka to find out.

We spent several days in Eureka, the seat of Humboldt County (named in honor of the famous Prussian traveler, explorer, geographer and naturalist, Baron Alexander von Humboldt, who never visited the area) and went to a number of other towns, including nearby Arcata, Ferndale, Fortuna and Trinidad, all mentioned by Villani.

After returning home, I wrote my story.

While reluctant to concede to Villani his higher rating of Eureka than our fair city, it didn't take long for us to realize that Humboldt County has many things that rival those of our Pioneer Valley. Because so many of these were so homelike, comparisons were, at once, easier and harder.

Despite dramatic differences in area, topography, flora, fauna and climate, the art towns of Humboldt and Hampshire County are remarkably similar. Eureka and Northampton are roughly the same size (28,000 people, and 31,000, respectively), and the good citizens of both have been engaged in the renaissance of city centers....

Like Northampton, Eureka has numerous galleries, new and used bookstores, music for every taste, live theater, artsy cinemas and a plethora of restaurants with mood-altering decor and first-rate kitchens that offer all kinds of cuisine. In addition to its counterpart's coterie of artists, artisans, writers, actors, musicians, restaurateurs, students, professors and culture mavens, Humboldt has its own gaggle of psychotherapists, masseuses and homeopathic gurus, boutique proprietors, real estate speculators, land developers, micro-brewers and growers, too. It should be noted that, while tobacco fields like those we know so well are nowhere to be found in Humboldt County, people far and near—and not just superannuated hippies,—pay good money to smoke what they grow out there, surely one of the best cash crops in the west!

Of course, Eureka and its county, like Northampton and its environs, also have some nagging problems. Town and gown relations are sometimes strained in Arcata, home to a large public university, Humboldt State, and the only place in California (and, most likely, one of the few in the country) ruled by members of the Green Party. Class divisions exist in many Humboldt towns and just beneath the surface there are unmistakable tensions between different cultural and sub-cultural groups, some quite specific to the area. There are those between the real natives, the remnants of aboriginal populations like the Yuroks and Hoopa, and the folks who long ago appropriated the title for themselves. Those latter-day "natives" are generally descendants of fur traders, homesteaders, and prospectors who moved in, staked and laid their claims in the middle of the nineteenth century. Residents of the area still include some scions of the timber barons and descendants of lumberjacks and sawyers who worked for them in the heyday of clear-cutting....There are fishermen who caught, canned and sold salmon by the millions until their activities were sharply curtailed by restrictions on what many still feel were their proprietary rights. There are ranchers and dairy farmers and those engaged in providing needed services of all kinds to support the infrastructure and individual businesses from garages and boatyards to motels and malls. Then there are those on whom Villani focused, latter-day pioneers from the Bay Area and L.A. who have been transforming the towns of Humboldt into havens for those seeking the very things he was looking for: stimulating environments of like-minded souls, good air, and affordable living. Their success in establishing a foothold on the North Coast and making a go of it has also been the greatest boon to what many of them say they hoped to avoid: an assault on their new-found Shangri La by a new wave of settlers and that worst-case scenario, the inundation of tourists! Most, however, have been able to go with the flow, to their own as well as the community's benefit. Not a few Chamber of Commerce-types told me that they are the key figures in putting the county back on its feet after years of decline.

Such talk sounded familiar. In a parallel move to what happened in Hampshire County some thirty years ago, many young people who came to Humboldt in the late 1960s and early 1970s stayed, some to continue their maverick, anti-establishment ways, many more to become creative and quite yuppified—if still eco-sensitive—entrepreneurs.[49]

There is a most satisfying addendum to this story. Three years after it was published, I saw a copy of the new edition of Villani's book proudly displayed in many bookstores and art galleries in Northampton. I don't know if the author ever saw my article but I was pleased to see that, this time, *Northampton was number one.*

As with so much of my serious work and many reviews and travel pieces, I wrote my story about Eureka and Northampton at our summer place on Cape Cod. Over the years there I had established a regular routine: running or biking in the morning, swimming and sailing or kayaking whenever the tide was high, then writing in the afternoon and evening. My exercising was rarely solo. When not busy, Hedy went with

---

[49]"Eureka!," *Hampshire Life*, October 3, 1997

me. But almost every time I'd go out, one of our dogs would accompany me. My most loyal companion was a boarder named Dante.

Dante, a Belgian shepherd, belonged to our daughter. For at least ten summers of his life, Lies would bring him up to Wellfleet and we would take care of him for the summer. He loved to run with me and swim with me, too. Unlike any dog we'd had before, instead of trying to climb all over me or swim a bit and then head for shore to wait on the beach, Dante would swim alongside me keeping my pace, picking up speed or slowing down when I did, turning when I turned, and ever so often glancing over at me as if seeking acknowledgment for his loyal companionship. It was quite amazing. And not just to me. To this day, people will stop me on the beach and say they remember how much they had enjoyed watching the two of us do long laps back and forth for up to an hour at a time. To give a sense of what a sport he was, I offer this very short story, based on a real experience.

> I have a friend named Dante. He has dark curly hair, has wonderfully expressive face and great personality. He is the sort of guy you can always rely on.
>
> If I call him, he will drop whatever he is doing and join me. It doesn't matter if I'm going for a walk in the woods or a ride in the car. He's always ready. He doesn't care if it's hot or cold, sunny or rainy. Unlike some of my other pals, he always wants to do whatever I am doing and he never asks me to do what he wants. In fact, he never says a word.
>
> The truth is that Dante is a dog—although I think he believes he is a person and a very sporty one at that. If I can do something, he seems to think he can do it, too. And usually he can. Dante can do almost anything.
>
> For example, he loves to run with me and swim, too.
>
> One day last summer he and I were out on our daily exercise adventure. I was jogging around the island where we live and Dante was running along beside me. As we passed the outermost point, I noticed a man watching us with his binoculars. He seemed more intrigued by Dante's loyalty than my prowess as a "mature" runner. I waved to the man. He waved back. When I turned around to see if Dante was still following, I again noticed the fellow on the beach seeming to focus on our every moves.

A half hour later we had circled the island and were about to go around again but, after a few hundred yards, I decided it was too hot. I stopped running and sat down on the sand. Wagging his tail, my pal Dante seemed to be saying, "Well, that was fun. What do we do now?"

He soon found out.

I took off my running shoes, stripped off my shirt and cap, and plunged into the water. Dante waited on the shore for about a minute, then, realizing this was not going to be a cooling-off dunk but a long swim, he dove in after me. He soon caught up and we swam together. He was doing a furious dog paddle that matched my pace, even in the waves. We followed the shoreline. We swam about a half-mile before we turned back.

As we approached the place where we started, the same man I'd seen watching us was sitting nearby. He still had his binoculars. He was looking at Dante, then at me, then back at Dante. As we came out of the water and walked toward my stuff, he called out to me.

"Hey, what the hell are you doing, training that dog for a canine triathlon?"

I looked at Dante, then at the man. Then I answered as honestly as I could. "You know, I would if I could but there is a problem. Dante is a great athlete. He can run and he can swim but—I hate to say this in front of him, he just keeps falling off the bike."

On a trip to Bergen, Norway, shortly after I wrote it, I had the manuscript of this story in my bag and left a copy with Elisabeth Halvorsen, a former graduate student. Shortly thereafter, she showed it her friend, the artist, Gro Skjeldal. Gro wrote me a note saying she loved the story and, while all the actions were easy to visualize, she would love to try to draw some pictures to accompany the piece. I was delighted. She asked me to send her a photo of Dante and I did. A few weeks later I received a bunch of cartoonish sketches, each one capturing a part of the tale: man and dog taking off from the house, the two of them (us) passing the guy with the binoculars, the plunge into the water, the long swim, and then the brief colloquy with the curious onlooker. All were amazing renderings and added much to the text. But the best and most evocative were the last two drawings.

The first showed the back of Dante's shepherd-like head with a comic book bubble over his head in which he is seeing himself high in the saddle speeding off on a bicycle. The second is a drawing of a bike lying on the side of a sandy road, one wheel a bit askew, and a bunch of dog prints heading up and over the dune.

For several months Gro and I wrote back and forth about turning this now-joint effort into a children's book. When I finally started seeking a publisher, I kept getting the same response. I was told it is a great story with wonderful illustrations but no kid will understand the meaning of "triathlon" and changing that would ruin the story. I now realize we should have pitched it to those who publish little books for athletes and/or dog lovers. Maybe someday.

Sometime during the last year of the 1990s, on the very cusp of the new millennium when everyone was talking about big events, great ideas, horrible disasters and the cascade of breakthroughs in science and technology throughout the twentieth century, the editor of the *Smith College Alumnae Quarterly*, invited a group of faculty members to think even bigger. He asked us to write brief pieces on what each of us thought was *the* most significant invention in the sweep of human history. After agreeing, I thought long and hard about it. I knew my colleagues were doing the same. There were so many things one could put down. But the *single* most significant invention, boy, that's hard. Then it suddenly dawned on me that there was something that really stood head and shoulders above all the others.

Wonder Bread.

I wrote about this unique contribution to culture, noting it's amazingly cheap cost and disarmingly bland and flavorless character, matched only by its incredible staying power attributable to the high content of preservative (probably some sort of embalming fluid) in its manufacture. But more important than its price, its tastelessness and its long shelf life, I stressed that, unlike all those *foreign* inventions, like Christianity, the printing press, the steam engine, Marxism, and the computer, the fact is that Wonder Bread is 100 percent American. It is a most iconic expression of the idea of something for everyone. And I said so. (I should note that, while Wonder Bread was my first choice for mankind's greatest invention, my second was academic tenure!)

VI

The 2000s: Moving On

THE START OF THE NEW DECADE—AND NEW CENTURY—was filled with promise and terror, both personal and global. For Hedy and me it was all intertwined.

Shortly after we said goodbye to the bloodiest century in history—the century in which her own parents and everyone else in her family save for her sister, Betsy, and a cousin with the same name, were murdered by the Nazis—we were startled to learn that Hedy had a pernicious form of breast cancer.

With the good fortune of getting a second opinion and some skillful surgery from an oncologist, Dr. Caroline Kaelin, Hedy was admitted into an experimental group at the Dana Farber Hospital in Boston. With a team led by Dr. Craig Bunnell, she underwent a ten month-long series of treatments involving chemotherapy, surgery, more chemo, radiation, and, above all, periodic infusions of the then-experimental drug, Herceptin. There is little question now but that the substance saved her life.

Fortunately, after a grueling year, wearing a blond wig and maintaining an amazingly upbeat manner—or putting up a good facade, she was back in to her pre-cancer rhythm, eager to continue her own work, travel with me to Holland, and then join me for the second fellowship at our favorite retreat, the Centro Studi Ligure per le Arti e Lettere in the little village of Bogliasco on the slope of the Mediterranean coast, near Genoa.

We arrived back at the Bogliasco Foundation's Villa di Pini on September 10, 2001. Early the next afternoon while unpacking books, sorting files and setting up the computers in the third floor study to which we were assigned, we were startled by rapping on the door. The housekeeper, huffing and puffing from running up the stairs, told us in rapid Italian that our daughter was on the phone from America and sounded upset. At least that is what we thought she said. Hedy ran downstairs to take the call. She was in time. Lies was still on the line. She told Hedy that there had been a terrible accident and that a big airplane had hit one of the towers of New York's World Trade Center. She said she was watching playbacks on her TV. Then the phone went dead. It took quite a while to reconnect and, when Hedy reached her again, Lies was still standing in front of the television set. As they spoke, there was suddenly a pause, then a gasp. In mid-sentence she said, "Oh my God...another plane just crashed into the Twin Towers."

Like so many Americans overseas and everyone back home, we were in a state of shock. We felt helpless. Our first inclination was to fly back to the States, but that was impossible because all planes were grounded. There was nothing we could do but huddle around the television set in the common room of the villa along with the other fellows, half of them American, half from other countries.

Among the small group of Americans was a former poet laureate of the United States, Mark Strand. Mark, who would become a close friend during our month in Bogliasco, later told me he had great difficulty writing anything during that trying time. I, who had never written any poetry other than doggerel, political clerihews and rhymes mimicking—often parodying—the rhythms of Kipling or Longfellow or the lyricists of Tin Pan Alley, was so upset on what came to be known as 9/11 that I found myself trying to express my thoughts in verse. I called my poem, "Evocation." A few weeks later, I shared it with Mark and some of the other fellows at the study center. One of them showed it to a woman on the staff who happened to own an art gallery in Genoa. She approached me a few days later and asked if she could publish it in English and in Italian along with an etching of the rugged cliffs it described. Of course

I agreed. It remains the only serious poem of mine ever to appear in print.

> Pine scent wafts on onshore breeze.
> Up the slope the trees move
> Almost imperceptibly,
> Matching the gentle pulse of surf below.
>
> There is serenity on the Golfo Paradiso.
>
> Little boats bob.
> Bigger ones loll.
> The sea is calm
> Except for the wavelets.
>
> At other times it is very different.
> Roiling surf, waves pounding
> Against the giant rocks,
> Against the bottom of the cliff,
> Reminders that peace is quite ephemeral.
>
> In the spring of 1945 men gave their lives
> Right near the place
> Where pine scent wafts on onshore breeze
> When tranquility became a raging storm.
>
> This morning from this peaceful spot
> I scanned the sea and smelled the air
> And listened to the far-off sound
> Of thunder.
>
> Bogliasco, September 11, 2001[50]

We took a breather after leaving Bogliasco and stayed for several weeks in the apartment of a Smith colleague in the town of Bordighera, very close to Ventimiglia on the Italian-French border. This respite enabled us both, but especially Hedy, to take things a bit easier and slow down our frenetic pace.

While based in Bordighera, we made a few short day trips to towns along the Italian Riviera and several more on the French side, the Cote

---

[50] *Evocation/Evocazione*, published in English and Italian, Galleria San Bernardo, Genoa, 2002.

d'Azur. We visited Monaco and the cities of Nice, Vence, Antibes, and Cannes. They all lived up to what we had heard of them, but the last proved a bit unnerving, especially along the beach where, despite the fact that it was late in the season, thousands of European vacationers and tourists were spread out on the famous beaches sunning themselves. Along the walkways people of much darker skin tones were peddling various wares. That night I wrote the following reflection. I called it "Conundrum in Cannes."

On the beach at Cannes
White folks lie in the sun
Frying.

The darker they are,
The better they feel.

On the beach at Cannes
Blacks folks ply their wares.
Trying to sell knock-off watches
And ersatz purses by Louis Vuitton and Gucci.
And *parapluies*.

But it rarely rains in the summer in Cannes.
And nobody buys *parapluies*
Or knock-off watches,
Or ersatz purses by Louis Vuitton and Gucci.

And so it goes—
Sunny day after sunny day.

White folks lie in the sun
Trying to get black.
Black folks sell knock-off watches
And *parapluies*,
Trying to survive.

From Bordighera we drove back to Bogliasco to see some friends and then wended our way to Salzburg where, once again, we would be participating in a conference. En route we stopped at a number of northern Italian cities and even managed to do a bit of hiking in the Dolomites. It was an exhilarating experience. Going up a rugged mountain trail had Hedy weeping with joy. It was truly a first for her—the first up-hill walk since she had been diagnosed with cancer. Reaching the summit was a double triumph.

I had hoped to finish editing the manuscript for my new book, *The Dispossessed*, while in Italy but finally completed the task at the Schloss Leopoldskron, home of the Salzburg Seminar in Austria. *The Dispossessed* was a concrete result of the year-long project I had organized and chaired called "The Anatomy of Exile" conducted at Smith College's Kahn Liberal Arts Institute during the 2000–2001 academic year.

The stated objective of the institute, founded in 1997, thanks to a bequest from a dedicated Smith alumna, Louise W. Kahn, class of 1931, was in the institute's own words, "To provide a setting in which faculty, along with students and outside experts, could collaborate on research projects of broad scope. In addition, a rich series of public events related to these projects would enhance the intellectual life of the college." Most exciting to me was that faculty and students would be given the opportunity to work together on common issues, celebrating and practicing interdisciplinary interaction in its best sense.

From the start it was decided that projects would be selected competitively, on the basis of applications from faculty members submitted to a board of their peers.

Illustrating the built-in range of possible topics, the title of the first program was "Ecologies of Childhood." The organizers were a professor of religion who had been the college chaplain and a child psychologist. An astronomer and a playwright who was a then-current member of the theater department would head the winning project in the second year, "Galileo in His Time and Ours." Its culminating public presentation was a play based on the trial of Galileo that was later restaged in New York City, called "Star Messenger." Mine was the next.

Since then there have been a number of year-long and shorter-term programs whose titles speak to the breadth of their range: "Symmetry and Asymmetry," "Evil," "Other Europes, Europe's Others," "Why Educate Women?" "Renaissances: A Multiplicity of Rebirths," "Altering Bodies

and Minds," "Plague," "Placing Space," and "Mothers and Others: Repro-
duction, Representation and the Body Politic."

Our project was to consider the meaning of dispossession from
many different perspectives historical, political, sociological and literary.
Once it was approved, it became my responsibility to select nine others
from the faculty to join the seminar. That I did by sending out an an-
nouncement outlining the general thrust of the project and inviting
those with special interests to tell me why they would be good members
of the group. From that body of applicants, I chose those I felt best
suited to the task. Then all ten of us sent word to the student body that
the Kahn Institute would be sponsoring a seminar on "The Anatomy of
Exile," with a brief explanation, encouraging them to apply. In the end,
ten students were chosen. It turned out that half of those in the faculty
group were foreign-born, some of them refugees; the same was true of
the student cohort.

We got together once in the spring before the seminar was to begin,
then starting in September, we met on a regular basis every Tuesday afternoon and for lunch together every Wednesday. In those sessions we
would discuss various aspects of our central concern, often addressing a
particular concept such as the meaning of exile itself or presenting
works in progress by individuals or subgroups of the whole, divided up
according to particular sets of common interests or fields of study. Many
others—artists and writers, filmmakers and foreign service officers,
refugee workers and representatives of newcomer-communities came to
Smith to take part in a variety of activities we sponsored: a series of lectures, including one by the music director of the London Chamber Or-
chestra, Adrian Sunshine, called "From the Ashes: The Music of
Theresienstadt;" theater performances written and directed by a faculty
fellow, Ellen Kaplan, on Bosnian refugees; and at the end, an original
cantata, "The Golden Door," by our Smith College colleague, composer
Ron Perera. Most ambitious were two three-day symposia, one at the
end of the first semester of 2000–2001 called "Forced Out: The Experience of Exile," the second at the end of the second semester, "The Rescue and Resettlement of Refugees," with a special emphasis on the role

of key figures in the twentieth century. There were several papers on individuals affiliated with Smith College living in several communities surrounding Northampton who had been instrumental in such activities, particularly in the 1930s and the 1940s, fighting fascism in Italy and National Socialism in Germany and its occupied lands and saving refugee intellectuals. Many of the latter were provided a haven in the Pioneer Valley of western Massachusetts.

Among those most prominent in the rescue effort was William Allan Neilson, the third president of Smith College and a leading figure in a number of campaigns for human rights, and a principal subject of my own research on those who took the expression about being "one's brothers' keeper" to heart.

A few more words about Neilson...

A Scottish-born Shakespearean and devotee of the poet, Robert Burns, former professor of English at Harvard, and co-editor of the Harvard Classics, William Allan Neilson came to Smith College in 1917, the height of World War I. With him was his German bride, Elisabeth Muser, who was hardly welcomed to Northampton with equanimity. Neilson dealt promptly with the local prejudices against having a Hun in their midst, as he would do with many other causes.

Over the years during which he headed the college, he not only set the institution on a course of internationalism, revised the curriculum, and in many ways put Smith on the map, but also used the bully pulpit of his office to speak out on important issues of the day. He vehemently opposed the execution of the anarchists Sacco and Vanzetti, fought against loyalty oaths, and, as noted earlier, became an active member of the board of the NAACP in 1930, and, in 1943, became the founding chair of the NAACP's Legal and Defense Education Fund.

On *Kristallnacht*, November 9, 1938, at a mass meeting in Northampton President Neilson spoke to the crowd. "This is what we have to do. We have to say 'I will not stand by and be silent before these terrible things. I will not forget my common humanity, the common element in the whole race. I cannot be contemporary with these events and have it said by my children that I lived through that and did nothing about it—

for no reason that I could honestly offer.'" It was a portent of things to come, and a key reason why we would focus the final symposium—and I would dedicate our book—to Neilson's memory. In *The Dispossessed*, I noted that:

> Whether railing against anti-alien legislation or aiding the dispossessed—as in everything else he considered important, William Allan Neilson, often described as a "Gladstonian liberal," and, sometimes as a "Jeremiah-with-a-brogue," was informed, outspoken and engaged. He thrived on diversity and on controversy long before the former became a buzzword and the latter something to fear. He was the sort of person Bobbie Burn's must have had in mind when he wrote, "The honest man, though ne'er sae puir, Is king o' men for a' that."[51]

Neilson—along with five other academic leaders—was one of the founders of the Emergency Rescue Committee (later to become the International Rescue Committee). Through a clandestine operation set up in Marseilles in 1940 under the leadership of Varian Fry, who has sometimes been called the "American Pimpernel," they set out to rescue two hundred and in the end managed to facilitate the escape of nearly two thousand foreigners and *apatrides* (stateless persons) and get them over the border into Spain and on to Portugal and finally to the United States. Among those Fry and his band of colleagues—who ranged from socialites to socialists and some pretty unsavory accomplices—managed to spirit out of France were such luminaries as Marc Chagall, Marcel Duchamp, Lion Feuchtwanger, Jacques Lipchitz, Wanda Landowska, Andre Masson, Ylla (the animal photographer), Lotte Leonard, Hannah Arendt, André Breton, Heinrich Mann (brother of Thomas), Golo Mann (Thomas's son), Walter Mehring, Franz Werfel and his wife, Alma Mahler, Gropius Werfel, Otto Meyerhoff, Hans Sahl, Max Ernst, and Giuseppe Modigliani.

Preparing the book based on the Kahn project presented me with a dilemma. There were so many good papers but they ranged widely over a large number of issues all clearly related to our central theme but

---

[51]See *The Dispossessed: An Anatomy of Exile* (Amherst: University of Massachusetts Press, 1995) 131.

often concentrating on different crises and different eras. After reading many submissions from Kahn fellows and some of the visitors, I decided to concentrate the focus on the period of the 1930s and 1940s. The period had been, in many ways, the centerpiece of the seminar, in the specific context of what it meant to be forced out, the role of those who provided care and succor and safe havens to the dispossessed, and the contributions and impacts that refugees had on their host societies.

The volume is bookended by two important contributions. The first is a foreword by the actress and activist and vice president of the International Rescue Committee, Liv Ullmann. It explains the roots of her concern about refugees.

> An era of inventiveness and creativity unmatched in human history, the story of the twentieth century was also indelibly marred by wars, atrocities, gulags and "ethnic cleansing," by the massacres of Armenians and Jews, Cambodians and Bosnians, by the transfer of populations as between Greece and Turkey, India and Pakistan; by hundreds of thousands who escaped from the Soviet Union and its satellites; refugees from Nazi-dominated Europe, and, after World War II, from China and Hungary and Cuba and Chile and Haiti and South Africa and, more recently from the various states of the former Yugoslavia. There were and continue to be conflicts in Northern Ireland, Sri Lanka, the Middle East, and many parts of Africa.

> More often than not the victims of despots and demagogues, of the captains of political cadres and tribal chieftains, and of terrorists of varied stripes were—and are—innocent civilians, men, women and children. While some are fortunate enough to escape the wrath of their persecutors, finding safe havens across the borders, only a relative few are able to get to a third country to start life over again. The vast majority of uprooted people are unable to escape. They, the internally displaced, are perhaps the most wretched sufferers of all.

> In my experience seeing refugees at first hand—and talking to hundreds of refugee workers (and to those who have studied both), I have been struck not only by their often desperate situations but by the critical roles played by those who are involved in providing relief to the dispossessed, those my friend Peter Rose has referred to as the "advocates," "caretakers," "gatekeepers," "guides," and "go-betweens" —all key players in offering assistance.

Declaring myself an advocate, it should not be surprising when I say that one of the most impressive things about the plan for this volume—and for the Smith College project on "The Anatomy of Exile," which was its incubator, was the emphasis placed on those special people who were engaged in the rescue and resettlement of refugees, especially in the dark days marked by the rise of fascism and Nazism. Not least among the groups cited is the International Rescue Committee, an organization that was created from the merging of two citizen groups, the International Relief Association, established in 1933, and the Emergency Rescue Committee, founded in 1940 by a small group of concerned citizens, writers, publicists and six university presidents, one of whom was Smith's William Allan Neilson.

That period is especially meaningful to me because my grandfather, Professor Halfdan Ullmann, was one who gave his life trying to save Jews in Norway—and died alongside those he had helped in the first concentration camp to be opened (and the last to be closed) in Germany: Dachau. But even this special connection has not made me, my former colleagues in UNICEF or my present ones in the International Rescue Committee, immune to the suffering of others. Indeed, reflections on my own loss, the courage of those closest to me, and the pro-active men and women who work in the field or behind the scenes, have only heightened my resolve to continue the campaign against bigotry and injustice and to do whatever can be done to aid the dispossessed. In my travels with UNICEF and the IRC to Southeast Asia, the Middle East, and various parts of Africa, I have seen the faces of those Peter Rose calls the "Madonnas of the Refugee Camps;" in my life in the arts, I have also been privileged to know and work with those he calls the "Maestros in Exile." Whether abjectly poor or illustrious, whether Northern or Southern, Western or Eastern, or middle-eastern, they have in common a desperate need for someone to give voice to their plights. This book is a fine example of responding to that desire. It is also a tribute to those who aided the dispossessed in the years from 1900 to 2000.

Those mentored by them are continuing the good work. But they need help. My help. Your help, too.

Liv Ullmann[52]

---

[52]"Foreword" to *The Dispossessed: An Anatomy of Exile* (Amherst: University of Massachusetts Press, 2005), vii–viii.

The last piece in *The Dispossessed* is a poem by Rubén D. Rumbaut, the late Cuban psychiatrist and father of one of the other contributors to the volume, Rubén G. Rumbaut. The senior Rumbaut's poem, called "A Psalm for Refugees: Lot's Wife," is an ode on the pain of leaving home and of longing for home. I thought it a fitting coda to both the volume published in 2005 and to the Kahn project. But it didn't end there.

We all enjoyed the reflected glory in the success of one of our student fellows, Sharmeen Obaid, a Pakistani woman who went on from Smith to receive two degrees from Stanford and become one of the premier documentary filmmakers in the world. Her first film, on Afghan refugees in Pakistan, came about in part because of her involvement in our seminar when she was in her senior year. Over the decade since she was with us looking into the meaning of dispossession and alienation, she has made many prizewinning films, none more powerful than *Saving Face*, winner of an "Oscar" in 2012 for the best documentary.

There were several other offshoots of our project, most notably two more seminars on a related topic: a short-term symposium on "Migration and the Resurgence of Nativism" sponsored by the Kahn Institute lasting three very intensive days in the spring of 2010, and another under the auspices of Five Colleges Inc.—a consortium of Amherst, Hampshire, Mount Holyoke and Smith colleges and the University of Massachusetts—which involved monthly gatherings throughout the academic years, 2010–11 and 2011–12. What was particularly rewarding to me was that all three of those seminars included more than half of the original faculty fellows who were part of the "Anatomy of Exile" project.

Once most of the work on *The Dispossessed* was completed, I began turning my attention once again to examining intergroup relations in this country and abroad, especially in the Netherlands, where I continued to spend a good deal of time. I also returned to travel writing.

Examples of the former are to be found in two essays on the specific subject of tensions between "insiders" and "outsiders" in the United States and in Europe, respectively. The first, "The Persistence of (an) Ethnicity," had begun as a review of the late Samuel Huntington's book, *Who Are We?* It focused on the resurgence of nativism in this country and, particularly, the animus directed at those from Mexico, a reprise of anti-immigrant sentiment that was so prevalent in earlier periods in American history. It was published in the Netherlands in a special book dedicated to a Dutch sociologist who wrote extensively about American society and culture, Rob Kroes, on the occasion of his retirement from the University of Amsterdam in 2005. At the end of my essay I noted that:

> I finished reading Huntington's jeremiad on a Southwest Airlines flight from Baltimore to Phoenix on September 23, 2004. The plane was filled to capacity. At least one-third of my fellow passengers seemed to be returning home from the great gathering of tribes in Washington, D.C. and the opening of the first National Indian Museum at the Smithsonian that had just taken place. Some of these truly real American were wearing bits of native gear in celebration of the persistence of their ethnicity; most wore tee shirts emblazoned with the logo of the big event in which they had just participated.
>
> As I sat there I thought of Huntington's claim that, "In its origins America was not a nation of immigrants, it was a society, or societies, of settlers who came to the New World in the seventeenth and eighteenth centuries," with nary a word about the fact that these settlers were interlopers who colonized a territory that had long been inhabited by people who also had their own rich cultures and indigenous characteristics.
>
> Still musing, I noticed that the rest of the passengers, including a number of Latinos, reflected the cross-section of citizens one expects on most transcontinental flights; the staff did, too. I turned back to the book and re-read Huntington's comment at the end of that chapter on the threat of the Mexican invasion and was again struck by his almost visceral reaction to the words of Lionel Sosa who had ended his own book, *The Americano Dream*, a compendium of advice to Hispanic entrepreneurs, with the words: "The Americano dream? It exists; it is realistic; it is there for all of us to share."
>
> Huntington's found this profoundly troubling, even repulsive. "There is no Americano dream. There is only the American dream created by an Anglo-Protestant society."
>
> I put the book down as the stewards, named Wong and Garcia, came by to offer drinks and some salty snacks that were typically

American—in more than one way. Included in the little box were peanut butter crackers, chocolate chip cookies, potato chips, and a bag of peanuts. On the latter it said "Celebremos tu Herencia" and "Southwest Airlines celebrates Hispanic Heritage Month."

Then, thinking more about what I was feeling on that crowded jet arrowing across the country, I suddenly recalled that long before Samuel Huntington asked his question, "Who are we?," the great African-American basso, Paul Robeson, asked it, too, way back in 1940. And I remembered his answer.

> *What's that, lady?*
> *Am I am American?*
>
> I'm just an Irish, Negro, Jewish, Italian,
> French and English, Spanish, Russian,
> Chinese, Polish, Scotch, Hungarian,
> Litvak, Swedish, Finnish, Canadian,
> Greek and Turk and Czech and double-check American.
>
> And that ain't all, I was baptized
> Baptist, Methodist, Congregationalist,
> Lutheran, Atheist, Roman Catholic,
> Orthodox Jewish, Presbyterian,
> Seventh Day Adventist, Mormon, Quaker,
> Christian Scientist
> And lots more.[53]

The second of the two essays I mentioned earlier is "Minus-Sum Games in a Land of Guilty Memories," an assessment of what was going on in Kroes's own society. It was published in the winter of 2007. Just as "The Persistence of (an) Ethnicity" was triggered by Samuel Huntington's *Who Are We?*, my commentary on the Netherlands also began as a review. It focused on Ian Buruma's *Murder in Amsterdam*. It was written at a time when a new word, *Islamophobia,* was showing up in more and more newspapers in the United States and overseas.

> Minus-sum games are contests in which all who play lose.
> A classic example is what happened in New York City during the struggles over community control in the racially charged atmosphere

[53]"The Persistence of (an) Ethnicity," in *Over (T)Here: Transatlantic Essays in Honor of Rob Kroes* (Kate Delaney and Ruud Janssens, eds.) (Amsterdam: VU University Press, 2005), 47–48.

of the 1960s. The context, as we remember, involved competing perspectives of conservatives, moderates, liberals, policy makers, poverty warriors, black militants and thousands of poor, frustrated people who lived in working class neighborhoods in New York and many other urban areas. At the time the political scientist Aaron Wildavsky explained the phenomenon in an article in which he facetiously offered a "Recipe for Violence."

"Promise a lot, deliver a little; lead people to believe they will be much better off, but let there be no dramatic improvement....Feel guilty about what has happened to black people; tell them you are surprised that they have not revolted before; express shock and dismay when they follow your advice."

These words have continuing relevance in this country and, substituting the words "black people" for "Muslim immigrants," even more significance today in many European countries, including the most open of them all, the Netherlands.

The Dutch writer, Ian Buruma, doesn't offer such an explicit formula in his dissection of the current situation in the Netherlands, but in his new book, *Murder in Amsterdam: The Death of Theo van Gogh and the Limits of Tolerance* (2006), but it wouldn't be a bad fit. Buruma's title refers to the cold-blooded assassination of a Dutchman with one of the most iconic names in the country, Theo van Gogh, a relative of the painter and one who shared a first name with Vincent's faithful brother. Its subtitle suggests something broader: a commentary on the dilemmas of diversity and the challenges of pluralism in a rapidly changing society.

Buruma is one of the most gifted, thoughtful and erudite journalists writing today. Author of a number of important meditations on modern times, such as his succinct assessment of German and Japanese responses to what he calls "the wages of guilt," here again he makes a number of interesting comparisons. This time the cultures are not those of former enemies but of Holland's people, "the ethnic Dutch" and others, especially those from North Africa and the Middle East....

Chroniclers like Ian Buruma tell us that Holland had a long and proud history of welcoming foreigners beginning with Sephardic Jews who arrived in the late sixteenth and early seventeenth century, many members of families who had fled the Inquisition in Spain. Then came the Huguenots after Louis XIV revoked their right to stay and worship in France in 1685. It was the Golden Age.

Writing about that era, Buruma notes that while Holland's reputation for hospitality is deserved, the spirit of tolerance didn't last, particularly in regard to welcoming outsiders. "The more recent immigration, particularly in the twentieth century, is a story of horror, opportunism, postcolonial obligations, and an odd combination of charity and indifference."

Alongside discussions of current conflicts, Buruma muses over how Jews were actually treated by many Dutch citizens during World War II. He cites the extent of collaboration with the NSB (Dutch Nazis) or, at the least, acquiescence to the demands of the occupiers. He reflects on how the revelation of the extent of complicity has tarnished the image the Netherlands as a haven for the oppressed and a nation of rescuers. It exploded the myth of unselfish heroism, doubtlessly reified by the general strike in February 1941, symbolized by the famous Dockworker Monument, and by Anne Frank's famous diary. Buruma confirms the fact that of over 80,000 Jews in Amsterdam at the outset of the war, only 5,000 survived. Of some 60,000 outside the main city, an equally small number made it through the war. The percentage of Jews from the Netherlands who perished in the camps was the highest in Europe outside of Poland.

In addition to a hardly sterling record of protection and resistance during the German occupation, there was also the bitter legacy of Dutch colonialism that had to be faced. And, as guilty memories of what was going on in the country in the 1940s began to be more openly reconsidered, the often sanitized and glorified history of colonization and its unraveling, not least the hardly benevolent treatment of Muslim rebels in Java in the last days of the Dutch Empire also began to be addressed.

After the war and decolonization of Indonesia and Surinam, things did begin to change. New migrants came to the Netherlands. In the first wave were many Dutch-speaking "repatriates" (so named because of their citizenship) from the former Dutch colonies. Then others, "guest workers" from the Middle East and North African, mainly from Turkey and Morocco, were encouraged to come to do the heavy lifting in a booming economy. Political asylees came, too, from Vietnam and Somalia and Bosnia and other war-torn states. The presence of these foreigners would soon challenge the resurgent spirit of hospitality and welcome and lead to unprecedented inter-group tensions.

Reading *Murder in Amsterdam* and pondering its historical passages, one can't help but think of what the French sociologist, Émile

Durkheim, called *anomie*, a shorthand term for a breakdown in the social order often provoked by dramatic changes for which members of society are unprepared.

Such a breakdown happened in many places over the century since anomie first entered our vernacular: the chaos in Europe following World War I, the worldwide Depression, the effects of Nazism and fascism on millions of victims, the disorientation of displaced persons after the war, and the upheaval that began in the mid-1960s when rebellious young people challenged the Establishment on both sides of the Atlantic. In the last instance, the parents of the rebels who were finally experiencing a semblance of normalcy and increasing affluence hardly knew how to react. Their confusion and anxiety was particularly dramatic in the Netherlands, where, reeling from unanticipated challenges to the status quo, many leaders in government, the academy, and the industrial sector acquiesced to the demands for a more open society and often for direct participation in decision-making at every level by those known as "Provos." They had successfully undermined the well-known Calvinist, Catholic, and secular/humanist pillars that were the principal supports of Dutch society.

In many ways, the cultural revolution the Provos unleashed, called by the writer Harry Mulisch "an Amsterdam revolt against the provinces," resulted in a sea change in the normative order. The nation officially became more accepting of diversity, and many experiments in a freer, more open system became institutionalized. Soon the Netherlands gained fame (or, to its critics, notoriety) for becoming the most liberal nation in Europe. Best known, of course, were its legalization of prostitution, decriminalization of the use of soft drugs, acceptance of the practice of euthanasia, and open-mindedness in regard to homosexuality. Less celebrated was the nominal acceptance of multiculturalism. I say "nominal" because, today, many say that divisions not only remained but, aside from the cosmopolites in Amsterdam and The Hague, there was never widespread acceptance of its full meaning in most parts of the country.

In recent years the Netherlands experienced another breakdown, this time the threat did not start with the rebellious progeny of old Dutch burghers and working-class conservatives but with the offspring of non-Dutch migrants, increasingly referred to by the invented and, initially at least, neutral word, *allochtoonen* (meaning something like newcomers but often used today as a pejorative term for outsiders).

Most of the Dutch Provos, like many of those who joined SDS and the Free Speech Movement in the United States, had been middle-class insiders who had sought and in many ways succeeded breaking loose from the confinements of their smug, self-righteous and stratified society where people took pride in minding their own business. Forty years after their appearance, some of the new provocateurs are members of the generation whose parents had migrated to the Netherlands, eager to work and hoping to enjoy the rights, privileges and welfare benefits the old Dutch bourgeoisie had come to take for granted. In certain ways, they were not disappointed. Whatever anxieties they felt, most seemed grateful for the chance to start life anew in a freer society than that which they had known before. Others, even when disillusioned, tended to feel and behave as if they were guests in someone else's home.

Often too old to learn the ways and difficult language of the new society, like millions of immigrants who came to this country at the turn of the twentieth century and after 1965, they frequently sought out others like themselves. Many found housing in "changing" neighborboods, dish cities that redefined the urban landscape. (They were so named because of the numerous satellite disks—*schotels* or large plates—set on rooftops and used to get better TV reception from their countries of origin.) Whether working or unemployed, those of the first generation found their personal solace in family and faith and links to homelands. Few had the energy or time for politics.

Those of the second generation frequently found themselves in a double bind caught between parental hopes (usually for them) and parental fears, especially about being enticed by what they saw as rampant permissiveness. They felt frustrated by the official promise of equality contrasted by the reality of increasing resentment of the society in which they were growing up and being educated and upon which they were often dependent for support. Fluent in Dutch, and far more attuned to the world beyond that of their kith and kin, many felt betrayed by their immigrant fathers and infuriated about the seeming hypocrisy of their prejudiced hosts. In many ways they became modern exemplars of what, over eighty years ago, Robert E. Park labeled "marginal men," and defined as "those whom fate has condemned to live in two societies and in two not merely different but antagonistic cultures."

Within the ranks of those no longer foreign but still alien—and increasingly alienated, a number of Muslim youth sought to resolve their frustration and their persisting estrangement by seeking some sort of redemption in ethnic pride and religious fervor, especially in Islamic fundamentalism. In a very real sense, they sought to turn the negativity of their marginality into a functionally positive response. Like those undergoing the ethnogenesis of black pride in this country, they began to revel in their differences, and exaggerate them, too, often becoming threatening specters to those who already knew them only in crude but fairly benign caricature. Some, perhaps many, influenced by charismatic and persuasive imams, underwent a true born-again conversion, eschewing their "errant" and "decadent" western ways, celebrating their Islamic heritage, and becoming more orthodox than their parents. This was manifest in many ways, including the denouncing of those in their ranks who fraternized with non-Muslims, a rise in attendance at mosques, and in the manners of dress by men who donned traditional garb paralleling the women with their headscarves, and sometimes, veils and full-body burkhas, all furthering the visible dichotomy between "us" and "them."

Within the host society growing anger at seemingly ungrateful behavior of the allochtoonen and their recrudescent radicalization, often turned from ethnocentric disdain to outright hostility, even among those who had been sensitized and socialized to avoid expressions of nationalism or racism and to cap their real feelings about "strangers" in their midst.

After the attacks on New York's World Trade Center and the Pentagon on 9/11 by Muslim extremists, the lid was lifted. People in the Netherlands began to think: Muslims are terrorists; Moroccans are Muslims; ergo, Moroccans are terrorists—or, at the least, potential terrorists.

More and more members of Dutch society bought into the syllogism. Among some of the most outspoken in their resentment of the Islamic challengers were several of the now-aging Provos of the 1960s and 1970s. Foremost among those voicing outrage early in the first decade of the new century was Pim Fortuyn, a sociology professor with political ambitions. Fortuyn was no typical stolid mind-my-own-business Dutchman. He was a populist rebel with several causes and many illusions of grandeur. He was an outspoken homosexual who favored all sorts of sexual freedoms, proudly boasting of his own exploits. He was a flamboyant dandy who wore fancy clothes and taunted environmentalists with his fur collared coats and jackets. He ridiculed Calvinist values of sobriety, piety, thrift, and probity, and he disparaged the sanctimoniousness of bureaucrats, leftist politicians and academics. Most significantly, he was a virulent neo-nativist, particularly hostile to Muslim immigrants, people he claimed were threatening to destroy his society.

Despite Fortuyn's outrageous behavior and extremist positions—or, perhaps, because of them—he had a large and rapidly growing grassroots following. Some pundits and many of his cronies claimed he might well have become Prime Minister, had he not been murdered in broad daylight in May, 2002.

With his death, Ian Buruma points out that Fortuyn's fame among an extraordinarily wide range of Dutch people turned into a sort of apotheosis. To many he was like a new messiah. (Departing from his generally cautious, investigative reportage, Buruma quotes from a dubious and very unscientific TV poll that claimed Fortuyn was voted the most popular Dutchman in history, outranking such luminaries as William the Silent, Rembrandt, and Erasmus. Spinoza didn't even make the list!)

The murder of Pim Fortuyn, a man ready to take over Her Majesty's wayward ship of state, was to be followed two years later by the assassination of another outspoken Dutchman, Theo van Gogh. Van Gogh was less a mutineer with a plan than a nihilistic anarchist. (If Fortuyn was the would-be crown prince of a purely Dutch society, van Gogh was its court jester.) Both lost their lives by those who felt they should die for their sins—and made it happen.

Fortuyn's background was working-class Catholic; Theo van Gogh's immediate family members were haut bourgeois Dutch liberals, but ones who did not easily fit into the pillared pigeonholes. They were at once Calvinist in demeanor, socialist in politics, and secular humanist. They were also principled activists. Proud patriots in the best sense of the word, several worked in the resistance during World War II. One of his uncles was executed for helping Jews; his maternal grandfather was jailed by the Nazis for similar activities. But Theo was not interested in this personal history, or, presumably, that of his country. From an early age he rebelled against his parents and what they stood for.

Anyone familiar with Vincent van Gogh's life knows he was an inwardly troubled man. His grandnephew was, by contrast, an extroverted troublemaker, a free-spirited, iconoclastic public figure and filmmaker, rabble-rouser and challenger to what on this side of the Atlantic we call political correctness. Nothing and nobody seemed beyond his contempt. This included Holocaust survivors and specific Jews like Job Cohen, the mayor of Amsterdam. It included Christians and those who saw Jesus as their savior. To Theo van Gogh, Christ was "a rotten fish from Nazareth." But his favorite targets were faithful Muslims whom he repeatedly mocked, insulted, and baited.

Fortuyn had been killed by Volkert van der Graaf, an ardent animal rights advocate; van Gogh was murdered by an Islamist jihadist, the son of Moroccan immigrants. His killer, Mohammed Bouyeri, was claimed to have been offended by many things van Gogh had said (he frequently and publicly referred to Muslims as "goat fuckers") and what he had done, none more egregious in Bouyeri's eyes that his support of the Somalian-Muslim feminist, Ayaan Hirsi Ali, whose short film, *Submission*, van Gogh had directed. The film, only eleven minutes in length, was intentionally provocative. Among other things, it depicted the body of a naked woman clothed in a see-through burkha and phrases taken from the Koran that demanded the subservience of women painted on the bodies of other unclothed females. A note pinned to his bullet-ridden body by Bouyeri railed against Ayaan Hirsi Ali and her blasphemous and traitorous behavior....[54]

Toward the end of his book Buruma turns to his subtitle, and notes that the welfare state is well established in most parts of Europe and many are quite proud of the cradle to grave benefits the system provides. But as Buruma rightly points out, taxpayers never expected they would have to share their benefits with large numbers of immigrants, especially with those who believe that they are entitled to state-sponsored care and then complain when they don't get as much as they believe was to be theirs.

"Immigrants appear to fare better in the harsh system of the United States, where there is less temptation to milk the state. The necessity to fend for oneself encourages a kind of tough integration." Here I think Buruma is a bit off-target. We have been far more successful in integrating newcomers, not because we offer them less (which is true), but because we do more than pay lip service to the idea of being connected by our hyphens rather than divided by them. Still, it would be Pollyannaish to claim that we are immune to many of the

---

[54]"Minus-Sum Games in a Land of Guilty Memories," *Congress Monthly* (January/February, 2007), 3–7.

troubling issues raised in his book. We aren't. Here in the U.S. we have our own paranoia about Islamic terrorism and a widening we vs. they dichotomy exploited by the Bush Administration and manifest in the restrictive implications of the Patriot Act and in America's own version of Germany's enabling acts of the 1930s. Many Americans are also asking, "Are there limits to tolerance?"

Buruma's answer to the question—and his coda—comes in the middle rather than the end of his book.

Tolerance, then, has its limits even for Dutch Progressives. It is easy to be tolerant of those who are much like ourselves whom we feel we can trust instinctively, whose jokes we understand, who share our sense of irony.... It is much harder to extend the same principle to strangers in our midst, who find our ways as disturbing as we do theirs, who watch fearfully as their own children, caught in between, slip from the paternal grasp into a new and bewildering world.

Then as a postscript, he could add words spoken to him by an Iranian-born Muslim friend and law professor at the University of Leiden, Afishen Ellian: "Citizenship of a democratic state means living by the laws of the country. A liberal democracy cannot survive when part of the population believes that divine laws trump those made by man." This is a most reasonable argument and few can gainsay its truth. But I am not sure a truly liberal democracy can survive when, by the same token, neo-nationalists like Pim Fortuyn and admirers of ultra-violence like Theo van Gogh (whose favorite film was Stanley Kubrick's *A Clockwork Orange*) have unbridled license to cry "Fire!" in that proverbial crowded theater, saying and doing whatever they want, distinguishing membership from citizenship in a society in which they alone claim ownership, and encouraging many to be intolerant of tolerance in the name of protecting the Volk from the Untermenschen, or its Dutch equivalent. Somehow such actions have an all too familiar ring.[55]

These may have been my first but would not be my last words on the subject. In fact, increasingly disturbed by the growing ethnic and religious conflicts going on within and between societies, and in a mood to revert to terser commentaries, after those two long essays, I wrote another poem. I called it "To Die For."

---

[55] Ibid., 6–7.

To die for what?

The cause.
The *Volk*.
For *Lebensraum*.
For glory.
For a shortcut to Paradise.

To die for whom?

The emperor, the czar,
The king, the country.
For Christ's sake.
Or Allah's
In crusades to rid the world of infidels.
Ours.
Theirs.

Obscenity begets obscenity.
And the orphans cry, "Stop the killing!"
But none pay heed.
They are true believers.
They just rattle their sabers and exclaim,
"*Gott mit uns.*"

While looking more deeply into the strains between the newest group of "strangers" and those who felt themselves to be the entitled owners of their special cultural heritages, I started to do more travel journalism than ever before. In some ways, I suppose, it gave me opportunities to escape temporarily from the intensity of what had become my principal subject of concern, clearly evinced by the telegraphic intent of the poem, "To Die For."

I continued to publish in hardcopy journals, but also began writing for two new web-based magazines, *Travelworld International*, sponsored by the North American Travel Journalists Association (also known as NATJA), and *SoGoNow*, a private enterprise based in Denver.

Toward the end of the decade, perhaps because I was critical of the mixed quality of what was being published in the second webzine, I told the publisher, Will Seccombe, that I didn't want to write for *SoGoNow* anymore unless there was some real editorial control. Then I got my comeuppance. While he didn't say it in so many words, what I heard from Seccombe was something to the effect of "Okay, Mr. Critic, *you* run the magazine." Ever a sucker for a challenge, I accepted the position as editor and held it, writing at least four cover stories and a monthly editor's column, for several years, during which I'm pleased to report we won a number of prizes, including peer-reviewed contests sponsored by NATJA. Unfortunately for me, for the stable of writers, and for our readers, when Seccombe left Denver for a new job in the public sector in Florida, the management of *SoGoNow* suffered and, after a rough several months of trying to get new sponsorship, it ceased posting anything.

Among the domestic venues discussed in stories of mine that appeared in *SoGoNow* in its heyday were a number on large and small New England towns, including our own two bases, Northampton and Wellfleet on Cape Cod; Scottsdale, Arizona and four places in northern New Mexico; Charleston, South Carolina, and nearby Kiawah Island; Sanibel and Clearwater in Florida; Little Rock, Arkansas; Oklahoma City, and Palo Alto. Other stories were datelined Barcelona, Madrid, and various cities in Andalusia; Cancun, Mexico; Belfast in Northern Ireland and Dublin in the Republic of Ireland; Salzburg and Vienna; Gothenburg, Sweden; Bergen, Norway, and many spots in Switzerland and in the Netherlands. I also wrote about doing more cruising in Penobscot Bay on old wooden schooners, spending a week on the Mediterranean on a very modern motor sailing ship, and fourteen days on a modern-day Northwest Passage by riverboat, going from Vienna, up the Danube, the Rhine-Main-Danube Canal then into the Rhine and on to Amsterdam with stops at ten cities along the way.

Three other travel stories—"Chianti Classico," on trekking in Tuscany (first published in *Travelworld International* in 2005), "Autumn in the Alps" (*SoGoNow*, 2007), on hiking on and around the Jungfrau in the Bernese Oberland of Switzerland, and "Panama: A Voyage of Discovery" (*SoGoNow*, 2008) about a week aboard a small, luxury catamaran affording the opportunity to go from Panama City to the islands near the Darien Jungle then through the Panama Canal ending in the town that was once the center of the slave trade in the area, Portobelo, gave me more visibility as a travel journalist, especially when each of the three won first place for the "Best Article Written for the Internet" for the year it was published.

In 2008, Hedy and I traveled to Patagonia, spending four days in Ushuaia, Argentina, the southernmost city in the world, then four more days cruising on the *Via Australis* through the Beagle Channel to Cape Horn and back through the Straits of Magellan to the small Chilean port city of Puntas Arenas. From there we went overland to Puerto Natales, the gateway to the Parque Nacional Torres del Paine, passing miles and miles of open pampas, and arriving at our next base of operations, the well-appointed and well-named three-year-old Remota Resort. Afterwards I wrote several pieces about that experience. One opened with a commentary on the majesty of the Patagonian panorama.

> Places are often best known—and best remembered by a particular image. Sometimes it is a man made structure: the great Mayan pyramid in Chichen Itza in the Yucatan, the Dome of the Rock in Jerusalem, the Taj Mahal, The Eiffel Tower; sometimes it is a creation of nature: the Grand Canyon, the Matterhorn, the Rock of Gibraltar, Yosemite's Half-Dome. Patagonia—that vast land, part Argentinean, part Chilean at the bottom of South America—has its own iconic symbol. It is known as the Torres del Paine, the Towers of Paine, sharp, vertical protrusions among big-shouldered mountains, rising out of rolling pampas. Close up they are awesome, formidable to all but the most intrepid climbers who rate them as very pinnacles of their obsession.[56]

While on that trip, our first to the area, we found out why those particular mountains are so alluring. But we also became enamored of another special feature of that very southern tip of South America, the thousands upon thousands of little human-like birds running around in tuxedos, as if they were getting ready for some gala event. I published a photo-essay about them. The idea came to mind during after-the-fact scanning of my pictures of their antics back in Northampton. I called it "Partying Penguins in Patagonia."

Not all my journalism in that period was graphically descriptive or particularly inventive. Some of it was quite analytical (read: sociological)

---

[56]From "Patagonian Panoramas," *Travelworld International*, January-February, 2010.

and some of it was definitely judgmental (read: critical). Perhaps the sharpest of all was an editorial I wrote in *SoGoNow* about the terrible treatment of marooned passengers by U.S. Airways during the aftermath of a snowstorm in Philadelphia, where nobody, including those with small children and those in wheel-chairs were given any assistance as they (and I) stood in line for nine hours. "Sometimes 'Customer Service' is an Oxymoron" got an even more positive response than some of my prizewinning stories and photographs.

Later in the decade I started cutting back a good deal on quick-take travel writing, preferring to concentrate on bigger projects and longer pieces. I am still at work on one that gets behind the scenes in the travel industry, a sort of sociology of tourism, and another focused on a cultural and commercial venture to bring Americans, Canadians, Australians and others whose ancestors came from Ireland and faux Irish, too, back to the auld sod to join in what was being touted as "The Gathering" in Ireland. I am still doing some writing in the genre, especially for *Travelworld International.* In 2010, the magazine had an incredible facelift by the gifted designer, Jerri Hemsworth, and now rivals the best of the on-line travel magazines.

Sometime around 1988 I had started culling through a number of stories that had appeared in *SoGoNow* and *Travelworld International* along with some published in print magazines and newspapers elsewhere to select a few of my own favorites and several others that seemed especially appropriate for reprinting in my new book, *Guest Appearances and Other Travels in Time and Space.*

Guest Appearances came out on April 4, 2003, the very day a series of special events relating to my pending retirement from Smith College after forty-four years on the faculty. (I would officially retire at the end of June).

Introduced by my long time colleague Mickey Glazer, I gave a sort of valedictory address.

In my talk I looked back and briefly sketched out some of what I have been elaborating upon here. In the audience were hundreds of colleagues, friends from near and far, including some I had known since childhood, and many former students.

After my speech, a debate of sorts took place. Eight of the many I had taught from the 1950s to the 2000s, five during their undergraduate days, two in the Diploma Program, and one from the Salzburg Seminar, were challenged to answer the question: "Do Sociologists Make Better Role Models?" The chair of the panel was one of the best and brightest in Smith's galaxy of stellar alums, my old student and now colleague, Andrea Hairston.

After the panel discussion there was a reception and, that evening, a dinner in the Faculty Club with about 150 guests. Throughout the evening, one person after another stood up to discuss some aspect of my life and work. It was overwhelming.

The next day I tried to put my feelings into words. I called what I wrote, "Panegyrics," a word I learned many years before but never had occasion to use. It refers to public praise. That day it seemed most appropriate.

> At memorial services
> Panegyrics fall on the deaf ears
> Of the deceased,
> And unseen friends
> Fill rows with tears of sadness.
>
> How lucky to be able
> To hear the accolades
> Before it is too late
> To see those who sing
> Their songs of praise—
> And feel their love.
>
> April 6, 2003

A few weeks prior to the last graduation ceremony before I would join the ranks of those kiddingly referred to at Smith by the initials OBND (said to mean "Out But Not Down—though most of us think it really means "Old But Not Dead!"), I had been asked by the director of graduate studies to take her place on the podium reading the names of those in various programs who would be receiving various master's degrees and diplomas in American Studies, the latter being my own special group. I was delighted to do it.

On commencement day, we marched into the Quad in brilliant sunshine then, for the last time before becoming emeritus, I sat down with my colleagues, heard the invocation, observed the presentation of the honorary degrees, listened to addresses by the president of the college and by the president of the senior class, and then observed the long parade of undergraduates individually receive their Bachelor of Arts degrees. While waiting to play my role, I kept ruminating about the days when I was a very junior member of the faculty. I was going to try to convey this here but suddenly remembered that I'd done it—or something similar—before. It was in an essay published as "Vivat Academia, Vivant Professores" in the *Chronicle of Higher Education* in 1986. My musing then had to do with an indoor convocation held at the beginning of the academic year not with commencement which, weather permitting, is always an outdoor event. Still, in many ways, in form and function the two events are pretty much the same.

Every year the college with which I am affiliated has an opening convocation. It is a half-serious, half-frivolous convention. Nearly the entire community gathers to hear an invocation by one of the chaplains, a choral piece or two sung by the world-renowned glee club, and a talk by the president. But there is more to it than this.

We on the faculty march in full academic regalia, a parade of robed, hooded, and sweating figures trying to appear solemn as we process into a hall filled floor and balcony with 2800 whooping, hollering, stomping undergraduates who arrived but minutes before....

With all the craziness, the annual ritual is, as we sociologists say, highly functional. At least that is how I tried to explain the elaborate pomp and curious circumstances to last year's group of foreign graduate students who had come to spend nine months with us studying American society and culture.

Men and women from very different worlds (that year's group was from Austria, Columbia, China, Croatia, France, Germany, India, Italy, Japan, The Netherlands and Switzerland), having been urged to attend all college functions, were astounded by what they observed. They wanted to know its *deeper* meaning.

I told them that the Convocation is like a rite of passage. Homage is paid to the Great Spirit (and the Board of Trustees and other benefactors). Old-timers reassert their fidelity and novices take their vows to Alma Mater. All are caught up in the fervor of the new beginning, in the excitement of being part of a special community. We reverently salute each other and our leader. (Last year a new bit of campus iconography was a ten-foot high banner that hailed Mary, hanging from the front and center of the balcony. It was a greeting to our new president, Mary Maples Dunn.)

As I spoke, I realize that I was not being entirely facetious. American academic rituals are a bit bewildering, even to those of us who engage in them. And truth to speak, while I find them all professionally fascinating, certain ones—like our convocation—are a bit much.

Then why do I participate? I don't have to. The colloquy with the foreign observers made me think about it.

I reflected on how many times in my early days at the college, when I was a very junior faculty member seated in the back row, catching only glimpses of the multitude between the mortar boards of my senior colleagues, shifting uncomfortably on a folding chair, and silently forswearing any future involvement in such a ridiculous activity, something would invariably happen that turned my annoyance into involvement, that would force me to relax and become something more than a reluctant participant. It wasn't the cheers of the throngs or their rhythmic clapping as we marched in, nor was it the words of the speaker. No, something else got me then. It gets me today.

What inevitably triggers the response that finally engages me and many of my colleagues, what proves to be the latent function of all this folderol, is the last number of the program. *Gaudeamus Igitur*. It is hoary to some, schmaltzy to many. And we love it. We especially love the last verse when the tempo picks up, the voices grow louder and the whole place resounds with "*Vivat Academia, Vivant Professors*." It makes *us* feel good.[57]

The fact is that "Vivat Academia" is *our* anthem: "Vivant Professores," *their* tribute. What more can I say?

Although I have been quite detached from the day-to-day activities of Smith since my retirement, I still put on my robe and hood and mortarboard and march, now with other emeriti in what we used to call "the long graying line" in most college ceremonies.

---

[57]"Vivat Academia, Vivant Professores," *Chronicle of Higher Education*, September 3, 1986.

I made the transition from full time teaching and almost full time moonlighting as a lecturer and travel journalist to that envious state of "permanent sabbatical" without too much trauma. Although I immediately missed—and still miss—my regular contact with both undergraduates and those special folks in the graduate program in American Studies I had directed for over thirty years, I found there were many compensating advantages of being an emeritus professor, foremost among them not having to attend meetings or grade papers.

I have heard it said that when professors retire the first September is the hardest. It is probably true. But I was so preoccupied with getting ready for a short-term appointment as a Senior Fulbright Specialist and visiting professor at the University of Vienna in the fall of 2003 that I hardly gave it a thought.

The appointment in Vienna was a kind of icing on the cake of a series of truly rewarding experiences working in Austria, mainly in Salzburg at the Salzburg Global Seminar. My first visit to the country had involved lecturing at several places in Vienna, the University of Graz, and at the University of Salzburg in the early 1980s. While in Salzburg I was invited to stop over and give an informal talk at the Schloss Leopoldskron, a Rococo palace built by the Archbishop of Salzburg in the eighteenth century which had changed hands many times. Between 1918 and the *Anschluss* in 1938, when Nazi Germany annexed Austria and took over the Schloss, it was owned by the great theater impresario, director and actor, Max Reinhardt, an Austrian Jew.

Reinhardt died in exile in the United States in 1943. In 1947, the building, taken back from the Nazis at the end of the war, became the home of the Salzburg Seminar, founded as an international program that would bring students from the United States and several countries in Europe, including those that had just been America's enemy, to study liberal democracy. Over the years, while that core program called American Studies continued, the agenda was expanded to include conferences on all sorts of cultural, political, legal and economic issues—including the one where I had been asked to speak.

After my talk, I met some of the fellows in the program that was going on and was then invited to have a drink in the *Bierstube* down in the cellar of the Schloss. My host, Majid Tehranian, a specialist in peace research then at the University of Hawaii, took me downstairs where we joined two people sitting at a table in animated conversation. One was Israeli, the other Egyptian. I listened to the two of them then entered the discussion. Neither had ever thought he would meet the likes of the person sitting across the table or if he did would have much to say to the other. It turned out that not only had they each had much to say, but there, in the neutral turf of the old Schloss and under the aegis of the Seminar, they discovered how much they had in common.

I was moved by the experience, the setting and the mission of the place, and vowed to figure out a way to become engaged in the work of the seminar myself. It would take me a while—almost twenty years, but when I did, I soon found myself deeply involved in three different Seminar-sponsored programs.

One was the still-ongoing American Studies Program for which I organized and directed two international symposia on the continuing challenge of religious, ethnic and racial pluralism. The first was in 2002 and focused exclusively on the United States; the second, ten years later, was far more comparative, examining the situation in the United States in relation to European debates over immigration and the rising tide of nativism and nationalism. What made the Salzburg seminars on the subject particularly challenging was the great diversity faculty members and the fifty fellows from twenty-five different nations brought to each of them.

My second Salzburg involvement was with its Universities Project, something quite different in character but equally rewarding. My participation was an unexpected opportunity afforded by the request of Smith's then-president, Ruth Simmons, who asked me to take her place at a gathering of American academics and foreign specialists on "global education" at a Dartmouth-organized meeting in Salzburg. I happened to be starting a sabbatical semester and was delighted to accept and to return to that favorite haunt.

The gathering was a bit lopsided. The Dartmouth people seemed to be playing catch-up, having suddenly climbed onto the global education bandwagon, whereas the foreign experts invited to meet with them were all extremely well versed on the subject and were a bit chagrined at the seeming naiveté of some of the members of the Dartmouth team. Most frustrating was the amount of time spent on defining what was meant by the subject which, to me, was mainly about the impact of global capitalism with its attendant cultural and social impact on all aspects of life in many parts of the world. (At the time there was little talk of other related matters, like the challenges to nation-states by movements rekindled by ethnic, tribal and, especially, religious connections. These would come to dominate discussions of globalization a decade later.)

By the second day of the three-day meeting I, too, was getting annoyed. I felt we were spinning our wheels and said so. Several of the delegates who were rectors of universities in different countries applauded my efforts to get things moving as did the Salzburg Seminar's director of education, Jochen Fried. Before the meeting broke up, Jochen, having heard me speak and also learning about my involvement with the Utrecht University honors colleges in the Netherlands, asked if I might be able to return to Salzburg a month later to attend a session of the recently established, Hewlett Foundation-funded "University Project" as a sort of unofficial member of the advisory group that was working with presidents, rectors and other high administrative officials from universities in the Balkans, in Russia and a number of former Soviet republics on the reshaping of higher education. The regular advisers were presidents and former presidents of American, Austrian, British, Czech, Finnish, German, Hungarian, and South African universities and senior administrators from several other countries.

A month after the Dartmouth conference I went back to Salzburg to work with Jochen and his colleagues on the UP board. There were several who had been at the Dartmouth Conference and they warmly welcomed me. Although I had never been a university administrator myself, they felt I could provide a useful perspective on higher education, especially in the liberal arts. I felt very comfortable there and was pleased to be able to make a contribution to their mission and to meet at least ten more times with them and with those they were advising during the remaining five years of the six-year grant. During the course of those many meetings all sorts of serendipitous encounters had fruitful spin-off effects. One of these occurred at a dinner when I sat next to Roger Svensson, a delegate from a government-supported Swedish foundation called STINT, the Swedish acronym for *Stifelsen för Internationalisering av Högre Utbildning och Forskning* (Foundation for International Cooperation in Research and Higher Education).

Svensson introduced himself and asked me where I was from. When I said, "Smith College," he asked if that was one of those liberal arts colleges in New England. I said it was, and he then started to tell me about his new project, conceived of by Sheldon Rothblatt, the Berkeley-based historian of higher education and longtime visitor to Sweden (and now close friend and neighbor, since he now lives half the year in nearby Amherst). Svensson told me that he and Rothblatt were eager to introduce Swedish academics to the best of undergraduate education. They hoped to forge links to several colleges where promising young Swedish professors might spend a semester on campus, attached to departments of their own disciplines, to observe, question, and get a feeling for how such institutions handle curricular issues, subject matter, and interactions with students.

While in no position to commit Smith to join the cause, I promised I would do my best to persuade administrators at the college to do it. When I got back, I immediately spoke to Ruth Simmons and the provost. After I agreed to serve as the liaison with the people in Sweden, to work with those who would come to Smith, and to monitor the program, the plan was approved. Smith became one of the key schools in the project, sponsoring, housing, and welcoming STINT fellows for the rest of the decade and well into the next one.

During that period the college also hosted several meetings of all STINT fellows then in the United States. At those sessions, professors from their host colleges and administrators from their home universities also came to Northampton to participate.

Just as my dinner with Roger Svensson had led to these activities, a meeting in a bar at a local hotel with one of the delegates to the first Smith-STINT meeting, Bengt-Ove Bostrum, vice rector of the University of Göteborg, Sweden's largest, led to another personal opportunity. At the end of the session, Bengt-Ove asked if I would be interested in spending some time at his institution meeting with members of his several faculties and giving some talks about liberal arts education as well as on my own field of research: race, ethnicity, and immigration. Like the character Paladin in *"Have Gun, Will Travel,"* I wanted to say, "Have Notes, Will Lecture," I desisted from blurting that out, but I did agree to go.

Two years later, I too became a STINT-fellow, the foundation underwriting Hedy's and my visit to Göteborg. In the interim Bengt-Ove had learned that Hedy was very much involved in issues relating to higher education and invited us both to speak in several venues, including the wonderful conference center he was developing in an old manor house. We met a number of fascinating people in the arts, humanities and social sciences, took a side trip to speak at the new Karlstad University hosted by a mathematician who had come to Smith as one of our STINT fellows, and developed a lasting friendship with Bengt-Ove and his wife. In every respect this new relationship was most positive and rewarding.

Once back home we learned from Bengt-Ove that while some of his colleagues were interested in the idea of the liberal arts approach to undergraduate education, most remained resistant to the idea of making significant changes in their institution or in many of its departments. This only made me more eager to continue on what was becoming a mission of my own: to expand the Dutch model of starting honors colleges within major universities as a way of introducing the best of our system abroad.

Numerous aspects of higher education had always intrigued me but one that I knew little about was the community college system. As the grant for Salzburg Seminar's University Project wound down, Jochen Fried started a new program and asked me to join him. Entirely different from anything else the Salzburg Seminar had done, and different from anything I had done, Jochen's plan was to bring selected community college students from the United States to the Schloss Leopoldskron for intensive weeks of studying "global citizenship."

I thought it was an intriguing but crazy idea. Imaginative, to be sure, but I wondered who would pay the high cost of such a venture; surely not the students who were among the most financially limited of those in any colleges in America. And even if ways were found to fund the project, I wondered how much those enrolled could get out of a program lasting only a week, no matter how intensive the curriculum would be. I needn't have worried. Backers were found, the program was launched, the students came, and Jochen was to be proven a most prophetic innovator. Hedy and I saw this up close when at Jochen's invitation, we joined the original faculty the first year. We have taught in one or two sessions every year since the program's inception. And there have now been almost sixty sessions.

Many students come to Salzburg from the multiple campuses of Miami-Dade Community College and the community colleges of the City University of New York, among the first two systems supporting what became known as the International Study Program or ISP (and, as of 2013, the Global Citizenship Program). Other colleges from Chicago to Texas to Kentucky—signed on as did several four-year institutions, most notably San Jose State University and a private, Jesuit school, the University of San Francisco. Most years there are four student sessions, one each for Miami-Dade and for the CUNY group, including Bronx Community College, the Borough of Manhattan Community College, Queensborough, Hostos, and, for a time, John Jay. The other sessions are more mixed.

The curriculum varies. Sometimes certain themes are set for a particular group, often depending on which American and European faculty members are available to teach in what is a very intense agenda of lectures, working groups, visits to the nearby former concentration camp at Dachau followed by discussions relating to that experience, and presentations by the members of each student contingent. Heady stuff, but, as we learned, it has an enormous payoff, for the vast majority of those who become student fellows in Salzburg go on to four-year colleges and universities and sometimes beyond. Each year we meet students we knew in Salzburg on the campuses of Smith and Stanford, the two campuses where we still spend most of our time while in the States.

One personal result of our early involvement with the ISP was the decision to give most of the books in my professional library dealing with race and ethnicity to the Bronx Community College, which in turn, established a Center for Tolerance and Understanding, to which others have also contributed. The Center continues to flourish.

I have stayed in touch with the faculty of the Bronx Community College and have recently worked with them to obtain a federal grant to introduce the curriculum that Jochen Fried, David Goldman, and Astrid Schroeder in Salzburg, and Andrew Rowan and others at BCC have developed to introduce in selected community colleges around the United States.

As mentioned early, several years after my appointment at the University of Vienna, I was once again invited to be a senior Fulbright specialist and visiting professor. This time it was in the Netherlands, at the Roosevelt Academy in Middleburg, located in the southwest corner of the country, the second international honors college attached to Utrecht University.

It was a great experience not only to be teaching at an institution with which I had been affiliated since its beginning, but to live with my Dutch wife for an extended period on Dutch soil.

We had a wonderful apartment above Galerie T, one of the finest art galleries in the country, and became good friends with Lia and Bert Hector, the owners. I often pause to look up at a wonderful acrylic painting on the wall of my study that Hedy gave me as a memento of our stay. Artist Maria Megen's broad brushstrokes in shades of red, yellow, green and stark white, while very modern in execution, it is still a very identifiable Dutch scene by the artist.

When I first visited the Dutch province of Zeeland where Middelburg is located, I was struck by how similar it seemed to Cape Cod. I was also taken by some important differences. In a short piece about these impressions, I began by noting that the Cape is a landmass flanked by ocean and bay, covered with scrub oaks and pines, lined with miles and miles of pristine beaches and fishing villages that have become resort towns each with its yacht harbors and boat yards, fish markets and flea markets, art galleries and souvenir shops, great restaurants and clam shacks. Locals, summer people, even day-trippers think there is nothing in the world quite like it. I went on to say:

> Cape Codders traveling to the southwest province of The Nether-
> lands, known as Zeeland, might be surprised to find there is such a
> place. The beaches and dunes, boat harbors and bike paths are so
> similar that it is hard to believe you are on the others side of the ocean.
> Aptly named Zeeland (Dutch for sea-land), like Cape Cod, it has
> a seaside character, a rich local culture, and an aura all its own, attract-
> ing many who own summer homes and many renters and day-trip-
> pers. Like the Cape, tourism is a critical aspect of the economy. But a
> stay of just a few days, even a few minutes, will open the eyes to things
> we would never associate with Barnstable County, like wooden shoes
> and cannabis "starter-kits" sold in open markets....[58]

Another place where I enjoyed the benefits of Fulbright-like bina-tional cooperation was Sarajevo, Bosnia-Herzegovina. My visits there were facilitated by a five-year State Department grant obtained by Jim Hicks, my successor as director of the American Studies Diploma Pro-gram at Smith. He hoped to establish a relationship between the college and the University of Sarajevo where he had spent a year on a Fulbright grant immediately after the end of the recent Balkan wars in the 1990s. I had been to Croatia, Serbia, and Slovenia, other states of the former Yugoslavia before the wars broke out, but had never been to Bosnia. The opportunity came soon after the cooperative program began.

Along with several other colleagues from our side, I went over to lecture at the University of Sarajevo and the new International Univer-sity of Sarajevo, established by Turkish backers, then, a few years later, returned to participate in a symposium, *Ex Uno Plures: American Studies*

---

[58]"A Dutch Treat for Cape Cod Lovers," *SoGoNow.com*, March 2007.

in the Balkans. Both trips allowed me enough free time to do my own exploring of a city that, like Cordoba in Spain and Thessaloniki in Greece, had long been of interest to me as a student of ethnic and religious pluralism who was always looking for examples of long-time inter-group comity among Christians, Muslims, and Jews.

Upon my return from my first visit I wrote a brief commentary for my Editor's Column in *SoGoNow.*

> I recently spent some time in Sarajevo. Within a few days there my mind and digital camera began to be filled with impressions. Stone bridges and stately minarets. Ancient cemeteries and leafy parkways. High-rise office towers and run-down neighborhoods. And incessant traffic. Downtown there are open-air coffee houses and internet cafes, smart boutiques, jewelry shops and carpet bazaars along a crowded walking street that begins at a building housing an eternal flame, a memorial to those who perished in World War II. On that promenade many women are garbed in headscarves and long dresses and others wear mini-skirts and sexy boots; all seem to be using mobile phones. There are movie theaters and ice cream buffets and bookstores advertising Dan Brown's *DaVinci Code* in Serbo-Croatian (Den Braun, *Da Vincijev kød*) and English volumes on recent Bosnian history.
>
> Striking evidence of that recent history, of a city—and a people— under siege, is also a part of the contemporary scene. Hulks of burned out houses still exist; so do pock-marked walls and "Wanted for Murder" broadsides with caricature pictures of the Bosnian Serb leader Radovan Karadzic and the Serb General Ratko Mladic held responsible for the brutality. Used 50 millimeter and larger shell cases are sold everywhere as mementos of the struggle, some turned into ballpoint pens or flower vases. They are sold as souvenirs alongside locally made copper coffee pots and cups.
>
> Ten years after the ceasefire there still are many such grim reminders of the war.
>
> But it is also clear that Sarajevo, the capital city of the newly independent state of Bosnia and Herzegovina, known locally as BiH, is on the slow road to recovery. This involves reuniting of families torn asunder by the conflict and the return of properties abandoned by fleeing refugees and appropriated by hostile forces. It involves the rebuilding of homes and shops and public buildings, such as the still-

standing but completely-gutted National Library where two million books were destroyed.

In parliament members debate the problems of trying to live within and go beyond the Dayton Accords. Everywhere there are citizens working hard to reclaim what had long been Sarajevo's claim to fame: its viability as a plural community....

It was not long ago that the newspapers and television screens were filled with stories of the break-up of Yugoslavia and of fighting between and within various communities in the former federation. Yet, while the federation was disassembling as one republic after another sought independence from Belgrade's hegemony, and while outlying parts of Bosnia were also becoming bitterly contested areas, until 1992 in Sarajevo at least, Catholic Croats, Orthodox Serbs, the few Jews who had survived the Holocaust, and the Muslim majority were still living together in relative peace, if not total harmony.

On April 6, 1992, the European Community and much of the rest of the world recognized Bosnia as an independent state. At the time, its principal city, already suffering outbreaks of violence, still reflected and often celebrated the variety of cultures in its centuries-old churches, synagogues and mosques; its inviting Turkish, imposing Austro-Hungarian, stark Communist, and international-modern architecture; its easternness and its westernness. But embers of distrust, fed by poisonous propaganda highlighting past conflicts over territory, religion, and political ideology, and the constant news of what was happening not only in Croatia and Serbia but within Bosnia itself—in Banja Luka and even nearer Mostar—was about to burst into a major conflagration. Sarajevo, the Olympic City, widely publicized as representing the confluence of cultures, the place where diversity meant strength, was besieged by the Bosnia Serb Army and a number of irregulars clearly supported by Belgrade. The encircled city became the site and symbol of disillusionment, disunification and destruction—and of courageous resistance, too.

An uneasy peace finally came in the still-controversial agreement in Dayton, Ohio, and signed by all parties to the conflict in Paris in November 1995. It has been struggling to come to terms with the terms and the meaning of the Dayton Accords ever since. Indeed, as recently as April 26, 2006, the first major attempt to revise them failed when the various factions in the Bosnian parliament refused to endorse recommended constitutional changes....

Speaking with members of the diplomatic community, university professors, government officials, shopkeepers and students, I learned that the wounds are deep and very visceral. One person after another told me of how differences of background and religion had been exploited, and how much economic competition and manipulation—subjects rarely mentioned in the western press—played a key role in exacerbating the tensions. They told me of fratricidal battles between long time friends and neighbors. They spoke of the reluctance of the great powers to intercede until it was almost too late. Said one new friend, "Few outside the area understood the complexity of the region's history and the real causes of the conflicts. They relied too much on the 'they-are-all-corrupt' sentiment imperiously expressed in Robert Kaplan's widely-read best-seller, *Balkan Ghosts*."

As I sat with a colleague from the University of Sarajevo in the midst of the old Jewish cemetery high above the city center, a sacred place with age-old stone slabs and more recent somber tributes to those who died in the Holocaust, I noted that many of the monuments were ravaged by shell holes. She explained that this was a favored place used by Serb forces to fire down on those below. It is a battle zone in the land of the dead.

Memories of the siege and the struggle to survive will not be easily overcome. Nevertheless, there is a feeling in the air—supported by sentiments most often expressed by young people, that, like the Phoenix, Sarajevo will arise from its ashes, reaching an uneasy entente among the various factions or at least containing centrifugal forces driven by kinship and ethnocentrism, reclaiming its special character and recapturing the spirit conveyed to the world just prior to the Winter Olympics of 1984, as a cross roads of civilization, a society where the whole aspires to be greater than the sum of its parts.

Good will and a readiness to think, act, and live in a spirit of reconciliation are clearly necessary, but they are not sufficient. Those seemingly most sensitive to the realities on the ground claim that economic growth is essential for sustaining hopes of political stability and inter-group comity. And even the casual observer notes there is little question but that such a possibility would be greatly enhanced by an infusion of interest and support from outsiders: business people, journalists, and travelers interested in getting to know a place that was so recently but a dateline on the evening news.

Sarajevo ought to become a destination for tourists as well. Those who go there will find what I have found, a place of familiar sights and smells that somehow merge into a new form, one that combines many characteristics of more popular and familiar destinations like Istanbul in the east and Vienna in the west. Without being overly optimistic, I believe that for all its suffering—or perhaps because of it, Sarajevo might be the city that will once again belie the wide-spread idea that in today's world a clash of civilizations is inevitable.[59]

The decade 2000–2010, filled with a myriad of experiences evoking every sort of emotion, had begun with a medical crisis in our family, Hedy's bout with breast cancer. Then there was my retirement, our involvement in all sorts of overseas activities, and a good deal of researching, reflecting, writing, and rewriting, ending with some far less scary but troubling medical matters of my own: five operations for glaucoma, another for a benign prostate problem, and a broken ankle on New Year's eve, 2009. I was never inclined to discuss my own health problems, but I have to say it was something that I thought a good deal about after turning seventy in 2003. I finally wrote about the subject in a story published in *Hampshire Life*.

Everybody who knows me knows I am a compulsive old jock. Every day for decades I have tried to keep fit by running or swimming or biking long distances. I watch my diet to control my weight. Even when I am out of town or overseas, I keep up my routine. Perhaps I should say "kept up" because, ever since I joined the ranks of the septuagenarians, I have been plagued by a number of medical problems, most which I had thought my daily regimen would stave off.

In my 70th year, the year of my retirement after nearly a half-century of college teaching, I began to listen to what my body was telling me. I also listened to my friends. Workout nuts like me, occasional exercisers, and couch potato-types, it didn't matter; they all seemed to have some sort of malady (often more than one). I know this because they shared their complaints and experiences with me and everyone else within earshot. And, I confess, I started doing the same.

"Yes, glaucoma. Unfortunately I know all about it. I just had surgery to correct it."

"The heart. Yep. He had a triple by-pass but seems to be thriving."

"No, not her hips, her knees. Both of them at the same time, too.

Unlike those earlier times, when somebody said, "How are you?"

---

[59]"Impressions of Sarajevo Today," *SoGoNow*, November 3, 2006.

the expression was taken as a simple, rhetorical salutation to be responded to with a perfunctory "Fine," often with the tag-line "And how are you?" and then, almost without skipping a beat, a move to other matters.

Today, we seniors take it as a real question and answer with a candor that evokes one of two almost predictable responses (usually depending on the age of the asker): a sympathetic nod only meekly masking a "Sorry-I-asked expression"—most notable in the responses of those younger than we; and a quid-pro-quo litany of counter claims from our peers and our elders. Not a few of the organ recitals are worthy of a Mel Brooks parody. Sounding like the 2000-year-old man, one hears all sorts of things about "being all right, except for..." liver problems and kidney problems and prostate problems. And we wince as one or another of the complaints hits pretty close to home.

Now to be sure, that is not all we talk about. Once the "How ya doin'?" and the medical colloquies are over, we move to other topics: books, films and film reviews, the state of the economy, politics, and recent and pending travel. And not surprisingly, we gossip about mutual friends, which, too frequently, bring us full circle. It doesn't take more than a word or two: "His heart."

Fifty years ago when I was a beginning graduate student at Cornell, I had a roommate, Arthur Siegel, who was a former editor of *The Daily Orange*, the newspaper of our undergraduate alma mater, Syracuse University. He was a fine and entrepreneurial writer with a wicked sense of humor. He was also a bit of a hypochondriac.

One day we were sitting on an off-campus park bench, surreptitiously listening to a bunch of old folks discussing their medical problems. On the way back to our digs, with eyes bright and a wry smile, he told me he had a great idea. He was going to start an unprecedented venture, a "Symptom-of-the-Month Club."

He stayed up for several nights pounding away on an old Royal typewriter, writing mock copy for a promotional brochure in which his charter subscribers were to be offered a free appendectomy or tonsillectomy (today it might be a hip replacement or tummy tuck) in return for a promise to order at least three diseases a year.

Somehow, what was hilarious back in 1954, isn't so funny these days. Maybe it is because so many of us have joined Arthur's club without even having signed up.

"And how are *you*?"[60]

---

[60]"Organ Recitals," *Hampshire Life*, October 22, 2004.

Voor
Joden verboden

DE PROCUREUR-GENERAAL
FUNGEEREND GEWESTELIJK
DIRECTEUR VAN POLITIE
FEITSMA

Seat dedicated in honor of
Rosa Parks
1913 - 2005

Este asiento está dedicado en honor de Rosa Parks

NO MAS MUERTES EN LA FRONTER
NINGUN SER HUMANO ES ILEGA

VII

The 2010s: Miles to Go...

IN 2010 MY SECOND TRAVEL BOOK, *WITH FEW RESERVATIONS*, was published. A compilation of stories about places visited and written about mostly in the years since my retirement. Around the time it was released, following a five-year hiatus from almost constant book reviewing, I agreed to write several review essays on two themes that had long been central to my concerns: race and social class in America. Two of these appeared in the journal, *Social Science and Modern Society*; the other in *Contemporary Sociology*. The first really brought me back to some of my earliest work. It was centered on an excellent book, *Freedom is Not Enough*, by the Brown University historian James T. Patterson on Daniel Patrick Moynihan's controversial report, "The Negro Family: A Case for National Action," which had come out nearly fifty years before and is still the subject of considerable debate.

From the time the report was published I felt it had been unfairly received, especially by many who would have benefited from its recommendations. To keep the issue alive, I had reprinted the entire "Moynihan Report" and several critiques of it in the second volume of *Americans from Africa*. To me—and now to Patterson—it was always a case of killing the messenger. Here is how he—and I—saw it in 2010 and the context of the longevity of the crisis Moynihan wrote about so long ago.

On August 15, 2010, *The New York Times* published a lengthy article on a just-released report describing the persisting test score disparities between high-achieving white and Asian students and lower-scoring Latinos and African Americans in the city's schools. "Experts have many theories," wrote Sharon Otterman and Robert Gebeloff, "but no clear answers about why national progress on closing the gap has slowed." Among their suppositions are "the worsening economic conditions for poor families and an increase in fatherless black households, social factors that interfere with the students' educational progress."

Déjà vu?

While many things have changed in relations between whites and non-white minorities and within the Latino and African-American communities themselves, certain problems persist in New York and other large urban areas—as they have for many, many decades.

In the late summer of 1964, the late Daniel Patrick Moynihan, then working as a high-ranking government researcher in the administration of Lyndon Johnson, sent a brief message to his boss, Willard Wirtz, U.S. Secretary of Labor. In it he stated: "It is my hunch that the American public is ready to face up to the proposition that unemployment is destroying the Negro family structure."

He was wrong. Few members of the public and fewer leaders were ready or willing to address the matter.

The fate of a now-famous (some would say infamous) report in which Moynihan fleshed out his arguments is a classic case of trying to kill the messenger carrying bad news. In its 53 pages, the author described continued discrimination at almost every level of society, a dearth of jobs, a welfare system that was out of whack, and the relationship of these matters to a crisis in the family life of poor African Americans. It was assumed that a plan for remediation would come later from what Moynihan, the Department of Labor, Congress, and the president—all claiming to be committed to righting egregious historic wrongs—would design. The deliberations were scheduled to begin with a conference, "To Fulfill These Rights," called by President Johnson himself.

It was not to be.

At the time the report was first released and then attacked, I thought that few people—including some of Moynihan's most vocal detractors—ever read the document very thoroughly, if at all. Instead, upon hearing about the report, many immediately rushed to judge it. They misconstrued the intention of the exercise, maligned its author, and ignored its central message. Thus, they played a major part in curtailing a truly open debate about the multiple results of institutionalized inequality, including those relating to the fragility of families under stress, and about the double role black women often had to play as mother and breadwinning head-of-household, described in the short-hand of social scientists as "the Negro matriarchy."

This missed opportunity is a central theme of prize-winning historian James T. Patterson's comprehensive new book, *Freedom is Not Enough*. There he reminds us that what quickly became known as the "Moynihan Report" (its official title was *The Negro Family: A Case for National Action*) was all but stillborn and then ignominiously buried with scornful condemnation of outsiders who blamed victims for their dire straits.

Early in his book Patterson quotes from the part of the report where Moynihan states his thesis: "...the principal effect of exploitation, discrimination, poverty, and unemployment on the Negro community has been a profound weakening of the Negro family structure....The process has reached the point where the problem is feeding on itself—the situation is getting *worse* not better." He notes that, in preparing the document, Moynihan, his colleague, Paul Barton, and others on the staff relied heavily on a number of empirical investigations, both qualitative and quantitative, that had been carried out by black scholars, northern and southern over more than half a century. These began with W.E.B. DuBois's early study, *The Philadelphia Negro* (1899), and the work of such African-American social scientists as Charles Johnson, Horace Cayton, St. Clair Drake, Hylan Lewis, Allison Davis and, perhaps most influentially, E. Franklin Frazier, author of *The Negro Family in Chicago* (1932), *The Negro Family in the United States* (1939), and *Black Bourgeoisie* (1955). Every one of those writers—and many others—commented on family problems, often referring to female-headed households and describing the struggles of young black males. The research of white psychologists, economists, anthropologists, historians and sociologists had come to similar conclusions. Notable were the works of John Dollard, Gunnar Myrdal, Hortense Powdermaker, Stanley Elkins, and Nathan Glazer.

Members of the various academic cohorts were not alone in their contentions. Some black literary giants like James Baldwin and a number of political leaders also raised the issue of the crisis in the Negro family, including such prominent figures as Martin Luther King, Bayard Rustin, A. Philip Randolph, and Malcolm X.

Malcolm X is remembered for many things, none more important than his statement, "The worst crime the white man has committed is to teach us to hate ourselves." And it is not surprising that those who sought to alter the situation all agreed that it was essential to address the impact of widespread institutional discrimination and to change negative images of those who were being left behind. They especially emphasized the need to find ways to counter the internalization of disgrace suffered by too many African-American children, especially males, growing up deprived of positive role models. Whether stated in so many words or not, it was clear that they felt there was a pernicious sickness pervading the ghettos: "*a tangle of pathology.*"

For the record it should be noted that it was that single straightforward phrase, as related to this social sickness and used by Moynihan, that many found most offensive. The troublesome label, "a tangle of pathology," was not his. It was borrowed directly from the black psychologist Kenneth Clark's, *Dark Ghetto* (1965), a book whose author had relied on many of the very same sources cited by Moynihan. But those four words, when expressed by Pat Moynihan, perhaps more than any others, led to his being labeled a naive and insensitive outsider—and worse.

In retrospect, it is evident that a number of factors may have contributed to the way the report was received, not least the times themselves. In the mid-1960s the entire country was in the throes of a dramatic sea change on many fronts. Moynihan's initial memo was sent off within months of the heady days of August 1963, the time the March on Washington for Jobs and Freedom, the occasion when Martin Luther King, Jr. gave his memorable "I Have a Dream" speech.

In his presidential inaugural address on January 8, 1964, Lyndon Johnson, doubtlessly inspired by Franklin Roosevelt, declared a "War on Poverty" and outlined measures that promised assistance to those left behind. That initiative, followed by the passage of the monumental Civil Rights Act of 1964 and the Voting Rights Act of 1965, seemed to augur a new birth of freedom. But many, including Pat Moynihan, knew that "freedom was not enough."

Already rent with mounting strains between traditional integrationists and those wanting a more aggressive and more "Afrocentric" approach, the civil rights movement and the larger society soon suffered a major breakdown. It was a time when white liberals were being eased or pushed from positions of leadership, and when it was said, in the words of Ron Karenga, "Face it, there are three kinds of people in this country, white people, black people and Negroes. Negroes are black people who act like white people."

Karenga's not-so-coded message says a great deal about why Moynihan's words were so hard for many black academics, politicians and community leaders to acknowledge, even if they accepted his basic premises. And this is to say nothing of their white liberal counterparts who had become super-sensitive to the accusation that they were a major part of the problem—perhaps even more than the real bigots—and certainly not part of the solution. David Riesman tersely commented on the reaction of many who had become principal targets of the ire of angry African Americans. "To understand black narcissism is one thing, but to feed it in a frenzy of white masochism is something else." And he was right. But instead of staying the course, many whites backed away from the fray itself.

This was also a time when attention and funds were already being shifted from the War on Poverty to the one in Southeast Asia. And to make matters worse, the onset of urban rioting in a number of cities further dimmed prospects for change instead of serving as an urgent bellwether.

The din of charges and countercharges filled the streets, the college campuses, the airwaves, and the halls of Congress. The President and his minions began to back away from earlier promises, further exacerbating the tensions and the search for scapegoats.

Moynihan, never a shrinking violet, condemned the most militant advocates of Black Power and what he called their "frenzy of arrogance and nihilism." These words, like so many others he used (such as "benign neglect," by which his defenders said he meant, "Let's cool the temperature, stop talking so much, and start acting") served only to fan the rhetorical flames of those out to discredit the gloomy report and its author.

Two years after the release of the report, Lee Rainwater and William Yancey published a book, *The Moynihan Report and the Politics of Controversy.* Others followed with assessments of their own. Patterson details the critiques of some of them, especially those of Christopher Jencks, Herbert Gans, William Ryan, Garry Wills and Peter Steinfels. These writers all claimed or implied that Moynihan gave support, if not explicitly, then implicitly, to those who saw the problem as a clear example of the inability of blacks to get their own houses in order, thereby being largely responsible for their enduring inferior position. Even sharper criticisms were put forth by other academics, including Carol Stack, a white anthropologist, Herbert Gutman, a white historian, and a number of black social scientists, including Benjamin

Payton, Andrew Billingsley, John Blassingame and Joyce Ladner. Most of those in the latter group wrote of the remarkable 'resilience' of the black family as an institution—first in slavery, then in freedom—and expressed the view that it was being discredited, even dishonored, by Moynihan's emphasis on its "pathology."

To say that no one stood up for Moynihan would be an overstatement. Patterson writes how, in the immediate aftermath of the controversy about the report and then sporadically over the next three decades, Moynihan's message would be restated and defended by a rather catholic cadre of supporters, including James Q. Wilson, Thomas Pettigrew, Charles Silberman, Reinhold Niebuhr, and James Coleman and, in time, by such influential blacks as activist Benjamin Hooks of the NAACP, commissioner and later chair of the U.S. Civil Rights Commission, Mary Berry, economist Glenn Loury, and sociologists William Julius Wilson and Orlando Patterson. They felt (and many still feel) that Moynihan's report was hardly a *noblesse oblige* exercise by an uninformed do-gooder. It was, instead, a candid description of an attempt to diagnose one of the most significant results of the increasingly anomic conditions that pervaded ghetto-areas, the sort of persisting white-black gulf highlighted by aforementioned recent story in the *New York Times* and also what William Julius Wilson would later identify as the widening gap in Black America, a growing chasm between upwardly mobile, well-educated African Americans and those who were left behind, variously referred to as 'the underclass' and 'the ghetto-poor.'

Like the mysterious corpse that wouldn't die, in recent years the Moynihan argument has had a sort of resurrection, a second life. In an oft-quoted statement, Moynihan once said, "Everyone is entitled to his own opinion, but not his own facts." Now those same facts have become a principal subject of discussion in a number of conferences of black leaders, some sponsored by major African-American organizations that had long been critical of Moynihan's perspective. Even some of those who long saw him as a *bête blanche*, grudgingly began to admit that his report should never have been treated the way it was. His thesis has become a central theme in books and speeches by such influential figures as Bill Cosby, Alvin Poussaint, Al Sharpton, and the current President of the United States, who proudly identifies himself as an African American.

While acknowledging that things have changed quite dramatically in terms of access to opportunity, all have said that many inner-city blacks, crippled by poverty, violence, and dysfunctional families, are still unable to cross the threshold. What is striking is the admission that, while it is necessary to recognize that racism is still a problem, I agree with Patterson that it alone is not sufficient to explain the continuing alienation of so many, thoughts clearly expressed by Barack Obama himself.

Patterson notes that in *The Audacity of Hope* (2006), written by the President while he was still a senator, Obama "made a point of reminding people of Moynihan's prescient warnings about the rise of out-of-wedlock pregnancy among the black poor, deploring what he called 'the casualness toward sex and child-rearing among black men that renders black children more vulnerable—for which there is no excuse.'" In the eleventh and final chapter of *Freedom is Not Enough*, its author also points to the fact that, so far, President Obama has done little to address this persisting case for national action....[61]

I ended my essay with some personal observations about the writer of the "Moynihan Report."

Moynihan was never a radical, though some of his ideas regarding such matters as a negative income tax led to many to see him as a closet socialist. To me, he was more a living oxymoron, at once a liberal-pragmatist and a neo-conservative, a man who was difficult to pigeonhole but rather easy to caricature.

He was one of a kind: a tall, red-faced, white-haired, tweedy and somewhat foppish Irish-American with a gift for gab and a penchant for hyperbole (he was not raised in Hell's Kitchen, as he sometimes claimed). Often portrayed as a garrulous, oversized leprechaun who suffered from the malady known as foot-in-mouth disease, he was also seen as a pixyish politician, a donnish legislator, and as a canny mediator. Last but not least, he was the quintessential outsider-within. This last characterization is my own. It is definable as one who peers into closed rooms and not only knows but understands what he sees. The problem is that insiders resent it when such a trespasser then turns what he learns into an exposé.[62]

---

[61]James T. Patterson's "Freedom Is Not Enough: The Moynihan Report and America's Struggle Over Black Family Life," *Social Science and Modern Society*, March-April (2011), 361–366.
[62]Ibid., 366.

Reading Patterson's book and rereading Moynihan's original report reminded me of something I'd written many years earlier. It was an attempt to offer three very different perspectives on race relations in the United States, circa 1975, on the very eve of the country's bicentenary. It was published as an addendum of sorts in what became a college-level version of the textbook mentioned earlier, the one I wrote with my co-authors, Mickey and Penina Glazer.

Instead of stating the different perspectives one by one, I made up a "trialogue," a discussion among three faux sociologists who were asked to join Tom Kelly, on his television panel, *Weekly Forum*. I began with Kelly introducing his guests, "all noted for their work on American society and culture." The first was Professor Cyrus Wyckham, teacher at "Warren University" in Washington, D.C. A specialist in political sociology, Wyckham, I said, had recently published a two-volume work, *Freedom and Control: The American Contradiction*. The second was Janice Fischer, professor of sociology at "Blaine College" who had "written extensively on American social structure" and was well known for her book, *Meritocracy and Democracy: A Functionalist's Analysis*. And the third was Professor Terry Jordan, a sociologist on the staff of "St. George University." Also a teacher of courses on American social structure, with an emphasis on the American people themselves, she was, I said, the author *of Peasants to Parvenus* and *The Plural Society*.

The interviewer then asks each to state his or her positions, beginning with Professor Fischer. Here is some of what I imagined they said:

Fischer: I see American society as a functioning system whose mechanisms are constantly at work trying to solve major social issues. I should stress that all sociologists know how problematic it is to maintain the social order. There are constantly new members to be socialized, deviant behavior to be controlled, tensions to be managed, needs to be met, decisions to be made, resources to be allocated, physical and social environments to be adapted to. This is such a complicated undertaking that it is impressive that any modern industrial society can continue functioning at all while providing the freedom to its members that ours does. It can only do so if there is substantial agreement on basic values and structural arrangements to support them.

The U.S. is effectively held together by such cultural and social factors.

The Founding Fathers created a unique set of social institutions whose norms underscored the values they felt were pertinent in achieving what sociologist Seymour Martin Lipset has called "The First New Nation"….What was created was a system, or series of systems, designed to carry out both lofty and mundane goals. While few of the founders anticipated the changes that would affect the course of national development—the influx of millions of immigrants, the challenge to the practice of involuntary servitude, the problems of urbanization and industrialization—they did provide the cement in the mosaic that was to become the modern United States. That cement—the core values of the society—has been amazingly resilient.

A society must be judged by the extent to which it establishes and maintains a meaningful equilibrium among its various parts. This depends in large measure on a general agreement about what the priorities should be and how to achieve them. In judging American society, I would say that the structures have served their functions well and that we have an extraordinarily stable society. [She then offers several concrete examples – including the stability of the society in the face of President Kennedy's assassination and Nixon's forced resignation and ends her "opening" with the following statement]:

In contrast to some of my colleagues, I would argue that the persistence of "the American Way" is based far more on the will of the people, the masses of people, than on pressures by some powerful elite of bankers, politicians, and military leaders. We can test that assumption by asking the people their views. The majority will agree with my own that, by and large, we are doing very well.

Moderator: Professor Fischer has argued that this country is basically sound, that the American system, for all its problems, works. What do you say, Professor Wyckham?

Wyckham: Professor Fischer is what we sociologists call a functionalist. To me functionalism avoids asking certain very serious questions. I see society—any society—from a rather different point of view. Take our Bicentennial. Every sociologist knows that such events are patriotic rituals. Traditional societies reaffirm their members' values and their group solidarity at annual group rites and festivals. Lately, worried about our future, Americans have been subject to a bombardment of rhetoric about our glorious past and our allegedly stable society. Tonight I'd like to introduce another function to this ritual—

one that is perhaps more appropriate. I'd like to propose a little more introspection in confronting the overwhelming problems that surround us. Frankly, I think the issue is one of survival, and I want to point to the critical problems that may spell our decline.

The first is racial violence. Despite the Supreme Court decision in 1954 ordering desegregation of public schools and despite the vast civil rights movement of the 1960s, I see little evidence that our racial problems can be solved—or even that the system is working toward solving them. We are faced with the widespread belief that busing children from black ghettos to decent white schools leads to violence, riots, and hatred, and further encourages the white exodus to the suburbs. Many blacks are still confined to the decaying centers of cities and are increasingly alienated. They hold little hope of improving their lot. The same is true of millions of Puerto Ricans, Chicanos and Native Americans. This despair has brought us the highest rate of violent crime in the history of the nation—from terror in city subways to gun battles on Indian reservations. Perhaps even worse is the hopelessness and apathy that pervade broken neighborhoods and families.

I think we have neither the will nor the way to solve the problems of race, urban decay, and national violence. As a sociologist I would say that the social structure inhibits meaningful change. The socialization process transmits the beliefs and values of the past to the social participants of the future. This is true in any society. It means that the social structure perpetuates itself. Unfortunately, the values that most members of our society hold do not encourage them to make sacrifices to achieve equality or justice—or even support the Bill of Rights. The results of some studies show that many people rejected the contents in the Bill of Rights when they appeared, reworded, on a questionnaire.

Our society is dominated by the profit motive. Great power is concentrated in the hands of corporations and their military and political allies. It may be in their interest to overthrow unfriendly governments in foreign countries, but it isn't in their interest to increase the power and opportunities available to poor people here or abroad.

Most of the rest of us are trapped by our commitment to the system's values and rules. [He then offers several examples of his own before continuing.] Even among those who see poverty as a manifestation of the stratification of our society, rather than the fault of the poor, few blame those in power for this structural inequality. We accept the system, so we go on defending the interests of the powerful against the weak.

...We used to worry about destroying ourselves through a nuclear holocaust. That's still a possibility, but I think we are more in danger of choking ourselves to death from smog, poisoning ourselves from cancer-producing materials in the water supply, or spraying ourselves to death with aerosol cans. Cigarette companies don't care about lung cancer. They care about profits. Oil companies have used the oil shortage to raise prices and profit margins and to lobby for tax benefits and unrestrained offshore drilling. They don't care about the rest of society. Profit is the name of their game. I'll close by saying the problems are getting worse—and bigger. Unfortunately, the solutions are not keeping pace.

Moderator: You sociologists differ as much in your interpretations of modern American society as the historians on last week's program did in their view of its past. Professor Wyckham's society is very different from Professor Fischer's, wouldn't you say so, Professor Jordan.

Jordan: Frankly, no. Their differences represent two basic perspectives on society that sociologists have debated for years. To my way of thinking, my two colleagues would look at any society from either a "consensus" or a "conflict" view. No, they are not looking at different societies; they're looking at this country from different angles and theoretical—and political—positions.

To me the United States is not so easily praised or damned. It is a tension-ridden social system, and in those tensions lay both its promises and its problems. This has been true for a long time. The United States is a vast land. It is many peoples with many voices. It is a nation of contradictions. It is held together by powerful interests that often appear more concerned with the private good than with the public welfare. But it is also a place where the dream of mobility has proved to be more than a slogan, more than a catch phrase. It is also a society that can and has changed.

Changes in American society have rarely come about through the good will of those in power. But they have occurred. The pressure of the people has been the primary motivating force. What was not accomplished at the ballot box was often accomplished in the streets. Voices in the wilderness—labor agitators, civil rights demonstrators, feminists, student radicals who first met with hostility and violence, were not easily stilled. In time—often a long time—others joined them. Little movements grew into great campaigns and, time and again, employers, government officials, and representatives of other powerful sectors of society began to make concessions. Most interesting to me is the willingness of opponents of change to change themselves, once they recognize that the force of public opinion is running against them.

There are areas where progress has been slow. And there are areas where we have not yet found the way or the will to make broader changes that will affect all who suffer from some of our greatest problems. Our cities are decaying and unmanageable; our environment is becoming polluted; economic recessions have caused thousands of publicly and privately employed citizens to be laid off... Perhaps such problems are so enormous that we cannot deal with them all. But so far such a view is not widespread in our society. There is still a fundamental optimism about our ability to deal with adversity.

Moderator: You feel, then, Professor Jordan, that the American people think they are capable of solving their problems?

Jordan: I do. While many Americans are frightened of what they see around them, the still seem to have a fundamental belief in the soundness of the system....But, as I tried to point out, the problems that confront us today are far greater and more ominous than those we have faced in the past.

Fischer: I disagree. The problems of today are not greater; they are different. There were very great problems in the earlier days of this country, and most were solved quite successfully. They were solved because of a common spirit that almost everyone—rich and poor—felt. It was a spirit or a belief that no problem was too big to handle.

Jordan: You really think Americans can do just about anything?

Fischer: Perhaps I was overdramatizing, but I do think that too much is said about how we've failed and not enough about the strengths and successes of this country....I am concerned by those who continually promote the idea that there are no common interests, that there is no strength in the social fabric. I think they give people false expectations that complex problems are the fault of a wicked conspiracy. I think it is irresponsible to undermine the emotional bonds that give us a sense of interdependence. The hyphenated Americans—Irish Americans, Polish Americans, Jewish Americans, and even Black Americans feel it. At the core of whatever they are is something that binds them. After all, why do blacks prove to be among the most patriotic citizens in public opinion polls?

Jordan: [interrupting] I'll tell you why. It's not because they're black but because they're southern. Southern Protestants, to be more accurate. And they're poor. Take those three variables and you've got a winning combination for political conservatism. Of course, they're not conservative when it comes to racial or bread-and-butter issues. But on anything else, they're conservatives. [She then cites several examples.] Studies of sexual attitudes and behavior reveal greater acceptance of "permissiveness" among members of the middle class than among the working class. Opinion polls about desegregation and rights of minorities reveal more support for these values among members of the middle class....

Wyckham: But that doesn't mean that working-class people are enamored with the system. Their conservatism may simply reflect a fear of the changes that other, more powerful people are always advocating at their expense. They stick to the straight and narrow because they are not really able to strike out at the source. They are taught to believe their problems are personal rather than political...[63]

They go on for much of the rest of the hour arguing back and forth. As they approach the end, the moderator asks Jordan to comment on something she had said about ethnic group progress, women's liberation and, lastly gay rights.

Jordan: ...Gay liberation, a movement that began in the late 1960s, has brought about profound changes not only in sexual behavior but also in attitudes toward it. As a result of pressure and publicity from people who no longer accept social views of what are proper and improper sexual relationships, homosexuals and their supporters have gained recognition for their cause.

Fischer: I'd like to comment on something that Terry Jordan suggests but doesn't say. It is an important sociological point that relates her examples to something about which I feel quite strongly. While it is true that changes of all kinds have occurred in recent years—the three she mentioned are but a sampling—many people seem to feel that these changes demonstrate the willingness of our society to stretch its tolerance limits to satisfy the needs of individuals who feel left out or discriminated against. That society is willing to do so is true. But it is

---

[63]"A Sociological Debate," appears in Peter I. Rose, Myron Glazer and Penina Glazer, *Sociology: Inquiring into Society*, (Canfield Press, 1977; second edition, St. Martins Press, 1982).

also true that the reason authorities are willing to do it—whether they be employers, college administrators, or government officials—is that they see acquiescence as a means of preserving the system.

Wyckham: Exactly.

Fischer: Wait, Cy, I'm not finished. You see, you think it's a bad thing to try to absorb the dissidents. I don't. I think it's essential to the well-being of a society that reforms be orderly and at a pace that the society can absorb. If not, the entire equilibrium of society can be upset, and chaos cannot benefit any group.

Wyckham: That's my basic disagreement! I think there is a real question about whether you can gradually patch up a failing welfare system, an alienated labor force, or a swollen military establishment, given the highly uneven distribution of power we have. Sure, the country will stay afloat a while longer, but it's destined to sink. That's the United States as we head for 1984. Not George Orwell's totalitarian regime but a ship stuck together with band-aids.

Making your sort of concession to protesters simply cools them down. It's clever. Any attempt at genuine revolutionary change is dampened by expanding what's acceptable. The outsiders—Blacks, women, homosexuals, and others—are taken into the fold and, feeling grateful for admittance, lose their zeal to overturn the system. What I think is less visible is the seething anger that most black people still feel in their slums, the potential violence that may explode in a way we can't control—not because changes will have occurred too rapidly, but because unemployment, poverty, and racism will have continued at their present levels. And...

Moderator: I must get to the last question, since time is fleeting. Where are we going from here? I gather from Professor Wyckham's last remarks, he thinks we're going nowhere, that the period some have called "The American Era," is coming to a sad ending.

Wyckham: Not sad. Just an ending. As you know, I have little faith in this society. It uses warfare to build itself up and welfare to keep people thinking everything is just fine. It is built on a mystique of individualism that is belied by the fact that the little guy can never run an even race. The United States was founded on lofty values and ideals, which no one can fault: life, liberty and the pursuit of happiness. But it never seems able to realize its own proclaimed destiny. It is a society crying for a real revolution—not one like the war of 1776. That was really just a civil war between British monarchists and British-American republicans. I'm talking about a true revolution. And yet I fear it will never occur. There will be protest, violence, rebellion, but it won't come to anything...The people are forever being told that they really have the best of all possible worlds. You'd no doubt say the fabric is too strong.

Fischer: I think you just admitted something that many of us have tried to say. Like it or not, the American system is an integrated society, and it's going to last a very long time....It values its heritage and also its future orientations, a belief that the past was good, the present is better, and the future will be better still.

Jordan: I think we're in for some rough sledding and our famous future orientation will be undergoing some rude re-orientations in the years ahead. In recent years the raw wounds of this society have been exposed. Our tensions and fears have been express. We've suffered— through misadventure, mismanagement, or sheer bullheadedness— in foreign policy and domestically. But we've also proven that we can deal with defeat, disillusionment, even corruption in the highest places. As many people said in the wave of relief after the Nixon impeachment hearings: "The system works."

Moderator: Our time is up. Once again, we're left with a variety of views and no clear answers to our questions. What the three guests have done is provoke our thinking about the nature of our society.... I leave you with some questions I posed to them before we went on the air. Is the United States an integrated society? How does it deal with its many problems, and how should it deal with them? What are the responsibilities of those in its mainstream? And what is the future of those on its margins?[64]

The mock TV show was later reprinted in my book *Mainstream and Margins* (1982) and, of all the essays in it, it was this one that seemed to be most intriguing to readers, especially colleagues who were teaching contemporary sociological theory and ways to apply it to racial and ethnic relations circa 1980. I have to say that as rewarding as that was it was nothing compared to my astonishment when, after doing readings of the piece on various campuses—sometimes having faculty friends on the campus reading the different parts, I would be asked by students

---

[64] Loc. cit.

where they might find the books I mentioned, that is, the made-up ones that had been written by my three invented professors Fischer, Wyckham, and Jordan.

While reflecting on the years between the publication of Moynihan's policy paper on "The Negro Family" and the publication of Patterson's book about it, I turned to two other books I'd promised to review for social science journals in 2012, *Made in America* by Claude S. Fischer and Charles Murray's *Coming Apart*. I couldn't avoid a sense of special satisfaction. As you will see, although being advanced nearly forty years later, some of the arguments made by Claude Fischer and my fictitious Terry Jordan, have a striking similarity; so too do those of Charles Murray and Claude Fischer's namesake Janice Fischer—a persona and name I created years before I'd ever heard of Claude—or of Charles Murray for that matter.

In *Made in America*, Claude Fischer describes the persisting strength of the middle class. Murray's *Coming Apart: The State of White America, 1960–2010*, is about its pending demise. Fischer argues that despite a long history of exploitation of workers and discrimination against various minorities, major changes in industry and demographics and legislation would alter some of the most entrenched mind-sets about who we are and the meaning and rights of citizenship. Many of these changes would be accommodations to pressures and threats brought about by political differences, economic necessity, and the vigorous social action of minorities and other interest groups. We witnessed this very phenomenon in the shift in attitude—or, at least, strategy—toward Latinos in the immediate wake of the Republicans' defeat in the presidential election of 2012. Whether attributed to responsiveness or cooptation or to the realization that everything is not, after all, just fine, I agree with Fischer that again and again the old limits of tolerance have been stretched and more and more outsiders have been brought into the mainstream, adopting what used to be called middle class values and trying to live by them.[65]

---

[65]"Yankees and Other Ethnics: The American Evolution," *Contemporary Sociology*, 40 July (2011), 409–412.

In *Coming Apart*, also published in 2010, Charles Murray, best known as the co-author of *The Bell Curve* (1994), a highly controversial book on race and intelligence, focused only on whites but his claims were almost assured to raise the eyebrows of skeptics. They certainly did in my case. I wrote:

> When I first read Charles Murray's new book about white America coming apart at the seams, I was immediately reminded of two other recent volumes on that growing shelf of books about the breakdown of American society and the dire consequences of a nation rent with polarizing differences. The first was Arthur M. Schlesinger Jr.'s, *The Disuniting of America: Reflections on a Multicultural Society* (1991), a book about what its author saw as the increasing balkanization of a polity that seemed to be inexorably moving from its glory days of *E Pluribus Unum* to *E Pluribus Plures*. Schlesinger had highlighted the catalytic role of the rise of black power and the powerful influence of certain Afro-centrists, abetted by naïve liberal allies, in instigating the whole process. The second was Samuel Huntington's *Who Are We? The Challenge to America's National Identity* (2004).
>
> In *Who Are We?* the author of *The Clash of Civilizations* (1996) was now writing not about those who want to uphold the Western Tradition in the face of growing Islamic fundamentalism but about something more akin to Schlesinger's worry about those corporate pluralists who were contributing to the demise of the real America. Sam Huntington strongly felt and said in so many words that the old Anglo-Protestant establishment—his people and his values—was under siege by alien elements (meaning non-WASPS) and their un-American ideologies. In language echoing that of nativists of earlier eras who railed against the Irish, the Chinese, the Poles, Italians, Greeks, Slavs, East European Jews and other "swarthy orientals," Huntington's principal nemeses were the latest group of "unassimilable foreigners," the Mexicans.
>
> Charles Murray also believes that white America is beset with challenges. But he is neither a disillusioned liberal like the late Arthur Schlesinger, nor a neo-nativist like the late Sam Huntington. W. H. Brady Scholar at the American Enterprise Institute, he is a self-proclaimed libertarian who firmly believes in what the sociologist Michael Lewis once styled as "the individual-as-central sensibility." His message is that a general decline in morality (manifest in various

forms of communal and family breakdowns), an increase of dependence on government support, and the personal failures of more and more citizens to uphold the "founding virtues of industriousness, honesty, marriage, and religiosity," have severely weakened the very core of the American ethos. Unless something is done to stop this systemic angst, we are heading down a slippery slope of national decline. He argues that this country "can remain exceptional only to the extent that its people embody the same qualities that made it work for the first two centuries of its existence. The founding virtues are central to that kind of citizenry."[66]

I think that while he raises some troubling questions, he is way off base when claiming that the conflicts are not the fault of those in power but the failures of those who have brought about their own estrangement, manifest in a new form of downward mobility and a new sobriquet, "the new lower class." It is not that our values are screwed up, but that the structure of our modern society is hardly geared toward accommodating the causes of stagnation and, too often, downward mobility.

To claim that it is all or mainly a function of a deterioration of their industriousness, honesty, the erosion of family values, the decline of religiosity and faith without noting the critical role of social and economic circumstances is as blatant a case of blaming the victim as one can imagine.

There is little discussion of the fact that many of the problems may be a function of the disappearance of opportunities for blue-collar employment caused by the decline of heavy industry, the outsourcing of such forms of manufacturing as that of garments and shoes and the new demands of an increasingly technical society. Especially for formerly steadily employed workers in factories that required little education and on-the-job skills, the conundrum of coping with the overwhelming reality of being laid off and then bombarded by more responsibilities than they can handle make it hard to accept the argument that it is moral degeneration that underlies their unhappy placement in their new and sad estate.

I was struck by the fact that Murray briefly cites the work of two well-known Wilsons: E. O. and James Q., the latter whose own perspectives on values and character he seems to find most simpatico,

---

[66] "Systemic Angst in a Polarized America," *Sociology and Modern Society*, November-December (2012), 554.

but that he never mentions the one Wilson who offered one of the most critical explanations for the growing anomie among the depressed members of the old working class, William Julius Wilson. That Wilson is the author of *The Declining Significance of Race* (1978), a book that described the widening gap within the African-American community between those who were making it (many of whose values regarding work, family, and faith would likely be indistinguishable today from those Murray sees as the ones being abandoned) and those left behind. The latter group became the subject of Wilson's *The Truly Disadvantaged* (1987). Both books are very germane to Murray's concerns. But the most important contribution to the issues raised in *Coming Apart* are to be found in Wilson's 1996 volume, *When Work Disappears: The World of the New Urban Poor.*[67]

Reading and writing about books such as Patterson's, Fischer's, and Murray's helped me get ready for the next item on my agenda, preparing a seventh—and fiftieth anniversary—edition of my first book, *They and We*. As I explained in Chapter Two, that book, first published in 1964, was my own early attempt to offer a brief overview of racial and ethnic relations in the United States in the context of changing attitudes but persisting forms of discrimination against certain minorities. The new edition will doubtless include some of the thoughts reflected in the passages from my reviews excerpted in this chapter. It will also address my growing concern with several other matters.

First among them is the persistence of what I once styled the "leap-frog phenomenon," the pattern of new, often poor immigrants to the United States moving in, on, and over African Americans, as happened in many major cities—New York, Philadelphia, Chicago, and Detroit at the turn of the twentieth century, then again after the Immigration Reform Act of 1965, which reopened the guarded gates of this country, and several times since as newcomers such as Koreans, Chinese, and other East Asians and then Cubans and other Latinos, seemed to be repeating an old pattern familiar to historians, sociologists and political scientists, who also described the earliest manifestation of this phenomenon. As I write it is predicted that thirty years from now the number of citizens of

---

[67]Ibid., 554.

Hispanic background will be twice that of African Americans (30 as opposed to fifteen percent of the population, respectively). Perhaps as significant will be a consideration of the implication that when this happens white people will cease to be a statistical majority in the United States, a confirmation of the fears of old Americans like Samuel Huntington who see themselves as "damned Yankees." and of others who used to be referred to as white ethnics but have moved from the margins into the mainstream of society.

The second subject is more closely related to my recent work which compares perspectives on migrant populations in the United States with those in Europe, in particular what I see as the bifurcated concerns of many nativists and neo-nativists in this country in regard to two cohorts: Latinos, especially Mexicans, and those who are all placed under the single rubric, "Muslims." From preliminary research it seems that while members of both newcomer groups are perceived by some as threats to people in this country, those in the first one, even when called "unassimilable" (that word that dominated the anti-immigrant sentiment in much of the ninetheenth century and the early twentieth centuries), are seen mainly as an economic threat. Those in the second are seen as an existential danger, one that carries the specter of terrorism. And every act of violence by individuals identified as Muslims exacerbates the tendency to tar their coreligionists with the same brush.

While I am only beginning to explore this issue, I suspect that instead of the two cohorts being separable as appears to be the case in the minds of many in the United States, such a distinction between migrants and Muslims is rarely made in Europe. In part, such conflation makes sense because the homelands of so many newcomers in Europe—though far from all—are from North African countries, or from Turkey, Pakistan, Bosnia, and a number of Arab lands, that have predominantly Muslim populations. The large presence of such people offers ready-made scapegoats for all the ills of societies that are dealing with a severe economic downturn. This is most evident in the portraits painted by growing nationalist groups and political parties found in almost every European country.

Getting a firmer understanding of such phenomena are topics I intend to pursue in the years ahead. A good start on the second one was another symposium I organized. "Resistance and Readiness: Immigration, Nativism and the Challenge of Racial, Ethnic, and Religious Pluralism in the U.S. and Europe Today." It took place in Salzburg in September, 2012. This time the emphasis was far more comparative than that of the conference I had run there ten years earlier, a reflection of my own growing interest in exploring and discussing the similarities and differences in the reactions to outsiders and to "strangers" already in the midst of American and European societies. While aspects of European xenophobia and discrimination against racial minorities, especially against colored immigrants was something I first witnessed and wrote about in the 1960s, only recently have I begun to revisit and more systematically explore the subject.

The program for the Salzburg seminar took a number of its themes from those focused at the three-day faculty symposium at the Kahn Liberal Arts Institute at Smith College in the spring of 2010, one that was explored further in Five College-faculty seminars during the academic years 2010–2011 and 2011–2012. There the participants explored, as we would again in Salzburg, issues of identity; differences between the concepts of citizenship and membership (i.e. true acceptance); the social, economic, cultural and political roots of distrust and their manifestation in discriminatory behavior as well as in cultural expression in literature, film, and art—and on the Web; labeling and scapegoating; the varied meanings of "marginality;" reactions to discrimination, including defensive insulation and recrudescent movements of intense in-group solidarity, "tolerance"—and the limits of tolerance. In the last instance much effort went into wrestling with conflicts over civil and human rights and the conservative ethnic and religious traditions of certain groups of both citizens and migrants. We also compared and contrasted ideological campaigns of anti-Semitism with prejudice against Muslims, a subject of special interest to me, and one of growing concern around the world.

Six months after the 2012 symposium on migration issues in the United States and Europe, Hedy and I were back in Salzburg once again, this time working with students from Miami-Dade Community College, there for a short course and seminar on global citizenship. Among the things we discussed was the destruction of the Jewish communities of Europe in the 1940s. Hedy spoke to the group about her personal experiences in Amsterdam during the war. The next day all were taken to Dachau, the former concentration camp and now memorial site near Munich. That night we had discussions about the persisting tendency to label and stigmatize people and the potential power of playing up differences between in-groups and out-groups and the consequences for the targets of such exclusion.

The following week we were off to lecture at the Lucian Blaga University in Sibiu, Romania, a charming old Transylvanian city. We were impressed by the enthusiasm of the students to hear our thoughts about American ideas and institutions and our struggles to move toward "a more perfect union," but startled to find how little they seemed to know—or, perhaps, how reluctant they were to talk about their own history—especially that during World War II when almost the entire Jewish community of Romania was destroyed by the Nazis and their allies.

Not long after returning from Sibiu, we spent some time in Thessaloniki in northern Greece. While in the area on a travel writing assignment in nearby Halkidiki, a seaside area with three long peninsulas of mountains, piney woods, and beautiful beaches; the birthplace of Aristotle and of Alexander the Great; and the site of the monasteries of Mount Athos, we tried to get a sense of the long history and abrupt demise of one of the most famous Jewish centers in the world. We had known something of the story of the Jews of Thessaloniki, whose roots go back before the Christian Era and where, for hundreds of years the main body of the community was made up of Sephardim who had fled Spain after the Inquisition in the late fifteenth century, enjoying good relations with Christians and Muslims until, like those in Romania, almost the entire Jewish population was rounded up, deported, and murdered in the Holocaust. In Thessaloniki, at least, there are many reminders of the role of the Jews and a genuine attempt to further an understanding of their critical role in the development of the city.

After leaving northern Greece, we managed a whirlwind first trip to Istanbul. It, too, was a place we had read about for many years but never managed to visit. We saw many of the famous tourist sites, including the Hagia Sofia, the Blue Mosque, the Basilica Cistern, the Topkapi Palace, the old Chora Church (now the Kariye Museum known for its incredible mosaics), the archaeological museums, the bazaars, and the Bosporus. It was all most interesting. Yet, in the limited time we had to interact with local people, what was most striking to me was the feeling that Kipling's terse statement that "East is east and west is west and never the twain shall meet" was belied at every turn. What will happen in the future is hard to predict. (As I write, the European Union is still debating whether to admit Turkey to its elite club while demonstrations taking place in the major cities are giving pause even to those disposed to grant accession. In flare-ups in Ankara, Istanbul, and Izmir, Turks who pride themselves on their country's long standing cosmopolitan secularism began challenging what they saw as an increasing bow to sectarian fundamentalism and the authoritarian rule by the prime minister, Recep Tayyip Erdoðan, and his dominant Justice and Development Party. Observers do not see these sorts of conflicts abating any time soon. Indeed, there is a widespread feeling that such events may be a portent of more upheaval in the months and years to come.)

Feeling we had only scratched the surface and eager to know more about Turkish society and politics, we left Istanbul very reluctantly, vowing to return someday soon. And we will, for though we move a bit slower these days, we intend to keep traveling and keep learning about different cultures and the characters who support them, about social institutions, social conflicts, and those special examples of true comity where peoples meet.

Looking over what I have written in this and the six earlier chapters, I realize that that my potpourri of postmonitions may seem to be a swan song. I don't see it as that but as a commentary on my *first* eighty years! (On every birthday in our family, we always say *"bis hundret tsvantsig"*— Yiddish for "until 120," the alleged length of Moses's life, so I figure I have still have some years to go.)

I have written about many of the things I have done and seen, and mentioned many places and many people. In closing this compilation of reflections and ruminations, I planned to zero in on a subset of those whose acquaintances have been particularly memorable and, more often than not, long lasting. In addition to Hedy to whom the book is dedicated, and to our daughter Lies, our son Dan, his wife Susan, and their sons, Jordon and Robert, I realized that there are thousands of others we have gotten to know over our sixty years together. I tried to write down those to cite but even my short-list took up several pages and I found it impossible to cut further. Included were distinguished writers, artists and sculptors, editors and publishers. A great number were social scientists with whom I found a special affinity; others were friends in many other fields as well as politicians, university administrators, political activists, members of John F. Kennedy and Lyndon B. Johnson's cabinets, key figures in a number of international organizations and NGOs, and many, many former students.

Then, mulling over the fact that somebody might reasonably want to pin me down and ask, in the fashion of the old *Reader's Digest* editor, *"But among all those folks, who is the most unforgettable character you've ever known?"* I started through the list again. Then I thought, it's "none of the above." Instead it is someone I only met twice and first wrote about twenty-five years ago in response to a similar question actually posed to me by a newspaper reporter with Northampton's *Daily Hampshire Gazette*. At the time, I immediately thought of Mr. David. I would still put him first today.

> I met Mr. David shortly after arriving in Northampton [now 53 years ago]. I needed some repairs on a tweed jacket purchased six years before in a post-Christmas sale at a very "Ivy" men's store in

Ithaca, New York, where I was then a graduate student. The jacket, worn and patched with leather at the elbows was, along with the pipe I smoked, a youthful statement about the academic career on which I was embarking. It was also falling apart from the inside out.

I asked a friend where I might get the jacket repaired. He said there was only one decent tailor in town, Mr. David. And so I went to see him.

His tiny shop off Masonic Street had an aura of familiarity about it. I could feel it in the air. The place smelled of steam and ironing. It was strewn with pieces of material and spools of thread. It was dark, too, save for a spot of light emanating from a gooseneck lamp over a big sewing machine behind which sat a little old man.

"May I help you?" he asked. The accent also rang a bell.

"Yes," I said, "I'd like you to put a new lining in this jacket."

He took it in his hands, lowered his glasses from the top of his forehead almost to the tip of his nose, inspected the whole thing very carefully, shook his head, and said, "Mister, it wouldn't pay. It would cost you thirty dollars, easy. Do yourself a favor. Get a new jacket."

"But I like this one. It's, well, something special."

He looked up at me, smiled, and said, "What are you, a teacher?"

"Yes," I said. He sighed, then said, "All right, all right. Leave it. I'll see what I can do."

A week later I returned.

"Is my jacket ready?" I asked."

"Yes," Mr. David said. "It's all fixed. Gimme, uh, two dollars."

Surprised by how little he was charging, I said, "Only two dollars?"

"Yes, just two dollars."

I paid him and took the jacket. I looked it over and noted that instead of replacing the lining, he had mended every rip and tear. I was impressed—and very grateful for his kindness. I didn't know what to say. I stood there for a few moments looking at him.

Then he spoke again. "So, you're a teacher. A good profession. The best. I know a lot of people like you. Professors, too."

No longer able to contain my emotions, I said, "And I know people like you. You remind me of my grandfather, my mother's father."

Mr. David looked up at me, tilted his head, and rather quietly asked, "Was he a tailor?"

"Yes," I answered.

"Jewish?"

"Yes."

Now grinning, he asked, "From Poland?"

"He was."

"Tell me son," Mr. David leaned closer and asked, "Was he a Socialist?"

"Of course," I replied.

Mr. David beamed. So did I. We shook hands and laughed, and, promising to come by soon, I bade him goodbye.

As I walked back to the campus, I decided I would visit him the following week. It was not to be. Two days after I picked up my jacket, I learned that he had died.

When I read the news in the local paper, I was very sad. Mr. David (I never learned his whole name until I read the obituary) was the link between my old world and my new one.[68]

That was written in 1988, but the sentiment remains.

Twenty years later I wrote a different sort of nostalgic memoir. Today I see it as a sort of lyrical coda to this compilation of postmonitions.

> *"Oh give me land lots of land, under starry skies above,*
> *Don't fence me in."*

I thought of that lyric a few weeks ago while riding my bike past JFK Middle School in Northampton.

Odd connection? Not to me.

It brought me back to a time over sixty-five years before when I would ride from home to a junior high school in Syracuse, New York, with my head full of then-current music, especially my favorite, one of Cole Porter's only cowboy songs, "Don't Fence Me In." Now, many years later the memory sparked two thoughts. First, the words of the song were prescient or, perhaps, prophetic for I would spend much of my adult life traveling. No fences would bar my wanderlust. Second was the realization that like many people, I often associate particular tunes with specific trips, venues or events, whether on rides to school or work or less frequent ones to far away places. Certain music, at least when I hear it, evokes times, sites, and activities; it enhances memory and contributes to a particular kind of travel—time travel.

For example, whenever I hear an old recording of Glenn Miller's band playing "In the Mood," I immediately see myself as a young boy

---

[68]"Mr. David," *Hampshire Life*, July 29, 1988.

sitting with my folks, listening to a big, boxy Zenith radio following the news of the progress of the Allied forces in the early 1940s. Whenever I hear "God Bless America," I can see Kate Smith's rotund image as I'd seen it in numerous newsreel clips during that same era.

The other day I heard Hoagy Carmichael's "Ole Buttermilk Sky" on my car radio. Suddenly I could see myself riding a chairlift for the first time while on a skiing excursion to the Laurentian Mountains of Canada. A bit acrophobic, I still associate the song with clinging to the upright rod of steel that held the rather rickety open seat as it swung in the wind taking me to the top of Mont Tremblant, all the while singing—over and over,

> *Ole buttermilk sky*
> *I'm a keepin' my eye peeled on you*
> *What's the good word tonight?*
> *Are you gonna be mellow tonight?*

That was in 1948.

Not too many years later it was "Stardust," that 1927 tune, that became "our song," as I commuted on a weekly basis from Syracuse, New York, where I was an senior in college to Rochester where my girl friend, later fiancé, now wife of nearly six decades, was living. We also loved "Harlem Nocturne." Whenever I hear it today, I am immediately transported back to 1953 and a smoky bar called The Orange, just off the university campus. And whenever I hear the words to that old Tenth Mountain Division song, "Give me skis and some poles and klister, and let me ski way up in Alta Vista," I am back with a bunch of fellow skiers drinking beer in a favorite hangout called Tecumseh or heading up to ski at what was then a new area, North Ridge.

We spent the academic year 1964–65 in the Midlands of merry old—and very cold—England. Wherever we went it was "A Hard Day's Night." Any time I hear any Beatles song, but especially that one, I am carried back to the house we sublet in Oadby, a suburb of Leicester, trying to fit into the strange environment of the British Midlands and working hard to adjust to life with funny money (pounds, shillings and pence), odd-sounding words in a language I thought I understood, boiled coffee with boiled milk, fish and chips, and pipes on the outside of houses so, as our neighbor explained, "The workmen can get at them when they freeze."

Certain tunes, many of them popular again owing to recent revivals, remind me of the late 1960s and early 1970s, driving from our home in Northampton to the little town of Chateaugay, New York, way up on the Canadian border to celebrate Thanksgiving or Christmas vacation with my parents. Once in the car, our daughter would urge us to sing. And we did.

> *Folks are dumb where I come from*
> *They ain't had any learnin'....*

> *June is bustin' out all over*
> *All over the meadow and the hill!*

> *It's that old devil moon*
> *That you stole from the skies.*
> *It's that old devil moon*
> *In your eyes.*

I saw *Annie Get Your Gun, Carousel,* and *Finian's Rainbow* on Broadway, but whenever I hear those songs, instead of visualizing the stage sets or the stars of the shows, I see us sitting in our little, blue 1958 Peugeot traveling through Vermont, along the coast of Lake Champlain and into the North Country, belting out those great tunes.

I long have had a fondness for Frank Loesser's Runyonesque musical *Guys and Dolls.* But each time I hear "Adelaide's Lament," I am immediately transported to a Smith College classroom sometime in the early 1970s. I am teaching a course, "Methods of Social Research." Trying to be inventive in preparing a mid-term exam in that pre-politically correct era, I ask my students to design a study to test the proposition:

> *"The average unmarried female*
> *Basically insecure*
> *Due to some long frustration may react*
> *With psychosomatic symptoms*
> *Difficult to endure*
> *Affecting the upper respiratory tract."*

(Hypothesis: Frustrated women get sick!)

My big regret was that I didn't come up with many more similarly evocative exam questions in the many other years I taught the course.

Listening to great calypso music in a Jamaican bar on one of my first trips to the Caribbean I found that what kept popping into my head wasn't the iconic record jacket with a picture of Harry Belafonte (though I saw that, too) but an eight-day canoe trip in the Adirondacks many years before as my bowman and I paddled to Belafonte's "Banana Boat" beat. Over and over we sang, *"Day-o, Day-o,"* gliding up the Fulton chain of lakes, on to Raquette Lake and Long Lake and the Saranacs in brilliant sunshine and pouring rain. (On the long portages, we sang about the Volga boatmen *"Yo-oh, heave ho!"*)

A few years ago we saw a very bad revival of *Fiddler on the Roof* on a San Francisco stage. Yet, hearing the lyrics of "Anatekva," especially the lines, *"Soon I'll be a stranger in a strange new place/Searching for an old familiar face,"* took me back in time once again—not to when I first saw the show in New York but to refugee camps in Southeast Asia in the early 1980s. While I don't remember singing the song or even thinking about it then, every time I've heard it since, it is not a shtetl in the Russian Pale of Settlement that first pops into my mind but a transit camp in Thailand filled with frightened and bewildered people about to leave their own worlds for an unknown future.

During a short period when we lived in Adelaide, Australia, Hedy and I and the kids never sang or heard "Waltzing Matilda," but I do remember humming the tune to *"Kookaburra sits in the old gum tree"* and conjuring images not of the local birds or the gum trees all around us but of the camp we ran ten thousand miles away where the song was a favorite round. I kept visualizing the campfire on the beach at twilight with the silhouette of Lyon Mountain above the lake and more than a hundred kids in a huge circle singing away. *"Laugh Kookaburra, Laugh Kookaburra/Gay your life must be."* I became very nostalgic.

Memories of the Galapagos and its particular fauna are fuzzier, at least in the head-tunes department. Maybe all I thought was *"Fish gotta swim/birds gotta fly"*—which may not be so far-fetched.

Sometimes the connections are far clearer. Several years ago, attending the Clearwater Festival at Croton-on-Hudson, I listened to the still active nonagenarian Pete Seeger sing the Weavers' anthem, "Wasn't That a Time," I was immediately back in South Africa during the worst period of apartheid and a particular day in Pietermaritzburg where I had gone to speak at what I had been told was an ecumenical

Christian seminary. When I got there, I found it surrounded by barbed wire. It was a school for black preachers. As I passed through the gate, all I could think of was:

> *The fascists came with chains and war*
> *To prison us in hate.*
> *And many a good man fought and died*
> *To save the stricken faith.*

Other sentiments—sometimes joyful, sometimes tearful—are reflected in songs conjured up from times long ago that evoke memories, moods, and social movements, such as when I marched in a peace parade led by Martin Luther King Jr. and joined him and thousands of others in singing the old civil rights anthem, "*We shall overcome.*" I can't hear that song today without being transported back to downtown Manhattan just months before his assassination.

My tune-connections are not always so heavy, though their imprints on the brain are also hard to shake.

For nearly two decades I have been going to Salzburg at least once and often twice a year to participate or teach in programs at the Salzburg Global Seminar located in a mid-eighteenth century rococo palace, Schloss Leopoldskron. While it is said that the locals can't get Mozart's *Eine Kleine Nachtmusik* out of their heads, I walk around the town and its surrounding areas humming, "*The hills are alive with the sound of music,*" just like the busloads of tourists who come to gaze at the palace and snap pictures of the building that was one of the settings of the famed musical about the Von Trapp family.

There is a variation on my theme of travel tunes. Sometimes a melody or the words to a song evoke a sense of *déjà vu* even on a first visit to a place I've never been to before. Call it pre-nostalgia. In such cases it may be that I've heard something so many times—"*The stars at night are big and bright/Deep in the heart of Texas,*" "*Oklahoma, where the wind comes sweepin' down the plain*"—that when I finally get there, it seems strikingly familiar. I'm sure that is how the folks staring at the Schloss Leopoldskron from across the lake are feeling when they see me waving to them from our third floor apartment. They may even imagine it's the Baron himself!

Finally, I have to say that on many occasions when I sit down to write at my desk in Northampton or the one in my loft-study in Wellfleet, like most writers, I often get frustrated. I swear under my breath. But then I get back to work, reminding myself of two seminal lines in a favorite Cole Porter lyric.

> *Good authors too who once knew better words,*
> *Now only use four-letter words,*
> *Writing prose,*
> *Anything goes.*[69]

---

[69]An earlier version of this appeared as "Travel Tunes" in *SoGoNow*, October, 2008.

About the Author

PETER ROSE, a sociologist, ethnographer, writer, world traveler, and sometime travel journalist, is Sophia Smith Professor Emeritus and Senior Fellow of the Kahn Liberal Arts Institute at Smith College. He studied at Syracuse University (A.B. 1954) and Cornell University (Ph.D. 1959) and taught at Smith College for 43 year. Over a long career that began at Goucher College in Baltimore, he served as a visiting professor at the University of Massachusetts,  Amherst, Clark, Wesleyan, the University of Colorado, UCLA, Yale and Harvard, and as a Fulbright professor in England, Japan, Australia, Austria, and The Netherlands. Recipient of the Medal of the University of Amsterdam, he was the first chair of the advisory boards of University College Utrecht and University College Roosevelt, both international honors colleges of Utrecht University. He has been a resident fellow at centers and institutes in Jerusalem, Beijing, Oxford, Bellagio and Bogliasco in Italy, and at the East-West Center in Honolulu, Harvard and Stanford. A long-time member of the Board of Trustees of the Salt Institute for Documentary Studies in Portland, Maine, he is also an active fellow and faculty member at the Salzburg Global Seminar in Austria where he continues to teach in its program on Global Citizenship and serve on its American Studies board.

He is the author of *They and We, The Subject is Race, Strangers in Their Midst, Mainstream and Margins, Tempest-Tost, Guest Appearances and Other Travels in Time and Space,* and *With Few Reservations,* and is editor of a number of other books in sociology, American culture, intergroup relations, ethnic history, and immigration and refugee policy.